HISPANIC AMERICAN LITERATURE
A Brief Introduction and Anthology

Nicolás Kanellos
University of Houston

The Longman Literary Mosaic Series
Ishmael Reed
General Editor
University of California, Berkeley

 **LONGMAN**

An imprint of Addison Wesley Longman, Inc.

New York • Reading, Massachusetts • Menlo Park, California • Harlow, England
Don Mills, Ontario • Sydney • Mexico City • Madrid • Amsterdam

Acquisitions Editor: Lisa Moore
Cover Designer: Kay Petronio
Cover Illustration: Rupert Garcia, "The Horse in Man." Copyright Rupert Garcia and courtesy of
artist and Sammi Madison-Garcia, Rena Bransten Gallery (SF), Galerie Claude Samuel (Paris), and
Daniel Saxon Gallery (LA).
Electronic Production Manager: J. Eric Jorgensen
Electronic Page Makeup: Kay Spearman/The Resource Center

Hispanic American Literature

Library of Congress Cataloguing-in-Publication Data

Hispanic American Literature: a Brief Introduction and Anthology / Nicolas Kanellos
    p. cm. -- (Longman Literary Mosaic Series)
    Includes index.
    ISBN 0-673-46956-5
    1. American Literature--Hispanic American authors. 2. American Literature--Hispanic American
authors--History and criticism. 3. Hispanic Americans--Literary collections. 4. Hispanic
Americans--Intellectual Life. 5. Hispanic Americans in literature
    I. Kanellos, Nicolas. II. Series.
    PS508.H57H55 1994
    810.8'0868--dc20
                                                                              94-44287
                                                                                   CIP

3/94

Contents

POETRY

DRAMA

Foreword

by Ishmael Reed, General Editor

I abandoned the use of textbooks early in my teaching career and developed my own "reader." I was frustrated with textbooks in which the preponderance of prose and poetry was written by people of similar backgrounds and sensibilities—the white-settler-surrounded-by-infidels-and-savages theme common to Euro-American literature. In these textbooks we seldom got information about how the Native Americans or the Africans felt. Female and minority writers were left out. There was slack inclusion of contemporary writers, and little space devoted to the popular American culture of our century. These textbooks seemed slavishly worshipful of the past, such that every mediocre line by a past "great" was treated with reverence while the present was ignored.

Of course, there are many worthwhile ideas to be gained from what in our sound-bite culture—in which complicated ideas are dumbed down for instant consumption—is referred to as "Western Civilization." But as Asian American writer Frank Chin points out when referring to the Cantonese model, after the ability of the Cantonese to absorb every culture with which they've come into contact, one doesn't have to abandon the styles of one's own tradition in order to embrace styles from other traditions. As I have mentioned elsewhere, the history of modern art would be quite different had not artists been receptive to or borrowed from the traditions of others. This creative give and take between artists of different cultures particularly characterizes the arts of the twentieth century.

Things have improved over the years, especially with the outbreak of textbooks labeled "multicultural," a term that has become a football in the struggle between the politically correct of the left and the right. However, even the new and improved multicultural texts appear to have added African American, Native American, Hispanic American, and Asian American writers as an afterthought. The same writers and the same—often unrepresentative—works show up again and again.*

The Longman Literary Mosaic Series

The HarperCollins Literary Mosaic Series was created as an antidote to this version of multiculturalism whose fallibility becomes evident when talented writers, well-known and respected in their communities, are ignored. The HarperCollins Literary Mosaic Series includes not only those writers who have made it into the canon but also writers undeservedly neglected in today's crop of texts.

---

* *For more information on the arbitrariness of this selection process, see Michael Harper's excellent Every Shut Eye Aint Sleep.*

In his autobiographical remarks, *Asian American Literature* editor Shawn Wong makes an important point that teachers should consider when adopting texts for their ethnic literature, multiculturalism, American literature, and introductory literature courses. Wong writes that his study of Asian American literature occurred outside of the university. "At no time," he writes, "in my English and American literature undergraduate education or in my entire public school education had any teacher ever used (or even mentioned) a work of fiction or poetry by a Chinese American or any Asian American writer." This observation could be made by all the editors of The HarperCollins Literary Mosaic Series: Al Young for *African American Literature*, Gerald Vizenor for *Native American Literature*, Nicolas Kanellos for *Hispanic American Literature*, and of course Shawn Wong for *Asian American Literature*. They had to go outside of the academy—which has committed an intellectual scandal by excluding these major traditions of our common American heritage.

The Series Editors: Pioneers for an Inclusive Tradition

These editors are among the architects of a more inclusive tradition. Indeed, this series is unique because the four editors are not only writers and scholars in their own right but are among the pioneers of American literature of the latter part of this century! It's hard to imagine a list of talented insiders who are as informed about the currents and traditions of their ethnic literatures as the editors of The HarperCollins Literary Mosaic Series. These texts provide teachers with an opportunity to employ material in their classrooms that has been chosen by writers who have not only participated in the flowering of their literatures but also have assisted in the establishment of a tradition for their literatures.

Al Young

Al Young is a multitalented artist who has distinguished himself as a poet, novelist, screenwriter, editor, and writing instructor. His presence is very much in demand at writing workshops and conferences. He has taught at a number of universities and colleges, including Stanford University, Crown College, the University of California at Berkeley, the University of California at Santa Cruz, Rice University, and most recently at the University of Michigan. Among his honors are a Wallace Stegner Writing Fellowship, a Joseph Henry Jackson Award, a Guggenheim Fellowship, an American Book Award, and a PEN/Library of Congress Award for Short Fiction. Al Young and I were editors of the Yardbird Reader series, which has been recognized as the first national publication of its kind devoted to presenting new multicultural literature.

Gerald Vizenor

Pulitizer Prize–winner N. Scott Momaday has said that Gerald Vizenor "has made a very significant contribution to Native American letters and also to American literature in general. He's innovative, he has the richest sense of humor of anyone I know, and in addition he's the most articulate person—he's a man to be reckoned with." Among his innovative novels are *Heirs of Columbus* and *Griever: An American Monkey King in China*. An American Book Award winner, Vizenor insists that the story of Native Americans in the United States should be told by Native Americans and not by intermediaries or translators. His *Native American Literature* anthology in The HarperCollins Literary Mosaic Series will provide students and readers with an entirely different slant on Native American literature from the one they have become accustomed to in standard texts.

Nicolás Kanellos

Author of a number of scholarly works and articles, Nicholás Kanellos is the founder and director of Arte Público Press, the oldest and largest publisher of United States Hispanic literature, as well as the *Americas Review* (formerly *Revista Chicano-Reguena*), the oldest and most respected magazine of United States Hispanic literature and art. A full professor at the University of Houston, he is a fellow of the Ford, Lilly, and Gulbenkian foundations and of the National Endowment for the Humanities. He is also the winner of an American Book Award and is a formidable essayist with an unrivaled knowledge of the intersections of African, European, and Native American cultures.

Shawn Wong

It is not surprising that Shawn Wong and Frank Chin, Lawson Inada, and Jeffery Chan have become known as "the four horsemen of Asian American literature" by both their admirers and detractors. One wonders how Asian American literature would look without their efforts. It was they who began the painstaking construction of a tradition whose existence had been denied by the academy. In *Aiiieeee! An Anthology of Asian American Writers* and its successor, *The Big Aiiieeeee! An Anthology of Chinese American and Japanese American Literature*, the four editors gave permanent status to an Asian American literary tradition. Wong is also the author of *Homebase*, the first novel published in the United States by an American-born Chinese male. This novel received the Pacific Northwest Booksellers Award for Excellence and the Fifteenth Annual Governor's Writer's Day Award. Among his many other honors, Wong has also received a fellowship from the National Endowment for the Arts. He has taught writing at the University of Washington since 1984.

Remapping Our Tradition

Although the four editors are from different backgrounds, the issues raised in their introductions are those with which a few generations of multicultural scholars, writers, and artists have grappled. With *African American Literature*, Al Young has both a literary and humanistic purpose. He believes that readers and writers will be able to learn from their exposure to some of the best writing in the United States that there are experiences all of us share with the rest of humanity. Like the classic critic F. R. Leavis, Al Young believes that writing can make people better. The writers included in Gerald Vizenor's *Native American Literature* are not outsiders writing about Native Americans or colonial settlers promoting the forest as a tough neighborhood full of high-risk people, a threat to civilized enclaves, but rather works by Native Americans themselves, beginning in 1829 with William Apess's autobiography, *A Son of the Forest*. Nicholás Kanellos's *Hispanic American Literature* represents a literary tradition, part European and part African, that existed in the Americas prior to the arrival of the English. The situation in Asian American literature, one of the youngest of American literatures, is as turbulent as that of the atmosphere surrounding a new star. Shawn Wong's introduction addresses the continuing debate over issues about what constitutes Asian American literature and the role of the Asian American writer.

The books in The HarperCollins Literary Mosaic Series give a sampling of the outstanding contributions from writers in the past as well as the range of American writing that is being written today. And the anthologies in this series contain a truly representative sampling of African American, Native American, Hispanic American, and Asian American writing at the end of this century so that students can become acquainted with more than the few European and European Americans covered by traditional texts or the same lineup of token ethnic writers found in the policy issue multicultural books. It should be welcome news to instructors looking for new ways to teach that such a distinguished group committed themselves to producing three-to-five-hundred-page textbooks that can either be used as the primary text in a course, supplemented with novels, combined for a single class, or used to supplement other texts that don't have the desired coverage of ethnic literature. While each book is designed to be brief enough for flexible uses in the classroom, each volume does represent the breadth of major literary genres (autobiography, fiction, poetry, and drama) that characterizes the literary contribution of each tradition, even if—as in the case of drama—the short format of the series would accommodate only a single example. The four volumes of The HarperCollins Literary Mosaic Series constitute nothing less than a new start for those who are interested in remapping our writing traditions.

Writing for Our Lives

The genius of the United States is not best or most in its executives or legislatures, nor in its ambassadors or authors or colleges or churches or parlors, nor even in its newspapers or inventors ... but always most in the common people. Their manners, speech, dress, friendships—the freshness and candor of their physiognomy—the picturesque looseness of their carriage ... their deathless attachment to freedom (Walt Whitman, "Leaves of Grass," 1855 Preface).

Whitman said that these qualities and others await the "gigantic and generous treatment worthy of it." Though American authors from the eighteenth century to the present day have talked about a body of writing that would be representative of these attributes of democracy, one could argue that "the gigantic and generous treatment worthy of it" is a recent and critical development because until recently many points of view have been excluded from United States literature. The Literary Mosaic Series also demonstrates that, for authors of a multicultural heritage, literature often provides an alternative to the images of their groups presented by an often-hostile media.

Of all the excellent comments made by Al Young in his introduction, one is crucial and strikes at the heart of why the writing is so varied in The HarperCollins Literary Mosaic Series. He writes,

> and if you think people are in trouble who buy the images of who they are from the shallow, deceitful versions of themselves they see in mass media, think what it must feel like to be a TV-watching African-American male. Pimp, thug, mugger, drug dealer, crackhead, thief, murderer, rapist, absentee father, welfare cheat, convict, loser, ne'er-do-well, buffoon. Think of these negative images of yourself broadcast hourly all over the globe.

When African Americans, Native Americans, Hispanic Americans, and Asian Americans write, they're not just engaging in a parlor exercise—they are writing for their lives. The twentieth century has shown that unbalanced images can cost groups their lives. That is why The HarperCollins Literary Mosaic Series came to be—to trumpet these lives, lives that are our national heritage. And once these voices have been heard, there is no turning back.

Acknowledgments

This is a series that has been taken the time, talents, and enthusiasm of its editors—Al Young, Gerald Vizenor, Nicolás Kanellos, and Shawn Wong—and I am excited that they chose to be a part of this project. In addition, the editors and I wish to thank those people who helped us prepare the series, particularly those instructors who reviewed this material in various drafts and offered their expertise and suggestions for making the books in this series even more useful to them and their students: Joni Adamson Clarke, University of Arizona; Herman Beavers, University of Pennsylvania; A. Lavonne Brown Ruoff, University of Illinois at Chicago; William Cain, Wellesley

College; Rafel Castillo, Palo Alto College; Jeffrey Chan, San Francisco State University; King-Kok Cheung, University of California at Los Angeles; Patricia Chu, George Washington University; Robert Combs, George Washington University; Mary Comfort, Moravian College; George Cornell, Michigan State University; Bruce Dick, Appalachian State University; Elinor Flewellen, Santa Barbara City College; Chester Fontineau, University of Illinois at Champaign-Urbana; Sharon Gavin Levy, University of Minnesota at Duluth; Shirley Geok-Lin Lim, University of California at Santa Barbara; Tom Green, Northeastern Junior College; James Hall, University of Illinois at Chicago; Lynda M. Hill, Temple University; Lane Hirabayashi, University of Colorado; Gloria Horton, Jacksonville State University; Ketu H. Katrak, University of Massachusetts at Amherst; Josephine Lee, Smith College; Russell Leong, University of California at Los Angeles; Michael Liberman, East Stroudsberg University; Paulino Lim, Jr., California State University at Long Beach; Kenneth Lincoln, University of California at Los Angeles; Marcus "C" Lopez, Solano Community College; Shirley Lumpkin, Marshall University; Barbara McCaskill, University of Georgia; Nelly McKay, University of Wisconsin at Madison; Lucy Maddox, Georgetown University; Thomas Matchie, North Dakota State University; Joyce Middleton, University of Rochester; Alice Moore, Yakima Valley Community College; Eric Naylor, University of the South; Jon Olson, Oregon State University at Corvallis; Ernest Padilla, Santa Monica College; David Payne, University of Georgia; Joyce Pettis, North Carolina State University; David Robinson, Winona State University; Don Rothman, Oakes College, University of California at Santa Cruz; Leonard A. Slade, Jr., State University of New York at Albany; Stephen Sumida, University of Michigan; Brian Swann, Cooper Union; John Trimbur, Worcester Polytechnical Institute; Hari Vishwanadha, Santa Monica College; Marilyn Nelson Waniek, University of Connecticut; Shelly Wong, Cornell University; Jackie Valdez, Caspar College; Richard Yarborough, University of California at Los Angeles.

Introduction

At this juncture in history, most academic and popular readers assume that Hispanic literature of the United States is a current phenomenon, having emerged during the last twenty-five years or so as an expression of Hispanic peoples' accepting and solidifying their "American" identity. In fact, the opposite is true: there was Hispanic literature in existence north of the Rio Grande before the United States was ever founded, and it was the political and geographic expansion of the United States that eventually resulted in the Hispanic literary tradition becoming encompassed within territories and states of the United States. But even in the nascent American republic, there were already Hispanic publications and literature as early as the 1820s, most notably purveyed by Spanish-language newspapers in New York City, Philadelphia, and New Orleans.

Forgotten Voices: Spanish-Language Literature in the Historical Past

The expansion of the American republic southward and westward was not accompanied by a willingness to recognize and incorporate the cultural patrimony of peoples living in those lands, except for the utilitarian appropriation and even usurpation of such technologies as farming, ranching, and mining. Consequently, much of the Hispanic literary tradition was suppressed, has been lost forever, or remains inaccessible to most readers and educators. Even today in intellectual circles of the United States an ignorance reigns regarding the earliest and most continuous history of literacy, writing, printing, and publishing in North America. The history of the book in North America, including that portion of our country that includes the Southeast and the Southwest, follows a trajectory of south to north, not east to west.

The general populace—and many teachers for that matter—may not be aware that the roots of Hispanic culture go deep even into such areas as New York City while it was still New Amsterdam and receiving exiled Spanish Jews. Or that the first highly literary book-length description of what eventually became the American South and Southwest was published as early as 1542 in Zamora, Spain: Alvar Núñez Cabeza de Vaca's *Account*. Or that the first epic poems written in a European language about colonizing these new and exciting lands were written in the late sixteenth century in Spanish by men of the pen, the cross, and the sword: Father Alonso Gregorio de Escobedo wrote *La Florida* and the Spanish soldier Gaspar Pérez de Villagrá wrote *La conquista de la Nueva México* (The Conquest of New Mexico). Few have considered the really good reasons for identifying works written in the Native American languages and Spanish as the true and authentic beginnings of the literature of the United States.

Hispanic literature, a literature created by the people proudly emerging from the fusion of Spanish, Native American, and African cultures, has always been part of the mosaic of the United States. True, only recently has there been any attempt to acknowledge Hispanicism as part of the national identity and as contributing to the national art and culture. But consider that, when the first English-language minstrels reached California, there were already full-fledged Spanish-language theatrical companies performing the high drama of Spain and the Americas. Spanish was the language of the first printing presses in the Southwest and of the first newspapers in Arizona, California, New Mexico, and Texas. But from the early 1820s on, Spanish-language periodicals publishing volumes of serialized novels, poetry, and short stories had also been firmly established outside of the Southwest as mentioned above. These periodicals established a tradition of publishing literary works that survived unbroken until after World War II. In retrospect, we can see that these publications disseminated and preserved an important body of Hispanic American literature that was developing at the same time that the works of Longfellow, Poe, Melville, and Twain were becoming the basis for an official "national" literature, one that was striving to develop a separate identity from the letters of the "mother country" England.

From the second half of the nineteenth century, Hispanics also began writing in English. Few of the works from this period in English or those many more in Spanish from the nineteenth and early twentieth centuries are currently available. Many have been lost forever, mainly because the writings of non-English-speaking citizens and immigrants were ignored and not deemed worthy of preservation by librarians, educators, and academicians. The literary expressions of the Hispanic *literate* and literarily oriented population were never collected, preserved, or made accessible to the broader society through the schools, libraries, and mainstream publishers, much less the oral literature of this period. How could the very institutions that were furthering the notion that barbarism existed west of the Mississippi and in the poor Spanish colonies of Cuba, Puerto Rico, and Santo Domingo further the idea of a thinking, sensitive, creative mestizo or mulatto culture? The racially degraded and impure Spanish-Native American-African cultures were anathema to Anglo-Americans. The whole ideology of expansion—the idea of Manifest Destiny—depended on an uncivilized, barbarous population in the lands colonized by Spain. How could the very same publishing industry that was enriching itself through dime-novel portrayals of the mongrel, heathen, and immoral Mexican, Hispanic, and dark races invest in a literature that was not supposed to exist in the first place much less exist in Spanish, a foreign tongue bastardized by racial mixing! The idea that Hispanic residents of the United States could write the King's English was, of course, even more far-fetched, out of the question and ludicrous—an idea which still strains credulity in many intellectual circles today as demonstrated by the genuine surprise in reviews across the country that greeted Richard Rodriguez's elegant prose in *Hunger of Memory*.

The Birth, Expansion, and Influence of Contemporary Hispanic American Literature

All of the above notwithstanding, Hispanic writing in English in the United States does go back to the mid–nineteenth century. But even in the 1920s when some Spanish-surname writers were breaking into such mainstream magazines as *Harpers,* and the *Saturday Evening Post,* there was no wholesale awareness of a Hispanic literary presence or heritage other than as some fanciful, picturesque curio of a romanticized Spanish past in California, Florida, and New Mexico. It took the broad civil rights and student movements in the 1960s, bent on reforming government, politics, and especially education, to begin to awaken the intellectual and literary establishment to the potential of Hispanic culture—what was called back then "the sleeping giant." And following the establishment in the early 1970s of ethnic studies programs, bilingual education, and a massive entry of Hispanics into colleges, mainstream presses rushed to publish a plethora of anthologies that spoke to the newsworthy moment of national strikes and boycotts by farmworkers, grassroots organizations, and militant political movements such as the Raza Unida Party, the Brown Berets, and the Young Lords Party. But, this interest from publishers and the popular media was as transitory as the headlines, and once again Hispanic culture slipped away from the national conscience.

It was really during the 1980s with the growing awareness in the media and business communities of burgeoning Hispanic populations, school enrollments, market potential, and voting power that finally a demand or "market" was identified for a literary culture that had always existed. Communities, schools and libraries began clamoring for materials that would better relate to their local constituents. It is true that Hispanics rapidly became and are becoming the majority population in the largest school systems and urban centers. And projections for the turn of the century suggest that the most populous states will be at least one-third Hispanic. But mainstream publishing, one of the last industries to recognize the potential of a Hispanic market and one of the most conservative segments of the "culture industry," has been unprepared and reluctant to serve this market and has abdicated its leadership to small grassroots and ethnic publishers and university-based presses such as Arte Público Press, Bilingual Review Press, Tonatiuh/Quinto Sol, and Editorial Universal, among many others.

It is from this base that the most noteworthy Hispanic writers have arisen. It is from this base only that an anthology such as this can be offered. Hispanic literature in the United States today thrives, for the most part, in academia and at the community level. Even though a writer supported by this base has won the Pulitzer Prize, little of this literature is available through bookstores or even libraries, where acquisitions often are haphazard and/or targeted exclusively for specific branches in Hispanic communities.

It is the hope of the editor and HarperCollins that the present anthology will assist in introducing Hispanic writers to broader audiences. It is the function of the entire Literary Mosaic Series to acquaint the United States with its true cultural base and the importance of creating a national identity out of its cultural diversity. Our desires are not based on a fad or a whim. This text and this series are an effort to provide the material that will awaken the country from its own "fantasy heritage" of a monocultural and monolithic past. Postcolonialist ideology and all forms of intellectual and creative apartheid are just as doomed in the world of tomorrow as are economic independence and militaristic superpowers. Just like the Soviet Union, we are certain to disintegrate as a country along the lines of rampant nationalism and racism unless we build on the strength of our pluralism. Only the United States has the ethnic base and the potential within its own boundaries to sympathize with and communicate with most of the peoples of the world. As a people whose ethnic and cultural makeup combines the heritages of Europe, Africa, and the Americas (some Spanish-speaking countries even have an Asiatic base), Hispanics are uniquely positioned to be the mediators of hemispheric and even global cultural and commercial transactions for the United States. As we move into a transnational world of European integration, the North American Free Trade Agreement, and many more such initiatives, our transnational peoples, our bilingual and multicultural literature, and the vision that literature bestows on the reader will become more crucial in identifying a place for the United States in the political, economic, and cultural geography of the twenty-first century.

Finding a Voice: The Lineage of Modern Writers

In the pages that follow, we have made an effort to bring together some of the most representative voices of contemporary Hispanic literature in the United States. Included are such pioneers as Tomás Rivera and Rolando Hinojosa, whose literary works and missionary proselytizing for a literary identity are greatly responsible for the creation of a Chicano canon. Despite their doctorates and careers at the highest levels of academia, in the early Chicano literary movement of the late 1960s and early 1970s their works were essential to creating a modern literary voice for small-town folk and even illiterate migrant workers. Their novels, stories, and poems led the way in creating a working-class identity and aesthetic for all Hispanic writers in the United States, an identity that recognizes that most Hispanics are still part of the working class in the fields or factories. This forging of a unique identity and style was accomplished in great part by close attention to the nuances and spirit of the language spoken every day, an attention reflected by the extensive bilingual work of both writers.

Other seeds of Chicano bilingual poetry were sown in the late 1960s and early 1970s, by an academic poet and by a prison poet, working in parallel in the Chicano civil rights struggle, and the student movements. Ricardo Sánchez began his prolific, outpouring while still behind bars; he drew from the tradition of oral performance and the lyricism that has always been a part of Hispanic popular culture in statements of love and protest. His success in having numerous volumes published and circulated both regionally and nationally, as well as his omnipresence in the civil rights struggles during the 1970s, served to inspire hundreds of barrio poets and performers to make poetry the most cultivated and influential literary genre among Chicanos. Alurista (Alberto Baltasar Urista), on the other hand, was a precocious student leader during this time and a talented scholar of pre-Columbian literature. He merged grassroots orality and performance with innovative written works created from within a historical and cultural framework that included Mayan and Nahuatl approaches along with English and Spanish models. Alurista took the bilingualism characteristic of Hispanic barrios and converted it into a literary language that explored all of the aesthetic possibilities of merging two cultures and linguistic codes. Some of his work is even trilingual in its evocation of pre-Columbian mythology and expression.

During the 1970s, women's voices began to break into print through Chicano literary magazines and oral performance as well. Most noteworthy were the contributions of Evangelina Vigil-Piñón and Lorna Dee Cervantes. The former really consumated the wedding of popular culture and sophisticated verse within the bilingual framework of her evocation of the San Antonio of her youth, while the latter inserted Chicano literature into feminist discourse through acutely sharp and well crafted English-language poems. While Alurista and Sánchez had access to book publication early on, Vigil-Piñón and Cervantes were limited during the 1970s to oral performance and to publication in small magazines such as *Caracol, Mango,* and *Revista Chicano-Riqueña,* which is now the *Americas Review.* It was not until the 1980s that they were able to publish their award-winning books—although they were very well known and influential among Chicano and Puerto Rican poets during the previous decade.

Contemporary Puerto Rican literature in the United States, nee Nuyorican writing, also made its appearance in the 1960s with a definite proletarian identity. But it was the urbanized culture of the children of dislocated tropical peasants that gave rise to a dynamic literature of oral performance based on folklore and popular culture as only a great cosmopolitan center can blend them into a kaleidoscope of sophisticated media manipulation and unschooled expression. Piri Thomas's passionate multivolume autobiographies in the poetic language of the streets and Nicholasa Mohr's developmental novel *Nilda* and her bittersweet sketches of family and community life in El Barrio (East Harlem) led the way toward the establishment of a new cultural and literary Nuyorican identity. This identity was as hip and sophisticated as the Big Apple itself and as alienated and seethingly revolutionary as shouts from urban labor camps and prisons. Miguel Piñero and the Nuyorican group of poets, some of whom were outlaws in the literal as well as figurative sense, embellished on the theme of urban marginalization and repression and made it the threatening dynamic of their bilingual poetry and drama. In so doing, they created a style and ideology that still dominates urban Hispanic writing today: working-class, unapologetic, and proud of its lack of schooling and polish—a threat to established society and mainstream literature. It is a literary movement quite reminiscent of Jean Genet, but at its inception totally unaware of and uninfluenced by him or any other "literary" movement.

Nuyorican poets such as Tato Laviera, Victor Hernández Cruz, and Sandra María Esteves did not seek written models for their work. They were far more attuned to and inspired by the poetry of salsa music and the recitations of the bards and town poets that had always performed news, history, and love songs in the public plazas and festivals of small-town Puerto Rico. In capturing the sights and sounds of their "urban pastoral," it was an easy, and natural step to cultivating bilingual poetry, to capturing the bilingual-bicultural reality that surrounded them, and reintroducing their works into the communities through the virtuosity that live performance demands in folk culture. El Barrio, the Bronx, and Loisaida (the Lower East Side) neighborhood audiences, made exigent by the technological sophistication of salsa records and performance as well as television and film, demand authenticity, artistic virtuosity, and philosophical and political insight. And Laviera, Hernández Cruz, and Esteves have reigned as masters for almost two decades. That they are accessible to far many more people orally through performance than through publication is no accident or a sign of lack of sophistication; it is their literary mission, their political and economic stance. In fact, it was a university-educated poet, a professor at Rutgers University who also hailed from the Puerto Rican barrios, that stimulated through example and entrepreneurial insight the publication of Nuyorican poetry in anthologies, magazines, and books as well as the showcasing of Nuyorican performance art at his Nuyorican Poets Cafe. As a mentor and outstanding avant garde poet heavily influenced by the Beat poets, Miguel Algarín solidified the Nuyorican literary identity and fostered its entrance into the larger world of contemporary American avant-garde literature.

In the theater, Nuyorican playwright Miguel Piñero's name emerges in the early 1970s about the time that the playwright and director Luis Valdez's plays were developing beyond the early labor theater that he had created in the late 1960s. Piñero was introduced to playwriting and poetry while in prison; Valdez was a migrant worker who obtained a master's degree but reversed his education in the canon by becoming a student and practitioner of folk and political theater. Both writers eventually revolutionized both commercial and grassroots theater by introducing the struggles, passion, and expression of people who had rarely been heard in the theater: Hispanics who were marginalized (prisoners, pimps, zoot-suiters, outlaws) and oppressed (housewives, cleaning ladies, factory workers, farmworkers). Piñero's success on

Broadway and on film, coupled with twenty-five years of Valdez's plays produced and toured by his El Teatro Campesino, reestablished the strength and importance of theater. In Hispanic urban culture, the theater had very much waned in Los Angeles, New York, San Antonio, and Tampa during the 1940s.

As Hispanic theater became more institutionalized in the1980s, there was a return to more conventional forms of drama. Even Mirian Coloón's Puerto Rican Traveling Theater left the streets to come indoors off-Broadway. Hispanic playwrights, assisted by workshops, festivals, and apprenticeships in New York, Los Angeles, and San Diego, returned to writing realism and comedy and musical comedy rather than artistic propaganda. The playwrights, however, still drew upon their roots to use daily barrio experiences as subjects. After cultivating many genres including poetry since the 1960s, Cuban American writer Dolores Prida became one of the leading creators of plays for university and Hispanic community venues. With a thorough knowledge of stagecraft and the standards of the New York commercial stage, Prida has produced everything from musical comedy to melodrama. Alongside Prida there are numerous playwrights cultivating the same broad range of genres in both Spanish and English for the community theaters in New York, New Jersey, Florida and the entire Southwest. For the first time since the 1930s, there is a healthy selection of Hispanic theater houses and programs to support the productivity of these writers.

During the 1980s, a new wave of Hispanic writers emerged, not from the barrios, fields, prisons and student movements, but from university creative-writing programs. Almost all were monolingual English-speaking and -writing: Denise Chávez, Sandra Cisneros, Judith Ortiz Cofer, Oscar Hijuelos, Alberto Ríos, Virgil Suárez, and Helena María Viramontes had honed their craft—some of them at elite institutions such as the Iowa Workshop—under the tutelage of such powerful mentors and sponsors as Vance Bourjuilly, Philip Levine, and Donald Barthelme. After leaving such privileged circles— where their admittance and presence was very much a function of their mastery of the English language, stylistic conventions and literary traditions on exclusively *Anglo-American* terms—they recovered their Hispanic voices and subjectivity rather than just blending into the plethora of characteristic voices and themes.

As can be seen from the above, the history of Hispanic American literature is rich and diverse, even more so if we were to go in depth into the literature produced in the Spanish language in the United States. Although many critics and scholars are unaware of this continuing Spanish-language tradition, it in fact is thriving today, as always, and may account for more written works than are presently written or available in English—but that's material for another, different anthology.

NOTE ON TERMINOLOGY

As with all peoples and ethnic groups, Hispanics in the United States have given themselves various names over time, as their identity shifted and as their social, cultural, and political contexts changed. The term Hispanic is the closest to the Spanish word hispano (short for hispanoamericano) which was and is used whenever Spanish-speaking people of diverse national and ethnic origins interact and live in the same communities. This was true, for instance, in the diverse Hispanic communities of New York that supported the Teatro Hispano theater house in East Harlem during the 1920s and of San Francisco where the newspaper *Hispano America* was published during the 1920s. Hispanoamérica refers to the countries in the Americas where Spanish is the national language. Latinoamérica refers to the countries in the Americas that speak Spanish, French, and Portuguese languages that derive from Latin. Latino, which is short for latinoamericano has also been used in ethnically and linguistically diverse circumstances by Hispanic communities in the United States to refer to all of the groups derived from Latin America. It is not as frequently used as hispano and Hispanic, because it can also include Haitians and Brazilians and other francophone peoples. Hispanic is a term also used by the government and in advertising as a handy way to group the Spanish-speaking-origins peoples of the United States together. Because it is used in that manner, some politicized groups take exception to the term; however, these very same groups misuse the term Latino, even ascribing to it some notion of Native American culture. Despite all of the foregoing, in many circles Hispanic and Latino are used interchangeably to refer to all Spanish-speaking origin groups in the United States.

The terms most used by peoples in the United States to refer to themselves is Mexican/Mexicano and Mexican American/Méxicoamericano. During the 1960s the Mexican-American civil rights, labor, and student movements resuscitated a term that dates back to the early days of Mexican immigration to the United states in this century: Chicano. During that time, the term (derived from an archaic pronunciation of Mexicano: Me-chicano) meant working-class Mexican immigrant. Because the students, laborers, and political workers of the 1960s saw themselves as working class, they began to use the term as a badge of political affirmation and positive identity. "Chicanos" were Mexican Americans with their political and cultural consciousness raised.

A similar evolution transpired when working-class Puerto Ricans born or raised in New York began to differentiate themselves from those raised on the island of Puerto Rico. The ones who were bilingual, bicultural and identified with the metropolis began calling themselves Nuyoricans (literally, New York Ricans). The term later was generally extended to all Puerto Ricans born or raised anywhere in the continental United States.

AUTOBIOGRAPHY

Piri Thomas

(b. 1928)
Puerto Rican

Piri Thomas is one of the most widely known writers of ethnic autobiography. His **Down These Mean Streets** *(1967) was so successful as a powerful chronicle of growing up in the barrio that it spawned a host of Puerto Rican imitators. Piri (John Peter) Thomas was born on September 30, 1928, in New York City to a Puerto Rican mother and a Cuban father. Thomas grew up during the Depression, facing both poverty and discrimination on the streets of East Harlem, where he began a life of theft, gang violence, and criminality. After repeated clashes with authorities, Thomas spent seven years in prison for armed robbery. In prison, he became an ardent reader, learned to take pride in his African and Hispanic heritages and began writing. It was writing that became his salvation since for many years he has been able to earn a very good living as a writer, lecturer, and performer of his works. Thomas has also been an inspiration to youths facing dead-end streets around the country and he has often participated in programs to assist inner-city teenagers. All of Thomas's works are highly autobiographical, dealing mostly with his experience of poverty, racism, and culture conflict. In addition to his highly acclaimed* **Down These Mean Streets***, he has published* **Saviour, Saviour, Hold My Hand** *(1972),* **Seven Long Times** *(1974), and* **Stories from El Barrio** *(1978). Thomas's works are of historical significance not only because they detail ghetto culture in the 1950s and 1960s, but also because they were among the first Hispanic works in English to be published by mainstream publishers, following an authentically American tradition of ethnic or immigrant autobiography. In the U.S. Hispanic tradition, his* **Down These Mean Streets** *initiated and epitomized the search for identity that was to characterize much of the literature during the 1970s.*

Seven Long Times
from

Prologue

Like I'm standing here and nuttin's happening. Diggit, man, what's in this here world for me? Except I gotta give, give, give, give. I'm tired of being a half-past nuttin'. I've come into this stone world of streets, with all its living, laughing, crying, and dying. A world full of backyards, rooftops, and street sets, all kinds of people and acts, of hustles, rackets, and eyedropper drugs. A world of those who is and those who ain't. A world of name-calling, like "nigger sticks" and "*mucho*" spics.

I'm looking at me and no matter how I set my face, rock hard or sullen soft, I still feel the me inside rumbling low and crazy-like, like I'm mad at something and don't know what is it. Damn it, it's the craps of living everyday afraid and not diggin' what's in tomorrow. What's the good of living in a present that's got no future, no nuttin', unless I make something. I fell into this life without no say and I'll be a mother-jumper if I live it without having nuttin' to say.

I know this world is on a hustle stick and everybody's out to make a buck. This I can dig, 'cause it's the same here on the street. I gotta hustle too, and the only way to make it is on a hard kick. I dig that—copping is the main bit and having is the main rep. You see, I'm really trying to understand and see where you're at.

How many times have I stood on my street corner, looking at your blippy world full of pros? At all you people who made it and got to be great, a real bunch of killer-dillers, I know about you. I've gone to the big school too. I've dug how to live too.

Are you willing to learn about me and what makes me click? Well, let me run it to you nice and easy.

Have you ever sensed the coming danger as on a bop you go? A rumbling of bravery, of *puro corazón*,[1] and gusto to the *n*th degree? Have you ever punched a guy in the mouth with a ripped-off garbage can handle, or spit blood from jammed-up lips? Have you ever felt the pain from a kick in the balls? Have you ever chased in victory in a gang fight supreme or run in tasteless defeat with all the heart you can muster? Have you felt the bond of belonging when with your boys you went down?

Tell me, did you ever make out in dark hallways with wet kisses and fumbling hands? Did you ever smother a frightened girl's rejections and force a love from her? Did you fill your dreams with the magic of what you wanted to be, only to curse the bitchin' mornings for dragging you back on the scene? Did you ever smoke the blast of reefers and lose your freakin' mind? Did you ever worry about anything at all—like a feeling of not belonging? Did you ever lover-dubber past this way?

Did you ever stand on street corners and look the other way from the world of *muchos ricos*[2] and think, *I ain't got a damn?*

Did you ever count the pieces of garbage that flowed down dirty gutters, or dig the backyards that in their glory were a garbage dump's dream? Did you ever stand on the rooftops and watch nighttime cover the bad below? Did you ever put your hand round your throat and feel your pulse beat say, *I do belong and there's not gonna be nobody can tell me I'm wrong?*

Say, did you ever mess with the hard stuff—cocaine, heroin? Have you ever filled your nose with the wild kick coke brought or pushed a needle full of the other poison and felt the sharp-dull burning as it ate away your brain? Did you ever feel the down-gone-high as the drug took effect? And feel all your yearnings become sleepy memories and reality become illusion—and you are what you wanted to be?

---

1. pure heart
2. many rich people

Did you ever stand, small and a little quiet-like, and dig your mom's and pop's fight for lack of money to push off the abundance of wants? Did you ever stand with outstretched hands and cop a plea from life and watch your mom's pride on bended knees ask a welfare investigator for the needed welfare check, while you stood there, getting from nothing and resenting it just the same? Did you ever feel the thunder of being thrown out for lack of money to pay the rent, or walk in scared darkness—the light bill unpaid—or cook on canned heat for a bunch of hungry kids—no gas—unpaid?

Did you ever sneak into the movies and dig a crazy set where everybody's made it on that wide wild screen? They ride in long, down shorts, like T-Birds, Continentals, Caddies. Such *viva*[3] smoothies, with the vines—the clothes—like you never ever saw. And, oh, man, did you ever then go out of the world to sit on the hard stoops and feel such cool hate and ask yourself, "Why, man? Why does this gotta be for me?

Have you ever known the coldness of getting busted. . .the scared, hollow feeling of loneliness as you're flung into a prison cell?

Have you ever heard voices inside you screaming *Don't bitch about being busted, turkey—you done broke the law and that's wrong* and had that truth eased off and another voice saying *Don't fret, little brother. How could you ever have done it right when everything out there in them streets was so goddamn wrong?*

So carry the burden with *mucho corazón* and try like hell to make the shadows of the prison bars go away by closing your eyes to the weight of time.

Hard days, long nights. Without a name, a number instead. Your love of color blighted by a sea of monotonous blues and grays. Warmth replaced by cold steel bars. Tiny, bleak cells surrounded by chilly concrete, mountain-high prison walls. Within is lost the innocence of a smile. . . . The leaves that flow are unsalted and the laughter is unreal. The days that eventually turn into long years are each terrible in themselves.

You don't want to hear me. I'll make you hear me.
You don't want to see me. I'll make you see me.

---

3.   glad-handing

Floyd Salas

(b. 1931)
Mexican American

*Floyd Salas is the author of three critically acclaimed novels and an autobiography.
Raised in Colorado and California in a family that traces both its maternal and paternal
ancestry to the original seventeenth-century Spanish colonizers of Florida and the
Southwest, Salas and his older brother entered the worlds of boxing and petty crime as two
of the few avenues open to them for economic survival during the Depression and World
War II. Salas later received a university education and creative writing fellowships that
opened up a new career for him, while his brother went on to one penitentiary and drug
treatment program after another. Never truly far from the underworld and the destruction
of drugs, Salas based his first novels on the drug, pachuco and prison cultures.*

His first novel, **Tatoo the Wicked Cross** *(1967), about a boy who becomes a killer in a
reform school, won the Joseph Henry Award and was called "the best first novel published in
ten years" by the* **Saturday Review of Literature.** **What Now My Love** *(1970) follows the
flight of three hippies after they get involved in the shooting of a policeman during a drug
raid.* **Lay My Body on the Line** *(1978) examines the uprisings at San Francisco State
University in the late 1960s through the eyes of an activist teacher and former boxer.*

His latest work, **Buffalo Nickel** *(1992), is an autobiography that reads like a novel. It
chronicles his dramatic coming-of-age in the conflicting shadows of two older brothers: one
a drug addict and petty criminal, the other an intellectual prodigy. Through intense,
passionate prose, Salas takes us through the seedy bars, boxing rings and jails of his youth
as he searches for his own true identity amid the tragedy that envelopes his family.* **Kirkus
Reviews** *called* **Buffalo Nickel** *a "piercing and eloquent coming-of-age story…
Beautifully written, gritty, and deeply human."*

from Buffalo Nickel

The Water Tower

His big plaster leg took up the whole back seat and he held his crutches next to
him. He was eleven and I was almost two. We were taking my brother Al home from
the hospital, where he had been put after jumping headfirst off a thirty-foot water
tower. I stared at him. He was a spectacular sight to me.

It was the deep depression of 1933. We lived in a mining town called Brighton
and my father was lucky to have a job. He had a job because he was a hard worker, the
best, a deputy sheriff's son who grew up on a ranch and knew how to get things done,
like blow coal out of the tunnel walls with dynamite, so other men could load it.

I remember that tower. My oldest brother, Eddy, who was thirteen and an
intellectual prodigy, swung me around by an arm and a leg up there and scared the

hell out of me. I caught my breath, got dizzy and nauseated and saw a damp, dark spot on the earth beneath the water spout under the tower.

When Eddy came to bring Al home to get a spanking for selling one of Dad's rabbits for a big jar of marbles, Al jumped headfirst from the tower. That's my first memory of my brother Al. It has set the tone for the rest of his life, as I see it: tragic, but with a stubborn streak of survival in it that has denied defeat.

Oh, he was fun, though. He took me to my first movie when I was three. It was in a red brick building across the dirt alley from our yard in the small town of Lafayette, Colorado. He took me right down to the first row, where we sat looking up. I remember being astounded by the size of the big cowboys in front of me. And somebody behind us was shining a big flashlight down on them. I kept looking back and forth from it to the spinning wheels of the stagecoach. It astounded me. I couldn't figure it out. It was real and not real, another spectacular sight.

Next, I remember this little suburb in Denver called Elyria, where my father worked in a packing plant. Al took me to a house where somebody stuck a rake under a front porch and pulled out little warm puppies. Then, he taught me to shoot little green buds off a tree like spit wads. I was still three then. Then, I remember him when I was four and we lived in a red brick, two-story building on Curtis Street in Denver. We lived on the bottom floor.

My birth broke my mother's rheumatic heart, it is said. She had my little sister three years later, so she had to sleep in the afternoons or she'd die. I remember her lying down in the bedroom. I had nothing to do and would wander around the house.

One day, I was rummaging around and I found the black suit with short pants and white silken shirt that my mother used to dress me in when we went somewhere. I liked it and put it on. Since I was dressed, I decided to go for a walk. I wandered a block down to Curtis Park, which was a big park with a swimming pool. I stayed there all afternoon, had all kinds of fun. I remember playing with these bigger boys who carried me and another little boy on their shoulders so we could wrestle and try to throw each other down. We were the arms, they were the legs. It was great fun.

Then I wandered to the other side of the park, where a woman in an alley told another woman I was the brother of Al Salas. He must have been thirteen at the time. I went back to the park and it must have gotten very late, almost dark already. Al appeared. He said he had been sent to find me and that I was going to get a beating when I got home. I can still see him lying down in the grass next to me: dark, wavy hair, strong-boned face, telling me very seriously that I better put a book under the back seat of short pants so the whipping wouldn't hurt so much. I took him very seriously, but the book was too big and didn't fit. I did need it, though, because the next thing I knew, I was running around in a circle in the kitchen, hollering, while my mother held onto one of my hands and switched me. Even then my brother knew how to lighten the punishment you got for being too free.

Al put the first pair of boxing gloves on me then. Some cute little blond kid who lived next door was in the kitchen with me. So he taught the both of us how to box or, rather, he put the gloves on us and had us slug it out on the linoleum floor. And we punched and punched at each other, getting all sweaty and red-faced. I remember it as a rainy day. That's why we didn't go outside. He kept stopping us and pouring hot water on the gloves so we could hit harder. It made the gloves heavier and they splat more when we hit each other. I didn't know then how many fights he was going to get me into during the years to come.

He taught me to tie my shoes, sort of. I don't know how old I was, but I didn't go to school, not even kindergarten, so I had to be four or five. We were living on Welton Street. Our house was pretty and bigger than the previous one, more lighted, too. It must have been cold outside, because we were inside again, and again he was watching me and my little sister. I kept going up to him to get my shoe tied. It kept coming undone. I watched him as he did it. He was getting tired of tying it. I knew he was annoyed. But a little while later, it came untied again. So I sat down and tied it myself and never asked him or anyone to tie my shoes again. He taught me that without even trying. Before it was over, he'd teach me a lot of things without trying, some good, some bad.

He protected me, too. I had a little dog by the name of Trixie, a little terrier. She was very pretty, black with perfect markings. She had a natural white collar around her neck, white feet, a white star on the back of her head, white tip at her tail and a white throat. She started barking one day at some Mexican kids about ten or twelve years old who had come into the backyard and grabbed my bicycle. When she threatened them, one of them hit her in the nose with a Vaseline jar. She started yelping and ran back to the house across the big back yard. I yelled, "They hurt Trixie!"

Al ran out of the house and, with all the neighborhood kids, chased those guys down to the ballpark on the next block, where Al tackled the guy who had hit Trixie. He then held him down and let me hit him in the face for hurting my dog. I leaned over the big kid, who stared at me with wide eyes, and touched him with my little fist. Then, satisfied, my brother let him up. The kid ran off across the baseball field and never came back to our neighborhood. My brother was a hero to me that day, as he would be on many other days.

The next thing I remember is my father taking me to a boxing match somewhere in Denver. As a small child, things seemed to suddenly materialize before me. There I was sitting next to my father watching the Golden Gloves. I was astounded again. Another spectacular sight. I saw a great big brown man get into the ring. Heavy flesh filled him out, rounding him off. He had black hair and black, narrow eyes. He was fighting a pink man who had hair on his chest. The bell rang and they ran out at each other. There was a big thud and the pink man flew backwards and landed on the mat. Everybody yelled and some stood up, then some man on the other side of my father said, "Who's that? He knocked him out." Another man, in a white jacket with a bony face, who was selling beer said, "He's an Indian!" Suddenly the cowboy movies I'd seen came to strange life again. Another spectacular sight. But that wasn't all. Then they brought out Albert, my brother.

I saw him go into the ring and stand opposite some kid with light brown hair who was built husky, like him. I got worried. He looked tough. Then, the bell rang and they ran at each other. My brother hit him, but got hit back. I jumped up on my seat and, standing on it, started swinging my arms like I was fighting, shouting, "Come on, Albert! Hit him, Albert! Hit him!"

He needed all my help, I could see. I forgot all about the people around me and threw all the punches I could, shouting all the time for him, shouting so much my father told the man on the other side of him, "That's his brother! That's his brother!" He said it a couple more times to other people who turned to look at me. Little kid, five years old, standing on a wooden seat, throwing punches for his brother. It paid off, though. When it was over, they raised my brother's hand. I was really happy. He had won.

I found out that he would fight again at the end of the week. I couldn't wait to go see him again. For some reason, however, we didn't. But the very next morning after the second fight, as soon as I woke up, I went into my brother's room and touched him, my eyes wide, my mouth open.

"Did you win?" I asked.

He shook his head and said, "No," then he laid back down, his wavy hair dark against the white pillow, his handsome face looking sad.

I was disappointed and lowered my eyes and shut my mouth and walked out. I was going to be disappointed in him a lot, too.

I did well in school. I could read before I even went to kindergarten. I remember my father reading the funny papers about a little kid my age riding down a snow slope on a sled, screaming, "Eeeeeeeeeeeeeee!" all the way across the page. My father made the sound and followed it with his finger. Picture and sound and letter came together and made words for the first time for me. The corner grocer's name was Freeeee-man. I could see the "e" in the word. I read it out after that. So, when I went to school, I could already do that part.

One night, when I was six, I went out into the back yard with Albert to get a pail of coal for the stove. I don't remember why I went with him. Maybe because my mother didn't trust him out alone. Maybe she wasn't home and he was supposed to stay with me. But when we were out by the coal shed, he suddenly said, "Do you want to go to the Epworth Gym with me?"

"Yes," I answered right away, thinking of another spectacular sight.

So, off we went on his new bicycle. My father bought it new for Al because he had stolen one and gotten in trouble over it. It had cost a lot of money for those depression days of 1937: sixty-five dollars. You could buy a decent car for that, then. He sold all the fancy parts off it, a piece at a time, until it was stripped bare, without fenders even. That disappointed me, too, because it had been so pretty. But off we went across town to the Epworth Gym, which was near Curtis Park, where we used to live and where I had so much fun the day I went for a walk.

We got there and Al took me inside. I remember playing around a while, even though I didn't know anybody. But then it came to be seven o'clock and all the little guys had to go home and the man put me out. I told him my brother was inside and that I had to wait for my brother. It got cold and the man kept telling me to go away. I kept saying I had to wait for my brother. But Al didn't come out. I waited there for two hours before he did. I remember how worried I was that he might run off without me. It was nippy, too, and I got bored, besides.

Al finally came out with all the big boys at closing time. The next thing I knew, he said to this other big kid about his age, "My brother can whip yours!" I looked up at this tall, skinny kid who had come out with the big boys. He was at least a head taller than I was.

They made a circle around us in the dark, with just the glow of streetlights shining on the residential street. "Fight!" Albert told me. I turned to face the tall kid, who immediately smashed me in the nose. Blood spurted out of it and stars filled my head. He almost knocked me down, and then he hit me a few more times. Albert stopped the fight, and tried to wipe the blood off my face.

Finally, when the blood stopped, Al said, "Here!" and gave me a buffalo head nickel. I took it, thanked him and got on the bike again. I was a little guy even for six and I fit handily on the handle bar in front of him. He pumped down the dark streets for a long time. I remember how cold it was and that my nose kept dribbling blood. I liked my brother, though. He had finally come outside at closing time, had stopped the fight, and had given me a nickel.

But when we were almost home, he told me not to tell my mother that we had gone to the Epworth Gym or that I had been in a fight.

"Okay," I said.

"Good," he said, then asked me, "Floyd, could you give me that nickel back? I need it."

"Sure." I handed it over to him.

He'd do that a lot to me, also, before it was over.

Al sure was fun, though. He'd take me with him when he had to go get a gallon of fresh milk from the dairy for our Sunday breakfast of pork chops and eggs. That was fun, walking hand in hand with him to pick up the big gallon glass jug with the thick yellow cream caked at the top. We'd stop and take a sip before we got home, and he'd say not to say anything. I didn't.

Maybe I thought he owed me something for the nickel, or maybe I was just naturally a predator. I remember my older sister Dorothy, who was seven years older than I and two younger than Albert, giving my little sister Annabelle and me dinner. She told us that she was saving a small bowl of preserved plums for Albert far up on a pantry shelf. I don't know. Maybe she thought I was a thief, or maybe she just wanted to get them out of sight and out of mind. In any case, I later sneaked into the kitchen and, using a chair, climbed up into the pantry and took down the bowl of plums. I can still see them, pale purple, swimming around in the juice. I ate them down. I was a sloppy crook, though, because the next thing I knew, Al, my fifteen-year-old boxer brother, was home. And Dorothy, who was a good housekeeper and baby-sitter, was showing him the empty plate. Al was right on me.

"Stole my plums, huh?" he said, and slapped me right across the face.

I yelled and started crying as I felt the blood gush out of my nose again. But he didn't try to comfort me this time, and neither did my pretty sister, Dorothy. I was a crook and, feeling sorry for myself, went into my bedroom, where I stood at the back window that overlooked the backyard and cried for myself, for the sting and the hurt. I dabbed at the blood with my mother's lace curtains. Then I got bawled out for that when she came home.

I told her, feeling full of self-pity, "Albert hit me!"

She said, "You shouldn't have wiped your nose on the curtains, anyway!" She knew I was a thief and didn't feel sorry for me either. That hurt a lot, too. Maybe that's why I never became a thief.

Albert did, though. I sensed it was about him when I came home from school and saw Mom walking back and forth in the kitchen. Her green eyes were all wet and pink as she walked back and forth from the table to the stove while cooking dinner. Her cheeks were pink, too, but they often were, because she had high blood pressure, and her skin would get so pink and white, it was almost transparent. This and the heat of the stove could make them burn. But next to her eyes, her cheeks looked worse, now. She sniffled every once in a while and I looked up at her. But she avoided my eyes when she turned back from the table and stepped toward the stove.

I was drawing on my chalkboard, which was located right next to the warm stove, with the colored chalks my father had gotten me. I didn't want her to hurt, but she kept me out of her world and I didn't say anything. I was well trained. Yet, I knew it was about Albert. He didn't come home that night. Often, he wouldn't be around for days at a time. The world was still a wonder to me. I didn't question its turning. My mother took care of all that. My life was well ordered and I never asked when

Albert disappeared or where my father was when he left somewhere for months at a time. She and he kept the worries of the world away from their children as much as possible. She kept a six-year-old child out now.

Soon after that, we took a Sunday drive to the town of Golden, some thirty miles away from Denver. Again, nothing was said to my little sister or me. But we saw Al there in a blue dungaree uniform, sitting with a hundred other boys out on the lawn, talking to their families in front of a big yellow building. I remember my mother making sure that she gave him a carton of cigarettes. Then, later, all the boys lined up and took down the flag, and we got in our '31 Model-A Ford and drove back through the settling darkness to Denver. I told my father all about how the Indians lived on the plains of Colorado, which I had learned in school, where I had gotten an unbroken string of A's. I never asked where Al was. I wasn't told and I didn't question. But I knew he was locked up, though it didn't look like those reform schools for dead-end kids I had seen in the movies.

The next thing I remember, it was summer. I was eight years old and skipping the last half of the third grade to enter the fourth. I was taken to a ranch near Pueblo, Colorado, called "Pinyon" for the pinyon-nut trees. My grandfather and grandmother lived with their sons in an old, long bunkhouse with only one separate room for them. The house was on land, I heard, that my grandfather had owned before his brother had lost it. His brother had been a college graduate who was county auditor and had power of attorney. He had gotten syphilis of the brain, went crazy and lost the family fortune to his cheating bank partner just before he died in 1927. This was twelve years later in '39. Now, my grandfather worked with his sons as a picking crew on other men's land. I didn't know this. I thought it was my grandfather's ranch and that all the horses were his.

I was surprised to see Al there, with his head shaved bald. It didn't take me long after my mother and father went back to Denver to learn that Al had escaped from Golden Reform School. I found this out because he stole my grandfather's new car for a joyride and wrecked it. Al was always pulling some kind of trick. I liked him, but I must have had some reservations already, because my Uncle Willy saw how much I liked my little dog, Trixie, and, smiling, asked, "Floyd, who do you like the most, Albert or Trixie?"

I looked up into his soft, gray eyes, then at Al, who looked away. "Trixie!" I said, and Uncle Willy burst out laughing.

from   **Buffalo Nickel**

The Boxing Match

My heart started pounding at the sight of the crowd, the roar of voices bouncing off the walls as I stepped into the hotel ballroom in Santa Clara for the smoker bout. To me, it was like walking into the Roman Coliseum. Puffs of smoke floated in clouds over the bald heads, the gray hair, the pink puffy faces and pot bellies, the eyes that were all looking at me!

I was in a new, shiny blue and silver Judson Pacific Murphy boxing robe with a silver sash. I was going to fight in front of a real fight audience for the first time. Al had decided I should box amateur with Babe Figuera's Judson Pacific Murphy iron foundry team, because I had gone to Alameda High School with half of them. Babe wanted me on the team, which was all right. But it also meant that I was going to have to keep boxing Ortega forever. I was afraid he was going to break my nose again tonight.

When we got close to the ring, which was set right on the floor in the middle of the ballroom and padded with mats, I could see Curly Upshaw and Roy, his older brother, a high-class pimp, too, with one of Curly's blond whores sitting on the other side of the ring. Al T. was there, too, in his dark tea-timers.[1] They gave me some support, but their presence also put pressure on me, because I knew I had to fight good for them. I was worried I'd look bad.

I could see them all watching me walk up. They made me feel so shy, I ducked my head and started shadowboxing like a welterweight amateur main eventer I'd seen kayo some guy in Vallejo. Babe had said, "That's the way you should fight, Floyd." Babe astounded me because the guy was so good and so tough. He even looked tough with hair on his chest and beard stubble. I never dreamed Babe would think I could fight like that. So, right now I copied the guy, the way he shuffled down to the ring. I tried to fall into it, get inside myself and keep the self-consciousness and fear off. I did not want to see all the eyes staring at me.

I shuffled forward on the balls of my feet, sanding the floor with the leather soles of my boxing shoes, my heels barely touching, hands flickering with subtle feints, barely suggesting punches, the twist of a wrist and turn of a shoulder for a hook, the knuckle point of my fist twice for two fast jabs. I teetered my head and rocked my shoulders to slip a punch and began to feel good. I slipped inside myself, safe from the crowd for the moment.

---

1.   sunglasses

But I was still scared. I still saw everybody looking at me, still knew they were there. I tried to concentrate on the feeling in my body, and it helped. I floated toward the ring, less a victim now. I could win this fight. I could beat Johnny, even if it was my very first amateur fight ever. I had beaten him in the gym only last week, and afterwards lots of guys had told me how good I looked against him, in front of him. Even Jack Mendonca's fighters said so. I could beat Johnny, I told myself, and squeezed my fists into tight balls in the twelve-ounce gloves. I gritted my teeth and set my jaw. I was going to win! I was determined to win!

I stopped shadowboxing and got scared again when I reached the ring and all eyes turned on me. I stepped through the ropes onto the mats set on the floor and into the bright lights all alone, tense, self-conscious. I walked in a blur to the neutral corner to sand my shoes in the resin box, then back to my corner, where Al untied my belt and slipped my robe off.

Now, I felt naked. The referee was beckoning me. Up close, he was a red-faced man with lines in his cheeks. Johnny stepped up. Babe Figuera, his eyes looking steel-rimmed in his glasses, was behind him, rubbing his shoulders.

With the bright lights shining down on us, Johnny looked like a tiny Atlas, like a miniature body builder at five-three, a hundred twelve pounds. He smiled stiffly at me. At nineteen, there was a toughness in the tight lines of his face from having to work so hard as a migrant farmworker when he was a child. He was supposed to be half Apache and had won every tournament he'd ever entered for two straight years, from boys club bouts to the Golden Gloves.

I could hear the announcer calling Johnny the Golden Gloves champion of California and then announcing my name and weight. But when the referee started mumbling instructions, all I could hear was my heart thudding against my chest: bu-bump! bu-bump! bu-bump!

When we got back to the corner, Al said, "He's going to try and get even with you for the whipping you gave him last week. So keep moving and keep fighting. Don't wait for him to pick his shots. Go get him. Beat 'im to the punch. Keep the pressure on him. He's not used to that."

He jammed my mouthpiece into my mouth and pushed me around to face Johnny at the sound of the bell. I froze with fright for a second when I saw him charging at me. But I caught my breath and danced away along the ropes, fast, running to get time to think. I skipped completely out of the corner and around to the other side of the ring, where I had a safe distance between us and I could see Johnny for the first time, really. Then, when I saw him chugging after me like a little locomotive, I knew I could hit him with a jab right away. All I had to do was beat him. Now I was thinking. Now I could fight. I wasn't afraid. It was just a fight. I'd been in lots of fights.

I was in another world when I skipped out under the bright lights on the balls of my feet to meet Johnny, my body sizzling as if the mats under my shoes were white hot, skimming over them toward him like a water mosquito. My hands were up and I peeked over the gloves in front of my face, my chin tucked into my left shoulder, my arms like two fence posts in front of my face and body, elbows covering my belly. My thighs were slim but muscular and popped out like turkey legs, knots of muscles above the knees. My calves were slim and muscular, too, with ridges of muscles outlining them.

I started firing with a jab as soon as I got in range to keep him off. But I was forced to jump back when Johnny charged with a flurry of hooks, overhand rights and lefts, grunting as he punched. He drove me around the ring, going all out to get me, trying to knock me out just as Al said he would. Johnny "The Killer" Ortega.

But I suddenly stopped and counterpunched with a quick one-two, left-right, and danced out again as Johnny charged in again. He was still throwing hooks with both hands, barely grazing me, only the slightest turn of my head making the punches slide off instead of connecting full force. And as soon as he paused after missing a couple, I leaped back in again with two jabs, pop-pop, then one-two, left-right, and leaped out again as the crowd started shouting.

Johnny chased me, kept coming and trapped me against the ropes, where he threw a barrage at me and caught me on the sides of the head. He kept punching, forcing me to fall inside the hooks and cover up, take the punches on the arms and shoulders and gloves as much as I could. I felt the sting of them on my face, my forehead, my cheekbone, but none were solid.

I could hear Johnny grunting with the swings, feel his weight pressing against me, leaning on me, keeping me trapped against the ropes. I shifted to my left and when Johnny pressed harder, I quickly shifted to my right and shoved Johnny by the left shoulder to his right, spinning out of the way and sending him sprawling over the second rope.

I heard the crowd cry out with approval as I danced back until Johnny was facing me again. Then I went in again, pop-popping with my left, and I shifted back a step to make the countering left miss and shifted back in with a left-right, one-two. I wasn't thinking of what I was doing. I was just doing what I'd been trained to do, what I knew I could do, anything to keep the fear away.

When Johnny charged, I waited and popped him with another jab, but caught one to the nose myself. It stung. I danced away, then back in with another jab, then back out again, out and in, again and again and again, jabbing, jabbing, jabbing, crossing with my right every time Johnny charged, stopping the charge, punching back every time Johnny punched, even when dancing back, throwing a flurry of punches as I backed up, short lefts and rights, all of them crosses, pumping them straight out in front of me, "Bam-bam-bam-bam-bam!" inside Johnny's hooks, catching the hooks to the forehead and temples, not letting any one punch get me in the face and landing every punch I threw square in Johnny's face until he finally backed off. Then I waited, facing him until I heard Al shout, "Go get 'im!" and I leaped in again.

But Johnny caught me with a right hook that stunned me. For just one second my sight blurred and Johnny fuzzed out of focus, and my head went "Bzzzzzzz." I caught another punch square in the face, and I grabbed Johnny's arms, tied him up and felt myself being pushed back against the ropes.

I could hear the excited voices of the crowd and knew I was hurt and in trouble. I held on desperately until my sight cleared and I heard Al shout, "Move! Move!" And I shoved Johnny back and danced away just as the bell rang.

Johnny walked away. When I got to my corner and sat down, I could see him on the other side of the ring, sitting on his stool. I met his heavy-lidded eyes with my own just for a moment. His eyes looked strangely at me. There was a question in them, the quizzical way he studied me that showed he was surprised, that he respected me for giving him, the Gloves Champ, such a battle in my very first fight. But there was no fear in his eyes. Ortega feared no one.

I was clear-headed now, but the rest of the fight was a blur for me. I started jabbing and connecting again, then let go with a sharp right when he started to come in and caught him right on the jaw. I heard the whole hall shout and saw Johnny stagger back, then just stand there staring at me with his arms down, mouth open, looking surprised.

I stared at him. His eyes were glazed. Yet, I just stood there, as surprised as he was. We stared at each other. Suddenly, I heard Al shout, "Go get him. He's all yours!"

And the whole crowd cheered as I leaped in as Al told me, but Babe yelled, too: "Hands up, Johnny!" and Johnny ducked his head down when I jumped in and started hooking over his head with both hands. We slugged it out there on the ropes. I could feel his punches but they didn't hurt me. And I could feel my gloves thudding against his face and body. I could hear shouts. My face was hot and my body was pouring sweat, moving like magic, without strain or fatigue, full of wind and endurance, punching, punching, punching, with all thought of fear and anxiety long gone. Everything was pure intuition, automatic. My whole body was behind and in every punch with fluid, effortless motion, without thought or feeling, firing punch after punch. It was thrilling.

Suddenly, the fight was over. There had been another round but I didn't even remember fighting it. I could hear the crowd shouting and cheering and clapping while the referee grabbed both Johnny's and my arms and turned us in a circle, calling it a draw. It was a draw. Al was in the ring, grinning, taking my mouthpiece out and throwing my robe over my shoulders. I felt a great sense of jubilation, with nervous skirmishes of fluctuating sound beating on my exposed, sweating face like quick blasts of wind. I couldn't think of anything to say. I couldn't speak. I just stepped through the ropes and down the aisle as if I were tip-toeing on air.

Victor Villaseñor

(b. 1940)
Mexican American

Victor Villaseñor is a novelist and screenwriter who has brought Chicano literature to the widest of audiences through his novel **Macho!** *(1973), through the epic saga of his own family in* **Rain of Gold** *(1991), and through the television screenplay of* **"The Ballad of Gregorio Cortez."** *The son of Mexican immigrants, he was born on May 11, 1940, in Carlsbad, California, and raised on a ranch in Oceanside. He experienced great difficulty with the educational system, having started school as a Spanish-speaker and dyslexic. Villaseñor dropped out of high school and worked on the ranch, in the fields, and as a construction worker. After attempting college at the University of San Diego for a brief period, he again dropped out and went to live in Mexico, where he discovered the world of books and learned to take pride in his identity and cultural heritage. From then on he read extensively and taught himself the art of writing fiction. During years of work in California as a construction worker, he completed nine novels and sixty-five short stories, all of which were rejected for publication, except for* **Macho!** *which launched his professional writing career.*

    Macho! *tells the tale of a young Native American's illegal entry into the United States to find work, a story following the classic lines of the novel of immigration. His second publishing venture was the nonfiction narrative of the life and trial of a serial killer,* **Jury: The People versus Juan Corona** *(1977).* **Rain of Gold,** *on the other hand, is the nonfiction saga of various generations of Villaseñor's own family and how its members experienced the Mexican Revolution and eventually immigrated to establish themselves in California. The saga is narrated in a style full of spiritualism and respect for myths and oral tradition, derived not only from Villaseñor's experience of growing up in the bosom of his extended working-class family but also from the years of interviews and research that he did in preparing the book.*

from   # Rain of Gold

The Confession

    "Okay," said Epitacio as he and Juan came walking down the busy street of Douglas, Arizona, "I feel lucky! Let's have a drink and double our paychecks!"

    Juan and Epitacio had been working at the Copper Queen Mining Company for over a month and they'd just been paid.

    "All right, whatever you say," said Juan, feeling good about his brother-in-law who'd returned across the border to get them.

    But Epitacio got drunk and lost both of their paychecks, then he refused to go home with Juan. The next day Epitacio didn't show up for work. Rumor had it that he'd taken off, gone back to Mexico.

Juan wasn't able to support his family by working only one shift at the Copper Queen, so he decided to change his name to Juan Cruz and get a second job on the night shift. After all, he was going on thirteen. He figured that he could hold down both shifts.

But, getting into line that night, one guy recognized Juan. His name was Tomás. He was seventeen years old and he had been in the poolhall the night Epitacio lost both of their paychecks.

Quickly, Juan winked at Tomás, signaling for him to keep still and not let on that he knew him. And it went easier than Juan had expected. Hell, the big, thick-necked *gringo*[1] boss couldn't tell him apart from all the other Mexicans.

"Hey, Juan," said Tomás, once they were inside the smelter. Molten ore moved all about them in great kettles. "You want to make some extra money?"

"Sure," shouted Juan above the noise of the smelter. "Why the hell you think I'm working a second shift? Because I love the smell of wet armpits?"

"Well, then, meet me at midnight on our taco break," winked the handsome young man. "And I'll show you a fine trick."

"Sure thing!" yelled Juan. So they met at midnight and ate together and Tomás explained to Juan the plan. First, they'd put a sack of copper ore alongside the outside fence so they could steal it later; then the next day, they'd sell it in town to an American engineer.

"How much we gonna make?" asked Juan.

Tomás had to smile. He liked his young friend's greed. "Oh, maybe six dollars each," he said.

"Six dollars!" shouted Juan. He only made a dollar for an eight hour shift as it was. "That's a fortune!" But then he thought again and he became suspicious. "Wait," he said, "just how do you know about this *gringo* engineer, anyway?" Juan was only twelve, but he had forty years worth of experience.

"Buddy," said the tall, good-looking young man, rolling his eyes to the heavens with great style, "I got my means." And he laughed a good, full, manly laugh, and Juan believed him.

They did it, and it worked beautifully. The next day they sold the ore to the American engineer in town for six dollars each. But, the following night, as they came up alongside the fence to do the same thing again, the lights came on and they were surrounded by sixteen armed men. The American engineer that they'd sold the ore to had set them up. He also worked for the Copper Queen. They were immediately taken to town, tried, found guilty and taken to Tombstone, Arizona.

"But I'm only twelve years old!" screamed Juan. "And my family will starve without me!"

---

1. Anglo-American

"Sssssshhh!" said Tomás. "You tell them that and they'll send you to a boys' place, and I won't be able to protect you! I got a plan. You just keep quiet and stick by me!"

So Juan stuck by his friend, saying he was eighteen, and that night in Tombstone, he saw what his friend's plan was. When the other prisoners saw them, and they came on them like wolves to rape the sheep, Tomás turned his ass up at them so they wouldn't beat him.

"Not me! You son-of-a-bitches!" bellowed Juan with all his might. "I'm from Los Altos de Jalisco! I'll castrate the first *puto cabron*[2] who touches me!"

That night, shooting broke out in front of the jailhouse, and a terrible explosion blew out the back wall. A Mexican on horseback yelled, "*Vámonos*, Aguilar!" Prisoners ran every which way as a dozen horsemen continued shooting. They had their brother on a horse, and they took off. Everyone else was left standing there, naked as plucked turkeys under the cold night sky.

Instantly Juan took off on foot after the horsemen through the *arroyo*[3] behind the jail. He ran uphill all night. And daybreak found him at the foot of a great mountain. But in the distance, there came a dozen armed horsemen, cracking leather. He took off as fast as he could through the cactus. It was his birthday, August eighteenth, 1916. He was thirteen years old, but the only presents the *gringos* brought him were well-placed bullets singing by his ears. Finally, they caught him, beat him, tied him to a horse and dragged him back to town.

By the time his mother, two sisters, his nephew and two nieces finally found out what had happened to him, Juan was in the Arizona State Penitentiary at Florence, Arizona.

His mother cried and cried. Luisa screamed and cursed and banged her head. Emilia couldn't stop coughing, and his nephew and nieces wept hysterically.

Then, the rich Mexican from Sonora, who'd driven Juan's family to the penitentiary to visit him, asked to speak to Juan alone.

"Juan," said the tall and thin old man once they were alone, "your mother is a wonderful lady. She's nursed me back to health with herbs and massage. I love her dearly, and I regard you as my own son."

Juan almost laughed at the stooped-over old man. Why, the son-of-a-bitch was an even smoother talker than the big bastard who'd converted Tomás into a woman.

"You see, Juan, I have a very high-spirited son like you. And I love him and I'd do anything for him. But you see, *mi hijito* killed a Texas Ranger." The dignified old man began to cry, leaning on his gold-headed cane. "I've been told that it was an honest battle, but the *americanos* don't see it that way and they're going to execute him."

---

2.   damn fag
3.   stream

Juan's heart came to his eyes. "I sympathize with you, *señor*," he said.

"I'm glad to hear that," said the old man, "because, well, I have a proposition to make you. I'll give your mother, God bless her soul, two hundred dollars in American money if you confess to the crime my son committed."

Juan couldn't believe his ears. He felt like spitting in the old man's face. Hell, he only had six years to serve for stealing the six dollars worth of ore. But for murder, shit, man, son-of-a-gringo-bitch, he'd be executed or be in for life.

"Calm down," said the old man, "please, and listen to my whole proposition. After all, they already have you locked up, so how much more can happen to you?"

Juan calmed down and looked into the eyes of the old man who, it was said, owned more cattle in the State of Sonora then the rails had ties.

"Your mother, look at her," he continued, "see how desperate she is. This is terrible time for us *mejicanos*."[4] He went on and on, and Juan didn't curse him and send him packing—as the *gringos* said—but, instead, he listened and looked at his mother and sisters and nephew and nieces over there by the far wall. Finally, Juan pulled down into his gut with all the power of his balls, his *tanates,* and spoke.

"Make it five hundred in gold!"

And so the deal was made, and a new trial was set for the murderer of the famous, Mexican-killing Texas Ranger of Douglas, Arizona. Juan Salvador Villaseñor—known as Juan Cruz—was found guilty and was sentenced to life imprisonment.

The big, fat Mexican cook from Guadalajara was the best man with a knife in the penitentiary at Florence, Arizona. He took Juan under his wing because they were both from Jalisco.

Two years before, the Mexican cook had won a lot of money in a poker game in Bisbee, Arizona. But then he'd been walking home when the three *gringos* that he had won the money from jumped him outside of town.

He was fat, so they'd made the very bad mistake of thinking that he was slow. Two died instantly, and the big Mexican had the third one down on the ground, ready to cut his throat, but the *gringo* kept crying for his life so much that the big Mexican finally decided to let him live on the promise that he'd admit to the authorities the following day that it had been a fair fight. But the next day, the third *gringo* went back on his word, saying that a dozen armed Mexicans had cut him and killed his two unarmed friends.

"So you see, Juan," said the fat cook, "I got life because I was soft in the head. If I'd killed him, no one would've fingered me."

The fat cook found out that Juan didn't know how to read, and he explained to Juan the power of the written word. "Look," he said, "the Mexican Revolution didn't

---

4.   Mexicans

start with Villa or Zapata, as so many people think. No, it started with the power of the words written by my friend, Ricardo Flores Magón. I learned from Flores Magón that if a man can't read and write, he's nothing but a little *puto* weakling!"

And so, there in the penitentiary, Juan's education began. He didn't want to be a *puto* weakling, so he worked hard at learning to read. His earthly body was locked up, but his mind was set free as a young eagle soaring through the heavens. The fat cook became his teacher, and Juan loved it. Juan ate better than he'd eaten in years, and life was wonderful except for the days when his mother came to visit him. Then Juan wanted out. He couldn't stand to see his mother's tears.

A year later, a new road camp was started outside of Safford, Arizona, near Turkey Flat, and prisoners got to volunteer. The big, fat cook warned Juan not to go because there'd be no guards with them at night and other prisoners would be sure to gang up on him and rape him like a female dog.

"Don't worry," said Juan, "I can take care of myself."

"But your reputation of having killed that Ranger won't protect you there," said the big cook. "Believe me, it's been my wing that's kept you from the fate that got your friend Tomás."

Tomás was now being bought and sold like a woman all over the prison to anyone who had the makings for half a dozen cigarettes. They'd knocked his teeth out and painted his ass for better service, it was said.

Juan looked at the big cook for a long time without speaking. "I'm going," he said. "It's my only chance to escape and stop my mother's tears."

"All right," said the big cook, "then good luck to you. And always remember, *un hombre aprevenido*[5] is a man alive. A guarded man is a man who's wary, cautious, and lives life as if he's lived it many times before."

"I'll remember," said Juan, "*aprevenido.*"

"Yes," said the big cook, and they shook hands, taking each other in a big *abrazo* like men do, and said farewell.

Five days later, Juan Salvador was in a Ford truck along with four other men chained by their feet to the bars of the iron cage. Two of the other prisoners were black-skinned, full-blooded Yaqui Indians with eyes as sharp as knives. Immediately, Juan liked them and he found out that they'd been put in prison for ten years for eating an army mule.

Getting to Turkey Flat, it turned out just as the big, fat cook had said it would. During the day they had armed guards on horseback all around them as they worked on the road over the mountain; but during the night, when they were locked up behind the barbed wire fence, there were no guards with them.

5.   a wary man

The things Juan learned in the first three nights were so awful—so completely inhuman—they would haunt him for the rest of his life. Here, men were worse than mad dogs. When he wouldn't let them rape him, they beat him with clubs; then they courted him with flowers as if he were a woman. When that didn't work, either, the big German pit boss and the black snake came at Juan in the night. But Juan was *aprevenido,* and he got the pit boss in the eyes with boiling coffee, but not before his big, black friend cut Juan's stomach open with a knife.

The last thing Juan remembered was the smell of his own intestines coming out of his stomach, between his fingers, as he desperately tried pushing the whole slippery mess back inside himself.

When Juan came to, he was in the tent hospital, and the big German and his friend were tied down to the beds next to him. They were screaming, foaming at the mouth, and straining against their ropes with all their might. The guards had castrated them, and blood covered their thighs. Juan pretended he was still unconscious and laid there quietly.

Later that same day, they brought in the two Yaqui Indians who'd been poisoned with canned food. For two weeks, Juan drifted in and out of death. The German raved and screamed. The big black died. The Indians never made a sound. Then one day, just at dusk, Juan heard the two Indians whispering, and they slipped away. Quickly, Juan got up and crawled after them.

"Turn to stone," one Indian said to him as they got out the door. He did as they told him, squatting down, and they were stones.

The guards walked right by, searching for them, but they didn't see them. Then the armed men saddled horses and took off after them. But they never moved. They just sat there, squatted to the earth like stone, moving a little and then a little more as they went down the mountainside and, finally, took to the creek.

For seven days and nights they walked and hid and ran. Juan never knew how they did it, but they'd turn into stone anytime anyone came near them.

Near Douglas, Arizona, Juan left the two Yaquis and went to church, waiting all day until his mother showed up for her daily prayers. They hugged and kissed, then she told him the news that his blind sister Emilia had died. They wept and prayed for Emilia to regain her sight in heaven. Then his mother got him a change of clothes and Juan took the name of his grandfather, Pío Castro. He immediately signed up with fifty other Mexicans to go north to work at the Copper Queen in Montana.

In Montana, Juan and his Mexican companions were put in with thousands of Greeks and Turks. The Greeks had never seen any Mexicans before and so, when they heard the other Mexicans call Juan "Chino" because of his curly hair, they thought he was Chinese, so they named him Sam Lee.

Sam Lee became Juan's official name. He lived among the Greeks and Turks for two years, working for the Copper Queen Mining Company in the winter, the railroad during the spring, and in the sugar beet fields during the harvest.

Then one day, a huge, brutally handsome Turk came to their camp. That night he stopped a fight between two armed men just by staring them down.

Immediately, Juan took a liking to this formidable-looking man of granite. He watched him set up a poker game that weekend and take everyone's money fair and square. The big man noticed Juan watching him and hired him to clean up the tables for him. They became fast friends. The big man's name was Duel. He told Juan that his mother had been Greek and his father a Turk.

"Here, inside the heart," he told Juan when they went out for dinner, "are the greatest battles a real man can fight. Blood to blood, a war is going on inside me that's ten thousand years old! The Greeks and Turks are mortal enemies! And I'm half and half, just like you with your Indian and European blood!"

Hungrily, he talked to Juan all night long, telling him of Greece and Turkey and the history of that part of the world. It was the first time in all his life that Juan had ever come close to a man who not only wasn't a Catholic, but readily admitted that he didn't believe in God.

Hearing this, Juan opened up his heart, too, and he sadly told the Greek-Turk how he, too, had left God at the Rio Grande.

"I knew it," said Duel, "the first moment I laid eyes on you. I said to myself, 'That boy, he's been to hell and back.' For no real man like us can believe in the puppet-God of the churches. The devil, yes, of course, but not God!"

And so that winter, Duel set up a gambling room in the basement of the best whorehouse in Butte which was owned by a famous English woman named Katherine. Duel made Juan his protege, teaching him the art of taking money from the greedy workmen who drank too much.

For the first time in his life, Juan saw cards as a solid business. He now realized that he and Epitacio had never had a chance in the world to double their paychecks back in Douglas. Why, he and Duel took money hand-over-fist every night, giving free liquor to the big losers and maybe even a girl. And the famous lady Katherine took her share, too. Over and over again, Duel explained to Juan that all of life was a gamble and so, "At gambling," he said, "a real man must be king!"

But there were problems. Especially with the local cowboys who didn't like foreigners taking their money. One night there was a bad knife fight. A big, powerful, raw-boned cowboy was going to cut up a girl that he blamed for losing all his money when, to everyone's surprise, Juan just stepped in, disarming the big cowboy with a number twenty-two cue stick and knocked him unconscious.

Katherine quickly gave the cowboy's two friends each a free girl and the tension broke. That night, after closing up, Katherine called Juan to her private room and thanked him for his quick action. The next day, she had her hair dresser cut Juan's wild-looking curly hair, then sent him to her private tailor.

Coming out of the tailor's shop wearing a new suit, Juan would never forget, as long as he lived, what happened when he saw his reflection in the window in downtown Butte, Montana. Why, he didn't even recognize himself, he looked so handsome and civilized.

That night back at the house, he was taken aside by Katherine once again, who presented him to the young girl whom he had saved. Her name was Lily, and she was beautiful. She was so grateful that he had saved her life that all night she purred to him like a kitten in love, teaching him things of the human body that he had never dreamed.

The next morning, he was taken in hand by the English woman again. They had tea together on fine china, and she spent the whole morning explaining to Juan the mysteries of life, love, women and good manners.

In the next year, Juan and Katherine became very close, and Juan came to respect her as the smartest and toughest woman he had ever known—except, of course, for his own mother—and she wasn't even Catholic.

But then Duel began to grow jealous of their friendship and one dark night, Duel got drunk and accused Juan and Katherine of cheating him out of some money. Juan denied it. But still, Duel drew his gun. The next thing Juan Salvador Villaseñor did was something he'd never stop regretting for the rest of his life. He had loved Duel, he really had, like his own father.

A few months later, Juan got a telegram from his sister Luisa in California, saying that if he wished to see his mother alive again, he'd better come home immediately.

The day that Juan left Montana by train, all the land was white. Only the tallest trees poked up through the blanket of snow.

Both Katherine and Lily stood at the depot, seeing him off. The year was 1922, and Juan Salvador was nineteen years old, but he looked more like twenty-five. He was well dressed, had a moustache, and the aura of a very cautious man, a man who'd lived many lifetimes.

"I'll be waiting!" called Lily.

"I'll be back!" said Juan.

Katherine only watched him go, following him carefully with her eyes.

Judith Ortiz Cofer

Puerto Rican

Judith Ortiz was born in Puerto Rico in 1952 into a family that was destined to move back and forth between Puerto Rico and Paterson, New Jersey. Her father, Jesús Ortiz Lugo, was in the Navy; he was first assigned to the Brooklyn Navy Yard and then other points around the world. After her father had retired from the Navy with a nervous breakdown in 1968, the family moved to Augusta, Georgia, where she attended high school and Augusta College. She later received a master's degree in creative writing at Florida Atlantic University. Cofer was also awarded a scholarship to do graduate work at Oxford University by the English-Speaking Union of America. Included among many other awards were fellowships from the Florida Arts Council (1980), the Bread Loaf Writers Conference (1981), and the National Endowment for the Arts (1989). **Silent Dancing: A Remembrance of a Puerto Rican Childhood** *(1990) has received awards from PEN and the New York Public Library.*

Judith Ortiz Cofer has published poetry in a wide range of magazines and in four chapbooks; she has two books of poetry to her name: **Reaching for the Mainland** *(1987) and* **Terms of Survival** *(1987). Her well-crafted poetry reflects her struggle as a writer to create a history for herself out of the cultural ambiguity of a childhood spent traveling back and forth between the United States and Puerto Rico. Through her poetry she also explores from a feminist perspective her relationships with her father, mother, and grandmother while considering the different expectations for the males and females in Anglo-American and Hispanic cultures. Her book of autobiographical essays and poems* **Silent Dancing: A Remembrance of a Puerto Rican Childhood** *(1990) follows this question in particular. Her novel* **The Line of the Sun** *(1990) is based on her family's gradual immigration to the United States and chronicles the years from the Depression to the 1960s.*

Tales Told under the Mango Tree

María Sabida

Once upon a time there lived a girl who was so smart that she was known throughout Puerto Rico as María Sabida. María Sabida came into the world with her eyes open. They say that at the moment of her birth she spoke to the attending midwife and told her what herbs to use to make a special *guarapo*, a tea that would put her mother back on her feet immediately. They say that the two women would have thought the infant was possessed if María Sabida had not convinced them with her descriptions of life in heaven that she was touched by God and not spawned by the Devil.

María Sabida grew up in the days when the King of Spain owned Puerto Rico, but had forgotten to send law and justice to this little island lost on the map of the world. And so thieves and murderers roamed the land terrorizing the poor people.

world. And so thieves and murderers roamed the land terrorizing the poor people. By the time María Sabida was of marriageable age, one such *ladrón*[1] had taken over the district where she lived.

For years people had been subjected to abuse from this evil man and his henchmen. He robbed them of their cattle and then made them buy their own cows back from him. He would take their best chickens and produce when he came into town on Saturday afternoons riding with his men through the stalls set up by farmers. Overturning their tables, he would yell, "Put it on my account." But of course he never paid for anything he took. One year several little children disappeared while walking to the river, and although the townspeople searched and searched, no trace of them was ever found. That is when María Sabida entered the picture. She was fifteen then, and a beautiful girl with the courage of a man, they say.

She watched the chief *ladrón* the next time he rampaged through the pueblo. She saw that he was a young man: red-skinned, and tough as leather. *Cuero y sangre, nada más,* she said to herself, a man of flesh and blood. And so she prepared herself either to conquer or to kill this man.

María Sabida followed the horses' trail deep into the woods. Though she left the town far behind she never felt afraid or lost. María Sabida could read the sun, the moon, and the stars for direction. When she got hungry, she knew which fruits were good to eat, which roots and leaves were poisonous, and how to follow the footprints of animals to a waterhole. At nightfall, María Sabida came to the edge of a clearing where a large house, almost like a fortress, stood in the forest.

"No woman has ever set foot in that house," she thought, "no *casa* is this, but a man-place." It was a house built for violence, with no windows on the ground level, but there were turrets on the roof where men could stand guard with guns. She waited until it was nearly dark and approached the house through the kitchen side. She found it by smell.

In the kitchen which she knew would have to have a door or window for ventilation, she saw an old man stirring a huge pot. Out of the pot stuck little arms and legs. Angered by the sight, María Sabida entered the kitchen, pushed the old man aside, and picking up the pot threw its horrible contents out of the window.

"Witch, witch, what have you done with my master's stew!" yelled the old man. "He will kill us both when he gets home and finds his dinner spoiled."

"Get, you filthy *viejo*."[2] María Sabida grabbed the old man's beard and pulled him to his feet. "Your master will have the best dinner of his life if you follow my instructions."

---

1. thief
2. old man

María Sabida then proceeded to make the most delicious *asopao*[3] the old man had ever tasted, but she would answer no questions about herself, except to say that she was his master's fiancée.

When the meal was done, María Sabida stretched and yawned and said that she would go upstairs and rest until her *prometido*[4] came home. Then she went upstairs and waited.

The men came home and ate ravenously of the food María Sabida had cooked. When the chief *ladrón* had praised the old man for a fine meal, the cook admitted that it had been *la prometida* who had made the tasty chicken stew.

"My what?" the leader roared, "I have no *prometida*." And he and his men ran upstairs. But there were many floors, and by the time they were halfway to the room where María Sabida waited, many of the men had dropped down unconscious and the others had slowed down to a crawl until they too were overcome with irresistible sleepiness. Only the chief *ladrón* made it to where María Sabida awaited him holding a paddle that she had found among his weapons. Fighting to keep his eyes open, he asked her, "Who are you, and why have you poisoned me?"

"I am your future wife, María Sabida, and you are not poisoned, I added a special sleeping powder that tastes like oregano to your *asopao*. You will not die."

"Witch!" yelled the chief *ladrón*, "I will kill you. Don't you know who I am?" And reaching for her, he fell on his knees, whereupon María Sabida beat him with the paddle until he lay curled like a child on the floor. Each time he tried to attack her, she beat him some more. When she was satisfied that he was vanquished, María Sabida left the house and went back to town.

A week later, the chief *ladrón* rode into town with his men again. By then everyone knew what María Sabida had done and they were afraid of what these evil men would do in retribution. "Why did you not just kill him when you had a chance, *muchacha?*"[5] many of the townswomen had asked María Sabida. But she had just answered mysteriously, "It is better to conquer than to kill." The townspeople than barricaded themselves behind closed doors when they heard the pounding of the thieves' horses approaching. But the gang did not stop until they arrived at María Sabida's house. There the men, instead of guns, brought out musical instruments: a *cuatro*,[6] a *güiro*,[7] *maracas*,[8] and a harmonica. Then they played a lovely melody.

---

3.   rice soup
4.   betrothed
5.   girl
6.   small guitar
7.   gourd
8.   instrument shakers

"María Sabida, María Sabida, my strong and wise María," called out the leader, sitting tall on his horse under María Sabida's window, "come out and listen to a song I've written for you—I call it *The Ballad of María Sabida*."

María Sabida then appeared on her balcony wearing a wedding dress. The chief *ladrón* sang his song to her: a lively tune about a woman who had the courage of a man and the wisdom of a judge, and who had conquered the heart of the best bandido on the island of Puerto Rico. He had a strong voice and all the people cowering in their locked houses heard his tribute to María Sabida and crossed themselves at the miracle she had wrought.

One by one they all came out and soon María Sabida's front yard was full of people singing and dancing. The *ladrónes* had come prepared with casks of wine, bottles of rum, and a wedding cake made by the old cook from the tender meat of coconuts. The leader of the thieves and María Sabida were married on that day. But all had not yet been settled between them. That evening, as she rode behind him on his horse, she felt the dagger concealed beneath his clothes. She knew then that she had not fully won the battle for this man's heart.

On her wedding night María Sabida suspected that her husband wanted to kill her. After their dinner, which the man had insisted on cooking himself, they went upstairs. María Sabida asked for a little time alone to prepare herself. He said he would take a walk but would return very soon. When she heard him leave the house, María Sabida went down to the kitchen and took several gallons of honey from the pantry. She went back to the bedroom and there she fashioned a life-sized doll out of her clothes and poured the honey into it. She then blew out the candle, covered the figure with a sheet and hid herself under the bed.

After a short time, she heard her husband climbing the stairs. He tip-toed into the dark room thinking her asleep in their marriage bed. Peeking out from under the bed, María Sabida saw the glint of the knife her husband pulled out from inside his shirt. Like a fierce panther he leapt onto the bed and stabbed the doll's body over and over with his dagger. Honey splattered his face and fell on his lips. Shocked, the man jumped off the bed and licked his lips.

"How sweet is my wife's blood. How sweet is María Sabida in death—how sour in life and how sweet in death. If I had known she was so sweet, I would not have murdered her." And so declaring, he kneeled down on the floor beside the bed and prayed to María Sabida's soul for forgiveness.

At that Moment María Sabida came out of her hiding place. "Husband, I have tricked you once more, I am not dead." In his joy, the man threw down his knife and embraced María Sabida, swearing that he would never kill or steal again. And he kept his word, becoming in later years an honest farmer. Many years later he was elected mayor of the same town he had once terrorized with his gang of *ladrones*.[9]

María Sabida made a real *casa* out of his thieves' den, and they had many children together, all of whom could speak at birth. But, they say, María Sabida always slept with one eye open, and that is why she lived to be one hundred years old and wiser than any other woman on the Island of Puerto Rico, and her name was known even in Spain.

"Colorín, colorado este cuento se ha acabado."[10] Mamá would slap her knees with open palms and say this little rhyme to indicate to the children sitting around her under the giant mango tree that the story was finished. It was time for us to go play and leave the women alone to embroider in the shade of the tree and to talk about serious things.

I remember that tree as a natural wonder. It was large, with a trunk that took four or five children holding hands to reach across. Its leaves were so thick that the shade it cast made a cool room where we took refuge from the hot sun. When an unexpected shower caught us there, the women had time to gather their embroidery materials before drops came through the leaves. But the most amazing thing about that tree was the throne it had made for Mamá. On the trunk there was a smooth seat-like projection. It was perfect for a story-teller. She would take her place on the throne and lean back. The other women—my mother and her sisters—would bring towels to sit on; the children sat anywhere. Sometimes we would climb to a thick branch we called "the ship," to the right of the throne, and listen there. "The ship" was a thick limb that hung all the way down to the ground. Up to three small children could straddle this branch while the others bounced on the end that sat near the ground making it sway like a ship. When Mamá told her stories, we sat quietly on our crow's nest because if anyone interrupted her narrative she should stop talking and no amount of begging would persuade her to finish the story that day.

The first time my mother took my brother and me back to Puerto Rico, we were stunned by the heat and confused by a houseful of relatives. Mamá's *casa* was filled to capacity with grandchildren, because two of the married daughters had come to stay there until their husbands sent for them: my mother and the two of us and her oldest sister with her five children. Mamá still had three of her own children at home, ranging in age from a teenage daughter to my favorite uncle who was six months older than me.

Our solitary life in New Jersey, where we spent our days inside a small dark apartment watching television and waiting for our father to come home on leave from the navy, had not prepared us for life in Mamá's house or for the multitude of cousins, aunts and uncles pulling us into their loud conversations and rough games.

---

9. thieves
10. "Colorín colorado [nonsense syllables], this story has ended."

For the first few days my little brother kept his head firmly buried in my mother's neck, while I stayed relatively close to her; but being nearly six, and able to speak as loudly as anyone, I soon joined Mamá's tribe.

In the last few weeks before the beginning of school, when it was too hot for cooking until it was almost dark and when mothers would not even let their boys go to the playgrounds and parks for fear of sunstroke, Mamá would lead us to the mango tree, there to spin the web of her *cuentos*[11] over us, making us forget the heat, the mosquitoes, our past in a foreign country, and even the threat of the first day of school looming just ahead.

It was under that mango tree that I first began to feel the power of words. I cannot claim to have always understood the point of the stories I heard there. Some of these tales were based on ancient folklore brought to the colonies by Spaniards from their own versions of even older myths of Greek and Roman origins—which, as I later discovered through my insatiable reading—had been modified in clever ways to fit changing times. María Sabida became the model Mamá used for the "prevailing woman"—the woman who "slept with one eye open"—whose wisdom was gleaned through the senses: from the natural world and from ordinary experiences. Her main virtue was that she was always alert and never a victim. She was by implication contrasted to María La Loca, that poor girl who gave it all up for love, becoming a victim of her own foolish heart.

The mango tree was located at the top of a hill, on land that belonged to "The American," or at least to the sugar refinery that he managed. *La Central*, as it was called, employed the majority of the pueblo's men. Its tall chimney stacks loomed over the town like sentinels, spewing plumes of grey smoke that filled the air during cane season with the syrupy thick aroma of burnt sugar.

In my childhood the sugarcane fields bordered both sides of the main road, which was like a part on a head of spiky, green hair. As we approached the pueblo on our way coming home, I remember how my mother sat up in the back seat of the *carro público*, the taxi, we had taken from the airport in San Juan. Although she was pointing out the bell tower of the famous church of La Monserrate, I was distracted by the hypnotizing motion of men swinging machetes in the fields. They were shirtless, and sweat poured in streams down their backs. Bathed in light reflected by their blades, these laborers moved as on a ballet stage. I wondered whether they practiced like dancers to perfect their synchronicity. It did not occur to me that theirs was "survival choreography"—merely a safety measure—for wild swinging could lead to lost fingers and limbs. Or, as I heard one of the women say once, "there are enough body parts in the cane fields to put one whole man together."

---

11. stories

And although trucks were already being used in most *centrales*,[12] in our town, much of the cane harvest was still transported from the fields to the mill in oxen-drawn carts which were piled so high with the stalks, that when you followed one of them you could see neither the cart driver nor the beasts in front: It was a moving haystack.

To car drivers they were a headache and a menace on the road. A good wind could blow the cane off the top of the cart and smash a windshield. But what most drivers hated was getting stuck behind one that would take up the whole road traveling at five miles per hour and ignore the horn, the mad hand-waving and the red-faced man shouting invectives. In later years this vehicle would be almost totally replaced by the open-bed trucks that were also loaded to the limit, traveling the roads of the Island at sixty or seventy miles per hour, granting no other vehicle (except police cars) right-of-way. The driver would keep his hand on the horn and that was all the warning a passenger car received. Pulling over as if for an emergency vehicle was usually the best plan to follow.

We sucked on little pieces of sugar cane Mamá had cut for us under the mango tree. Below us a pasture rolled down to the road and the cane fields could be seen at a distance; the men in their perpetual motion were tiny black ants to our eyes. You looked up to see the red roof of the American's house. It was a big white house with a large porch completely enclosed by mosquito screens (on the Island at that time this was such a rarity that all houses designed in that way were known as "American"). At Mamá's house we slept cozily under mosquito nets, but during the day we fought the stinging, buzzing insects with bare hands and, when we lost a battle, we soothed our scratched raw skin with calamine lotion.

During the first few weeks of our visits both my brother and I, because we were fresh, tender meat, had skin like a pink target, dotted with red spots where the insects had scored bull's-eyes. Amazingly, either we built up a natural resistance, or the mosquitoes gave up, but it happened every time: a period of embarrassment as pink "turistas," followed by brown skin and immunity. Living behind screens, the American couple would never develop the tough skin needed for Island survival.

When Mamá told stories about kings and queens and castles, she would point to the big house on the hill. We were not supposed to go near the place. In fact, we were trespassing when we went to the mango tree. Mamá's backyard ended at the barbed-wire fence that led to the American's pasture. The tree stood just on the other side. She had at some point before my time, placed a strong stick under the barbed wire to make an entrance; but it could only be pulled up so much, so that even the children had to crawl through. Mamá seemed to relish the difficulty of getting to our

---

12. sugar mills

special place. For us children it was fun to watch our mothers get their hair and clothes caught on the wire and to listen to them curse.

The pasture was a magical realm of treasures and secret places to discover. It even had a forbidden castle we could look at from a distance.

While the women embroidered, my girl-cousins and I would gather leaves and thorns off a lemon tree and do some imaginative stitch work on our own. The boys would be in the "jungle" gathering banana leaves they built tepees with. Imitating the grown-ups who were never without a cigarette hanging from their mouths, we would pick the tightly wrapped buds of the hibiscus flowers, which, with their red tips, looked to us like lighted cigarettes. We glued wild flower petals to our fingernails and, although they did not stay on for long, for a little while our hands, busy puncturing the leaves into patterns with lemon tree thorns, looked like our mother's with their red nail polish, pushing needle and thread through white linen, creating improbable landscapes of trailing vines and flowers, decorating the sheets and pillowcases we would sleep on.

We picked ripe guavas in their season and dumped them on Mamá's capacious lap for her to inspect for worms before we ate them. The sweetness of a ripe guava cannot be compared to anything else: its pink, gooey inside can be held on the tongue and savored like a caramel.

During mango season we threw rocks at the branches of our tree, hanging low with fruit. Later in the season, a boy would climb to the highest branches for the best fruit—something I always yearned to do, but was not allowed to: too dangerous.

On days when Mamá felt truly festive she would send us to the store with three dollars for ten bottles of Old Colony pop and the change in assorted candies: Mary Janes, Bazooka gum, lollypops, tiny two-piece boxes of Chicklets, coconut candy wrapped in wax paper, and more—all kept in big glass jars and sold two for one penny. We would have our reckless feast under the mango tree and then listen to a story. Afterwards, we would take turns on the swing that touched the sky.

My grandfather had made a strong swing from a plank of heavy wood and a thick length of rope. Under Mamá's supervision he had hung it from a sturdy lower branch of the mango tree that reached over the swell of the hill. In other words, you boarded the swing on level ground, but since the tree rose out of the summit, one push and you took off for the sky. It was almost like flying. From the highest point I ever reached, I could see the big house, as a bird would see it, to my left; the church tower from above the trees to my right; and far in the distance, below me, my family in a circle under the tree, receding, growing smaller; then, as I came back down to earth, looming larger, my mother's eyes glued to me, reflecting the fear for my safety that she would not voice in her mother's presence and thus risk overriding the other's authority. My mother's greatest fear was that my brother or I would hurt ourselves while at Mamá's, and that she would be held accountable by my excessively protective father when he returned from his tour of duty in Europe. And one day, because fear invites accident, I did fall from a ride up to the clouds.

I had been catapulting myself higher and higher, when out of the corner of my eye I saw my big cousin, Javier, running at top speed after his little brother, swinging a stick in front as if to strike the younger boy. This happened fast. The little boy, Roberto, ran towards Mamá, who at that moment was leaning towards my mother in conversation. Trying to get to his brother before he reached safe haven, Javier struck, accidentally hitting my mother square on the face. I saw it happening. I saw it as if in slow motion. I saw my mother's broken glasses fly off her face, and the blood begin to flow. Dazed, I let go of the swing ropes and flew down from the clouds and the treetops and onto the soft cushion of pasture grass and just rolled and rolled. Then I lay there stunned, tasting grass and dirt until Mamá's strong arms lifted me up. She carried me through the fence and down to her house where my mother was calling hysterically for me. Her glasses had protected her from serious injury. The bump on her forehead was minor. The nosebleed had already been contained by the age-old method of placing a copper penny on the bridge, between the eyes. Her tears upset me, but not as much as the way she made me stand before her, in front of everyone, while she examined my entire body for bruises, scratches, and broken bones. "What will your father say," she kept repeating, until Mamá pulled me away. "Nothing," she said to my mother, "if you don't tell him." And, leaving her grown daughters to comfort each other, she called the children out to the yard where she had me organize a game of hide-and-seek that she supervised, catching cheaters right and left.

When it rained, the children were made to take naps or play quietly in the bedroom. I asked for Mamá's monumental poster bed, and, when my turn came, I got it. There I lay four or five feet above ground inhaling her particular smells of coconut oil (which she used to condition her thick black hair) and Palmolive soap. I would luxuriate in her soft pillows and her mattress which was covered with gorgeously embroidered bed linens. I would get sleepy listening to the drone of the women's conversation out of the parlor.

Beyond the double doors of her peacock blue bedroom, I could hear Mamá and her older daughters talking about things that, at my age, would not have interested me: They read letters received from my father traveling with the navy in Europe, or letters from any of the many relatives making their way in the barrios of New York and New Jersey, working in factories and dreaming of returning "in style" to Puerto Rico.

The women would discuss the new school year, and plan a shopping trip to the nearest city, Mayagüez, for materials to make school uniforms for the children, who by September had to be outfitted in brown and white and marched off to the public school looking like Mussolini's troops in our dull uniforms. Their talk would take on more meaning for me as I got older, but that first year back on the Island I was under

María Sabida's spell. To entertain myself, I would make up stories about the smartest girl in all of Puerto Rico.

When María Sabida was only six years old, I began, she saved her little brother's life. He was dying of a broken heart, you see, for he desperately wanted some sweet guavas that grew at the top of a steep, rocky hill near the lair of a fierce dragon. No one had ever dared to climb that hill, though everyone could see the huge guava tree and the fruit, as big as pears, hanging from its branches. María Sabida's little brother had stared at the tree until he had made himself sick from yearning for the forbidden fruit.

Everyone knew that the only way to save the boy was to give him one of the guavas. María Sabida's parents were frantic with worry. The little boy was fading fast. The father tried climbing the treacherous hill to the guava tree, but the rocks were loose and for every step forward he took, he slipped back three. He returned home. The mother spent her days cooking delicious meals with which to tempt her little son to eat, but he just turned his sad eyes to the window in his room from where he could see the guava tree loaded with the only food he wanted. The doctor came to examine the boy and pronounced him as good as gone. The priest came and told the women they should start making their black dresses. All hope seemed lost when María Sabida, whose existence everyone seemed to have forgotten, came up with an idea to save her brother one day while she was washing her hair in the special way her grandmother had taught her.

Her Mamá had shown her how to collect rainwater—water from the sky—into a barrel, and then, when it was time to wash her hair, how to take a fresh coconut and draw the oil from its white insides. You then took a bowl of clear rainwater and added the coconut oil, using the mixture to rinse your hair. Her Mamá had shown her how the rainwater, coming as it did from the sky, had little bits of starshine in it. This starstuff was what made your hair glossy, the oil was to make it stick.

It was while María Sabida was mixing the starshine that she had the brilliant idea which saved her brother. She ran to her father who was in the stable feeding the mule and asked if she could borrow the animal that night. The man, startled by his daughter's wild look (her hair was streaming wet and she still held the coconut scraps in her hands) at first just ordered his daughter into the house, thinking that she had gone crazy with grief over her brother's imminent death. But María Sabida could be stubborn, and she refused to move until her parents heard what she had to say. The man called his wife to the stable, and when María Sabida had finished telling them her plan, he still thought she had lost her mind. He agreed with his desperate wife that at this point anything was worth trying. They let María Sabida have the mule to use that night.

María Sabida then waited until it was pitch black. She knew there would be no moon that night. Then she drew water from her rainbarrel and mixed it with plenty of coconut oil and plastered her mule's hoofs with it. She led the animal to the bottom of the rocky hill where the thick, sweet smell of ripe guavas was irresistible. María Sabida felt herself caught in the spell. Her mouth watered and she felt drawn to the guava tree. The mule must have felt the same thing because it started walking ahead of the girl with quick, sure steps. Though rocks came tumbling down, the animal found footing, and in so doing, left a shiny path with the bits of starshine that María Sabida had glued to its hoofs. María Sabida kept her eyes on the bright trail because it was a dark, dark night.

As she approached the guava tree, the sweet aroma was like a liquid that she drank through her nose. She could see the fruit within arms-reach when the old mule stretched her neck to eat one and a horrible scaly arm reached out and yanked the animal off the path. María Sabida quickly grabbed three guavas and ran down the golden trail all the way back to her house.

When she came into her little brother's room, the women had already gathered around the bed with their flowers and their rosaries, and because María Sabida was a little girl herself and could not see past the crowd she thought for one terrible minute that she was too late. Luckily, her brother smelled the guavas from just this side of death and he sat up in bed. María Sabida pushed her way through the crowd and gave him one to eat. Within minutes the color returned to his cheeks. Everyone rejoiced remembering other wonderful things that she had done, and why her middle name was "Sabida."

And, yes, María Sabida ate one of the enchanted guavas herself and was never sick a day in her long life. The third guava was made into a jelly that could cure every childhood illness imaginable, from a toothache to the chicken pox.

"Colorín, colorado..." I must have said to myself, "Colorín colorado..." as I embroidered my own fable, listening all the while to that inner voice which, when I was very young, sounded just like Mamá's when she told her stories in the parlor or under the mango tree. And later, as I gained more confidence in my own ability, the voice telling the story became my own.

Sandra Cisneros

(b. 1954)
Mexican American

*Sandra Cisneros was born the daughter of a Mexican immigrant father, who was from a family of means, and a Mexican American mother. She was raised and educated in Chicago, the youngest and only girl among six older brothers who were protective to the point of spoiling her. Cisneros graduated from Loyola University in 1976 with a bachelor's degree in English and went on to study and graduate with a master of fine arts in writing from the famed Iowa Workshop. Her first exposure to and training in literature was mostly with mainstream models; only after leaving the workshop did she begin to discover the world of Chicano and Hispanic poetry and writing. In 1983 she published a novel, **The House on Mango Street**, made up of short poetic prose pieces written in the ingenuous voice of a young girl that vividly depicts the culture of Chicago Hispanic families and their neighborhoods. Over the years, the book became an underground best-seller and was one of the first books to attract New York agents and publishing houses into the Hispanic literature being produced by the new crop of Hispanic graduates from writing programs. But Cisneros first made her debut as a poet, placing her poems in reviews and chapbooks. Her first true collection, **My Wicked Wicked Way**, was published in 1987. In 1991 Cisneros published a collection of personal narratives and stories, **Woman Hollering Creek and Other Stories** that, coupled with **The House on Mango Street**, solidified her place in the vanguard of Hispanic feminist writers.*

Ghosts and Voices: Writing from Obsession

I like to think one of the circumstances that led me to my writing is the fact I was born an only daughter in a family of six sons—two older, four younger. There was a sister, born next in sequence after me, but she died when she and I were both so young I hardly remember her, except as an image in a few blurred photographs.

The six brothers soon paired themselves off. The oldest with the second-oldest, the brother beneath me with the one beneath him and the youngest two were twins, genetically as well as socially bound. These three sets of men had their own conspiracies and allegiances, leaving me odd-woman-out forever.

My parents would be hard-pressed to recall my childhood as lonely, crowded as the nine of us were in cramped apartments where there were children sleeping on the living room couch and fold-out Lazy Boy, and on beds set up in the middle room, where the only place with any privacy was the bathroom. A second- or third-floor flat, but invariably the top floor because "noise travelled down," or so we naively believed, convinced it was wiser to be the producer of noise rather than its victim.

To make matters worse, we were constantly moving back and forth between Chicago and Mexico City due to my father's compulsive "homesickness." Every couple of years we would have to pack all our things, store the furniture I don't know where, pile into the station wagon, and head south to Mexico. It was usually a stay of a few months, always at the grandparents' house on La Fortuna, numero 12. That famous house, the only constant in the series of traumatic upheavals we experienced as children, and, no doubt for a stubborn period of time, my father's only legitimate "home" as well.

In retrospect, my solitary childhood proved important. Had my sister lived or had we stayed in one neighborhood long enough for a friendship to be established, I might not have needed to bury myself in books the way I did. I remember, I especially liked reading about "the olden times" because the past seemed more interesting than my dull present.

But in school we were also required to take books out of our class library. Since our school was poor, so were the choices. As a result I read a lot of books I might not have read otherwise; the lives of saints, or very stodgy editions of children's stories published in the 1890s—usually dry didactic, Horatio Alger–type tales which I enjoyed all the same because of the curious English.

About this time I began hearing a voice in my head, a narrator—just like the ones in the books—chronicling the ordinary events that made up my life: "I want you to go to the store and get me a loaf of bread and a gallon of milk. Bring back all the change and don't let them gyp you like they did last time." In my head my narrator would add: ... *she said in a voice that was neither reproachful nor tender. Thus clutching the coins in her pocket, our hero was off under a sky so blue and a wind so sweet she wondered it didn't make her dizzy.* This is how I glamorized my days living in the third-floor flats and shabby neighborhoods where the best friend I was always waiting for never materialized.

One of the most important books in my childhood (and still a favorite now) was Virginia Lee Burton's *The Little House*, a picture book that tells the story of a house on a country hill whose owner promises never to sell her "for gold or silver" and predicts his great, great grandchildren will live in her.

Stable and secure in the country, the little house is happy witnessing the changes of seasons and generations, although curious about the distant lights of the big city. The sun and changing moons across the top of the page as well as the alterations in the landscape and dress fashion, make us aware time is passing. Finally, the city that has been growing ever larger catches up with the little house, until she finds she is no longer in the country but eventually surrounded by tall buildings and noisy traffic. The inhabitants move away, and the little house, no longer able to see the stars at night, grows sad; her roof sags and the doorstep droops; the windows that serve as eyes, one on either side of the door, are broken. Fortunately the great granddaughter of the man who built the house rescues her in one of the best moments in the book. Traffic is halted on the busy boulevard for the little house to be wheeled away to the country and settled on a hill just like the one it originally sat on, happy and once again loved.

Wasn't *The Little House*, the house I dreamed of, a house where one family lived and grew old and didn't move away? One house, one spot. I read and reread that book, sometimes taking the book out of the library seven times in a row. Once my brother and I even schemed to keep it. If we lied and told the librarian we'd lost it, we would simply be fined the price of the book, and then it would be ours forever without the anxiety of the rubber-stamped due date. That was the plan, a good one, but never executed—good, guilty Catholics that we were. (I didn't know books could be legitimately purchased somewhere until years later. For a long time I believed they were so valuable as to only be dispensed to institutions and libraries, the only place I'd seen them.)

The Little House was my own dream. And I was to dream myself over again in several books, to re-invent my world according to my own vision. I dreamed our family as the fairy-tale victims of an evil curse, the cause of our temporary hard times. "Just for a spell," we were told, and in my head my narrator interpreted, "Just a spell."

"Don't play with those kids," my mama and papa warned. "Don't hang around with that kind. We didn't raise you to talk like that. That's how *gente baja* behave. Low class." As if it didn't have anything to do with us.

I dreamed myself the sister in the "Six Swans" fairy tale. She too was an only daughter in a family of six sons. The brothers had been changed into swans by an evil spell only the sister could break. Was it no coincidence my family name translated "keeper of swans"? I dreamed myself Andersen's "Ugly Duckling." Ridiculous, ugly, perennially the new kid. But one day the spell would wear off. I kept telling myself. "Temporary."

There were other books that spoke to me. Hugh Lofting's *Doctor Dolittle* series. Imagine being able to talk to animals. Didn't it seem as if they were the only ones who understood you anyway? And *The Island of the Blue Dolphins*, the survival story of a lonely girl who inhabits a one-citizen island. *Hittie: Her First 100 Years*, a century account of a wooden doll who is whisked through different homes and owners but perseveres. And *Alice in Wonderland* and *Through the Looking Glass* for the wonderful way of transforming the everyday into the fantastic.

As a young writer in college I was aware I had to find my voice, but how was I to know it would be the voice I used at home, the one I acquired as a result of one English-speaking mother and one Spanish-speaking father? My mother's English was learned in the Mexican/Italian neighborhood she grew up in on Chicago's near south side, an English learned from playmates and school, since her own parents spoke Spanish exclusively. My father, on the other hand, spoke to us in a Spanish of grandmothers and children, a language embroidered with the diminutive. To give you an example:

My mother: "Good luck I raised you kids right so you wouldn't hang around with the punks and floozies on the corner and wind up no good to nobody."

My father: (translated more or less from the Spanish): "Eat a little bit more, my heaven, before leaving the table and fill your tum-tum up good."

These two voices at odds with each other—my mother's punch-you-in-the-nose English and my father's powdered-sugar Spanish—curiously are the voices that surface in my writing. What I'm specially aware of lately is how the Spanish syntax and word choice occurs in my work even though I write in English.

It's ironic I had to leave home to discover the voice I had all along, but isn't that how it always goes. As a poor person growing up in a society where the class norm was superimposed on a T.V. screen, I couldn't understand why our home wasn't all green lawn and white wood like the ones in "Leave It To Beaver" or "Father Knows Best." Poverty then became the ghost and in an attempt to escape the ghost, I rejected what was at hand and emulated the voices of the poets I admired in books: big, male voices like James Wright and Richard Hugo and Theodore Roethke, all wrong for me.

It wasn't until Iowa and the Writers' Workshop that I began writing in the voice I now write in, and, perhaps if it hadn't been for Iowa I wouldn't have made the conscious decision to write this way. It seems crazy, but until Iowa I had never felt my home, family, and neighborhood unique or worthy of writing about. I took for granted the homes around me, the women sitting at their windows, the strange speech of my neighbors, the extraordinary lives of my family and relatives which was nothing like the family in "Father Knows Best." I only knew that for the first time in my life I felt "other." What could I write about that my classmates, cultivated in the finest schools in the country like hot house orchids, could not? My second-rate imitations of mainstream voices wouldn't do. And imitating my classmates wouldn't work either. That was their voice, not mine. What could I write about that they couldn't? What did I know that they didn't?

During a seminar titled "On Memory and the Imagination" when the class was heatedly discussing Gustav Bachelard's *Poetics of Space* and the metaphor of a house—*a house, a house,* it hit me. What did I know except third-floor flats. Surely my classmates know nothing about that. That's precisely what I chose to write: about third-floor flats, and fear of rats, and drunk husbands sending rocks through windows, anything as far from the poetic as possible. And this is when I discovered the voice I'd been suppressing all along without realizing it.

Recently, talking with fellow writer and friend Norma Alarcón, we agreed there's no luxury or leisure in our lives for us to write of landscapes and sunsets and tulips in a vase. Instead of writing by inspiration, it seems we write by obsession, of that which is most violently tugging at our psyche.

If I were asked what it is I write about, I would have to say I write about those ghosts inside that haunt me, that will not let me sleep, of that which even memory does not like to mention. Sometimes it seems I am writing the same story, the same poem, over and over. I found it curious that Cherrie Moraga's new book is titled *Giving up the Ghost*. Aren't we constantly attempting to give up the ghost, to put it to sleep once and for all each time we pick up the pen?

Perhaps later there will be time to write by inspiration. In the meantime, in my writing as well as in that of other Chicanas and other women, there is the necessary phase of dealing with those ghosts and voices most urgently haunting us, day by day.

Lecture, Indiana University, November 11, 1986.

Notes to a Young(er) Writer

When I was young(er), I wanted to die young, about 30—a suicide preferably—because I couldn't think of a more romantic way for a writer to die than young. And a suicide.

Now that I am *30,* any and all suicidal thoughts that ever entered my goofy head have permanently fled. I want more than anything to live—long enough to learn what I'm doing with my art, long enough so that I can rightfully say I am a writer.

The great Japanese artist Hokusai admitted that at the age of 78 he had learned a little about the structure of nature, but at 80 he would have still more progress, at 90 penetrate the mystery of things, and finally at 100 arrive at a marvelous stage.

I've only been writing since 1974, more or less, since I enrolled in my first writing class taught by a professional writer in my junior year in college. It's true I did write all the four years I was in high school, enough so that everyone knew me as the "poet," fanatically so that, ultimately, I became the literary magazine editor. And yes, I've mentioned in other papers my interviews that I used to write when I was in grade school, mostly things I kept to myself in a spiral notebook—never anything I showed to anyone. When did I talk to anyone and when did anyone ever talk to me?

But those years before that first college writing class, I was more a reader than a writer—an important first step to *becoming* a writer. I was getting myself ready to be a writer with the books I borrowed from the Chicago Public Library, the books I read instead of doing my household chores, instead of learning how to cook or taking care of my little brothers, instead of talking to the best friend I didn't have or the boys who never noticed me. I was reading and reading, nurturing myself with books like vitamins, only I didn't know it then.

What if that first creative writing class had never come around? What if I didn't go to college? Where would I be now? Maybe and most probably I'd still be scribbling my poems and stories in spiral notebooks, not showing them to anybody.

When I was growing up in Chicago, and going to college in Chicago, and not travelling anywhere except on CTA [Chicago Transit Authority] buses and subway trains, but desperately wanting to break loose, I liked to think of my favorite American poet, Emily Dickinson, who lived during the last century in a little town called Amherst and hardly travelled beyond. I liked to think of that extraordinary woman who in her later life never even strayed beyond the house and its gardens, but who wrote in her lifetime 1,775 poems. No one knew she was a poet until after she died, and then, when they discovered those poems handwritten on sheets of paper folded and stitched together, the world rang like a bell.

I used to think of her and she gave me inspiration and hope all the years in high school and the first two in college when I was too busy being in love to write. Inside, some part of me secretly clung to the dream of becoming a writer. But for many years what I didn't realize about Emily Dickinson was that she had a few essentials going for her: 1) an education, 2) a room of her own in a house of her own that she shared with her sister Lavinia, and 3) money inherited along with the house after her father died. She even had a maid, an Irish housekeeper who did, I suspect, most of the household chores. It's true Emily Dickinson baked and sewed for her sister Lavinia and her beloved brother Austin, but she baked and sewed because she wanted to, not because she *had* to. I wonder if Emily Dickinson's Irish housekeeper wrote poetry or if she ever had the secret desire to study and be anything besides a housekeeper.

Maybe she was a woman like my mama who could sing a Puccini opera, cook a dinner for nine with only five dollars, who could draw and tell stories and who probably would've enjoyed a college education but whose only taste of college was reading the books her children brought home from the university. Maybe Emily Dickinson's Irish housekeeper had to sacrifice her life so that Emily could live hers locked upstairs in the corner bedroom writing her 1,775 poems. That's what I'm thinking.

So I'm pretty lucky to be here today. I'm here because my mother let me stay in my room reading and studying, perhaps because she didn't want me to inherit her sadness and her rolling pin.

And I'm here because I didn't marry my first boyfriend, that pest who never gave me any time alone, something crucial to every writer—"aloneness" breeds art—and who couldn't understand why I didn't want what he wanted: marriage and a house in the suburbs. (Always knew I was smarter than him.) He never understood my desire to be a writer, my need to do something for my people. But of course, he wasn't Mexican, didn't grow up poor, and had no ambition to be/do anything in his life other than buy that house, put his feet up and sigh.

In some ways, when I looked at everybody else around me in college—the kids whose daddies were paying for their tuition, their little red sports car and their designer clothes—I envied them. How nice to think of nothing other than getting a job and making as much money as possible. How nice to think of no one but yourself. They didn't have any responsibilities. They didn't feel guilty and sad when they looked out the window of their sports cars and passed the poor tenement apartments of Uptown. What were the poor to them but a burden on their taxes? They had never had pancakes and peanut butter for dinner. What did they know of need?

When I think those kids are now the people changing history, the ones in government and business, altering and making our laws, it makes me sad. It makes me sad because they never feel compelled to change the world for anyone but themselves. No understanding of how hard it is to rise above harsh circumstances. Nothing. Like speaking another language.

But in many ways I feel luckier than them. I can write of worlds they never dreamed of, of things they never could learn from a college textbook. I am the first woman in my family to pick up a pen and record what I see around me, a woman who has the power to speak and is privileged enough to be heard. That *is* a responsibility.

I don't know when I first said to myself I am going to be a writer. Perhaps that first day my mother took me to the public library when I was five, or perhaps again when I was in high school and my English teacher forced me to read a poem out loud and I became entranced with the sounds, or perhaps when I enrolled in that creative writing class in college, not knowing it would lead to other creative writing workshops and graduate school. Perhaps.

I've been writing a little over ten years now, and, if there's anything I've learned, it's how much more I need to learn. I don't want to die young. I don't want to drive fast, or get on airplanes, or sit with my back to the door when I'm in a bar. For the sake of my writing I want a long life. There are so few of us writing about the powerless, and that world, the world of thousands of silent women, women like my mama and Emily Dickinson's housekeeper, needs to be, must be recorded so that their stories can finally be heard. I want a long life to learn my art well, so that at 78 I too, like Hokusai, can admit. "If God should let me live five years longer, *then* I might call myself an artist."

Lecture, "Second Annual Hispanic Achievement Festival," La Cumbre Santa Barbara Junior High School, October 22, 1986.

FICTION

Rolando Hinojosa

(b. 1929)
Mexican American

Rolando Hinojosa is the most prolific and bilingual of the Hispanic novelists of the United States. Not only has he created memorable Mexican American and Anglo characters, but he has completely populated a fictional county in the Lower Rio Grande Valley of Texas through his continuing generational narrative that he calls the Klail City Death Trip series.

Born in Mercedes, Texas, on January 21, 1929, Hinojosa was educated at first in Mexican schools in Mercedes and later in the segregated public schools of the area where all of his classmates were Mexican Americans. It was in high school that Hinojosa began to write, with his first pieces in English published in an annual literary magazine, **Creative Bits**. *Hinojosa left the Valley in 1946 when he graduated from college, but the language, culture, and history of the area form the substance of all of Hinojosa's novels. In 1969 he obtained his doctorate in Spanish from the University of Illinois and he returned to teach at Texas colleges. Hinojosa has remained in academia and today he serves as the Ellen Clayton Garwood professor of English and creative writing at the University of Texas.*

Although he has written throughout his life, Rolando Hinojosa did not publish a book until 1973. His **Estampas del Valle y otras obras** *(which he re-created in English and published as* **The Valley** *in 1983) was the winner of a national award for Chicano literature, the Premio Quinto Sol. From that time on he has published one novel after another that center around the lives of two of his alter egos, Rafe Buenrostro and Jehú Malacara, in individual installments that vary in form from poetry and dialogue to the picturesque novel and the detective novel. His titles in English alone include* **Korean Love Songs** *(1980),* **Rites and Witnesses** *(1982),* **Dear Rafe** *(1985),* **Partners in Crime: A Rafe Buenrostro Mystery** *(1985),* **Claros varones de Belken/Fair Gentlemen of Belken County** *(1986, bilingual edition),* **Klail City** *(1987),* **Becky and Her Friends** *(1989), and* **The Useless Servants** *(1993). His original Spanish version of* **Klail City**, *entitled* **Klail City y sus alrededores** *(1976), won an international award for fiction, from Cuba in 1976, the Premio Casa de las Américas.*

Into the Pit with Bruno Cano

"Hold your horses right there, Father. What do you mean you're not about to bury him?"

"Yeah, what about that, don[1] Pedro—everybody's entitled to at least one burial."

"Not from me, they're not."

"But you're the mission priest, don Pedro."

"Well, don Pedro?"

---

1. A term of respect used for elders

"Listen, you two: you want Cano buried? You bury him. The Church sure won't."

"The Church won't bury him?"

"Yeah, what do you mean that the Church won't bury him?"

(Smiling.) "Listen very carefully: I'm not about to bury him, and the Church certainly won't. Is that clearer now?"

"But you've got to."

"Look! He swore at me, and I'm a priest, but don't forget, I'm also a man—a full-fledged man—of the cloth, true, but a man, for all that."

"Who says any different?"

"Right, don Pedro—you're a man, and a good one—and a friend to Bruno Cano."

"Just hold it right there, you two. Not only did he swear at me, he then soiled—hear?—soiled my sainted mother's good name. Yes, he did."

"The man had been drinking, don Pedro."

"That's right, he was overwrought."

"Overwrought? Over—wrought? See here, the man yelled, shrieked, screamed bloody murder at me. And what did I do? I prayed for him."

"He was drunk, don Pedro. Come on, what do you say?"

"A short service, don Pedro. Shorter than short."

"No... I..."

"Go on, don Pedro."

"Look, we'll all have a drink afterwards. I'm buying."

"Well ..."

"Come on; we've got him over at Salinas' place; we'll take him to the church, and ..."

"No! No church. Absolutely not. No, no, no!"

"All right, all right, no church, then. Tell you what, though: from Salinas' place right to the cemetery."

"And what about the hole?"

"Don't worry about it, we'll get it done in time."

"All right, but listen very carefully, you two: from Germán Salinas' place to the cemetery, and that's it. Now, where's Jehú? I'm going to need him for the response. Remember, now, no church."

"No church."

"Thank you, don Pedro; I'll send someone to locate Jehú for you."

"No one's to know 'bout this. Got that? No one; fifteen minutes, and down he goes to ..."

"Thank you, don Pedro, you're most kind."

"Yeah, don't you worry none and thanks, 'kay?"

The two men left the rectory and headed for the center of town; they neither spoke to nor looked at each other or their fellow townsmen. When they came up to Germán Salinas' cantina, they found that Cano's body was still in the beer locker.

"Good, keep him there for a while longer. We bring good news, as the brother says. We got ourselves a funeral, boys; now, someone call the Vega brothers and tell them we want their biggest hearse, that's the maroon one with the gray curtains, got that?"

"Now, as for the rest of you, you know what to do: get at that hole and spread the word."

Don Bruno Cano, a native of Cerralvo, Nuevo León, Mexico, and a resident of Flora, Texas, U.S.A., a widower, childless, and with no visible or apparent progeny, died (according to the death certificate issued at graveside) of a myocardial infarct that left him like a possum in sull. Now, those who knew Cano au fond[2] said he died of other causes: greed, mostly, and an uncontrollable penchant for skinning his fellowman.

The night Cano died, he and a sometime friend of his named Melitón Burnias had agreed to dig up a plot of ground which belonged to doña Panchita Zurárez, bone healer, midwife, and general gynecological factotum (G.G.F.), and a fare-thee-well mender of pre-owned virgos belonging to some of the neighborhood girls of all ages; virginity is a strict requirement in Flora and thus, we have a simple case of supply and demand.

Now, Auntie Panchita did, in fact, own the plot used for digging, and the Flora types—to a man—said there was gold buried there or near there.

The *relación*,[3] a local usage for treasure, had been there, according to some, since 1) the time of don José Escandón, first explorer and later first colonizer of the Valley, who died with the title given him by the Spanish Crown: el Conde de Cerro Gordo, and whose honored name, etc., etc., 2) since the time of General Santa Anna (Antonio López de, 1795?–1876); Mex. Revolutionist and general; president (1833–1835; 1841–1844; 1846–47; 1853–55). Involved in the War for Texas Indep., the Mexican-American War; and under whose leadership Mexico lost the so-called Gadsen Purchase, not to mention the etc. and etc. and the etc.; 3) since yesterday, a conventional term when speaking of the Mexican Revolution (that grand and glorious Crusade for Justice, whose many advantages present day Mexico now enjoys, etc., etc.) when some greedy-blood-sucking-merchant types who brought gold with them escaping the armies of etc. and etc. And etc., too. Well, the upshot of all this is that

2. well
3. story

one day Bruno Cano and Burnias, a drink-here-a-drink-there, agreed to form an ad hoc partnership as others had in the past to look for the gold that was surely there, had to be there, etc., etc.

The clincher this time was that Melitón Burnias claimed and swore he had recently memorized some infallible prayers for making the earth surrender its buried treasure.

It's difficult to picture more unlikely partners than these two: Cano, plump and running to fat, pink in color, snug with a dollar, and a successful merchant as well as the sole owner of a slaughterhouse called "The Golden Fleece." Summary: one of Flora's most illustrious citizens. Not so Burnias. Burnias was somewhat deaf, on the short side, an indifferent careerist, and

thin and dry/dry/dry

as goat droppings in July.

To add to this, he was worse off than penniless: he was constantly, endlessly, irreversibly poor. He had high hopes, but he also had bad luck, as we say in Belken. For example, when Tila, his eldest girl, ran off with Práxedes Cervera, they were back within the week and, in tandem, the two carried Burnias out to the street and left him there. The man, and this is gospel, shrugged his shoulders, dusted himself off, and went to find a place to sleep, which he did: the watermelon patch. That same night, it rained like hail. Burnias, however, was not avaricious—didn't even know the meaning of the word—which may explain why Bruno Cano chose him as a partner in the search for the *relación;* the prayers came as a bonus.

And there they were, at Salinas' place, the two of them drinking away—with Bruno buying—when they were both brought back to earth by the cuckoo clock: eleven o'clock! Hey! We gotta get goin' here! So, out the two partners went to hunt for their picks and shovels and whatnot to try *their* luck at doña[4] Panchita's lot.

It must've been around three a.m. with Bruno digging and throwing dirt out and Burnias spreading it around the best he could when there came a sound like t-o-n-k! Bruno looked up and then continued to dig some more when t-o-n-k! and he dug some more and that tonk was followed by another and yet another.

"Melitón! Melitón! Didn't you just hear that? I think we're gettin' close!"

"What was that?"

"Close! I said we're gettin' *close here.*"

"A ghost? Near, did you say?"

"What? What did you say? A ghost? Where-a-ghost? Here?"

"There-a-ghost? Oh, *dear!* My God, my God, it's *clear!*"

"A ghost is clear? Is that what you said, goddamit? Melitón? What are you doing? Melitón! Answer me!"

---

4.   A term of respect used for elders

"A ghost? Bruno, I gotta get outta here!"

"A ghost? Did that idiot ... Jesus! Did he say a *ghost*! Jesus, save me, Lord!"

By this time, Burnias was headed straight for the melon patch and making good time. Cano, for his part, began to scream for help, but Burnias was out of earshot by then: he had cleared two fences clean, had jumped across three fairly wide puddles without trying, and he was then chased by most of the neighborhood dogs. One of them strayed off the chase and sniffed near the hole; Cano looked up, saw something, and he heard a growl. That did it: Cano not only heard the ghost, he had seen it!

The dog finished his business, turned around and scratched the ground around him, and some fell on Bruno.

"Help! Heeeeeelp! Help me, goddamit! Sorry, Lord. Jesus Christ, get me out of here! Help me, help me out there, somebody!"

It was close to five o'clock now, and here came don Pedro Zamudio, Flora's one and only mission priest, wending his way to matins when he heard Bruno's screams and cries and curses for help. Don Pedro walked in that direction, peered down the hole, and said:

"Who are you? What's going on down there?"

"Is that really you, don Pedro? This is me, Cano. Help me up, will-ya?"

"What are you up to in this part o' town?"

"Look, get me out o' here, and then we'll talk. 'Kay?"

"Are you all right? Did you injure yourself when you fell down?"

"What? No, no, I didn't fall down here ... Come on, help me up."

"All in good time, all in good time. Now, tell me, how was it you wound up down there, and are you sure you're not hurt in some way? I was sure I heard some scream ... "

(Interruption) "That was me, but I'm okay, really. Now, for God's sake, hurry up and get me the hell ... sorry."

"And what was it you were about to say, my son?" (Knowingly)

"Nothing, Reverend Father, sir—just get me out o' this hole. Please."

"Well, it's this way: I'd like to, but I don't think I can, you know. I mean, you *are* a little, ah, heavy, ah, a little fat, you know."

"Fat? Faa-aaaaat? Your Mama's the fat one!"

"My whaaaaaaat?"

"Your mother! That's who! That *cow*! Now, get me the hell out o' here! Do it!"

"Speaking of mothers (sweetly), friend Cano, maybe *yours* can get you out o' that hole!"

"Why, you pug-nosed, pop-eyed, overripe, overbearing, overeating, wine-swilling, son-of-a-bitch! You do your duty as a priest!"

"I will, my son, I will," he purred. With this, don Pedro knelt at the edge of the hole: First, a rapid sign of the Cross, and skipping the Our Father altogether, don Pedro started out on the one about ... "clasp, o' Lord, this sinner to your breast" and then Bruno let go with another firm reminder of don Pedro's mother. This time, the reminder was as plain as West Texas and the birds stopped at midtrill. For his part, don Pedro wearing a resigned beatific smile, dug deep and came up with his rosary and, rather unexpectedly, started on the Mass for the Dead; this was just entirely too much for Cano and what started as a low growl exploded into a high-piercing scream directed, variously, at don Pedro, his innocent mother, and any and all relatives dead, living, and to come. Cano then gathered another lungful of air at the time that don Pedro jumped up and extended his arms to form a cross, and, not to be outdone, screamed out: "... and *do* take this sinner to your ... " but Cano did not rejoin; in fact, Cano was still catching his breath or trying to, and by the time don Pedro finished his latest prayer, he leaned over the hole and asked, "Now, do you see? Prayers *do* bring inner peace, don't they? They've stilled your anger, my son, and tempered both our faiths. Rest easy, the sun will soon be coming up, and so will you."

Bruno was past caring. Somewhere just after one of the mysteries or one of Bruno's motherly recollections, Bruno stopped breathing and thus delivered his uneasy soul to the Lord, the Devil, or to don Pedro's mother. Or to none of the above.

As may be supposed, no less than thirty of us witnessed, so to speak, the sunrise tableau, but we'd all kept a respectful distance while the one chanted and the other ranted.

But, be that as it may, Bruno Cano was buried, and in sacred ground, to boot. To don Pedro's keen disappointment, the funeral was more than well-attended; and, the damn thing was over seven hours long:

Four orators showed up unannounced but dressed to the teeth: black flower, white hat, gold book, and serious as Hell. Then there were the four choirs (a boys' choir, a girls' choir, one made up of older women, members all of the Perpetual Candle, and the fourth one, an all-male choir from the Sacred Heart Parish from Edgerton; all four choirs were in rigorous white for the occasion, and one would have thought that this was Easter, but no such thing).

The Vega Bros. brought Bruno's body in that wine colored hearse of theirs; the one with the gray curtains. Besides don Pedro, there were twelve of us who served as acolytes, and there we were, in white-collared black chasubles heavily starched with backsides to match.

People from all over the Valley got word that something was up in Flora and there they came in trucks, bikes, hitchhiking, while the more enterprising ones from

Klail leased a Greyhound that already had some people in it who had boarded the bus back in Bascom, and they too joined the crowd.

Three candymen appeared and immediately opened up shop: it was a hot one, and they started selling sno-cones left and right. The crowd was later estimated, quite conservatively, I thought, at some four thousand. Some didn't know who was being buried. Most didn't care, of course, had never heard of Cano, but you know how things usually turn out: people'll use anything for an excuse to get out of the house.

As for don Pedro, well, he had to take it, and he came through with no less than three hundred Our Fathers, between Hail Marys, Hail Holy Queens, etc. And, when he began to cry (anger, hysteria, hunger) the crowd understood, or thought it did: they dedicated *their* prayers to don Pedro and to don Pedro's dear, departed friend, the respectable what's-his-name. At this juncture, up jumped the orators again having gotten their respective second winds, and each repeated their eulogies and then they began to compete with one another until a time limit was set; this helped to settle them down.

The candymen couldn't keep up with the demand, and each one ordered another hundred pounds of ice; the ice company charged more for delivery and thus the price increase was passed on to the consumer who was not getting any more syrup, the candyman having run out almost from the start. It mattered little since the people didn't care, and one could hear the chant for blocks around: ice, ice, ice, they cried.

Not to be outdone, the choirs, having run through all their songs and hymns, sensed a God-given opportunity and crossed the line to join forces with the others, and the first thing you know, they broke out with *Tantum Ergo*[5] which was out of place and worse, "Come, Good Shepherd, Celestial Redeemer ..." heard only around Easter time. Finally, the four groups began taking requests.

Now, despite the heat, the dust, the pushing, and the shoving, the crowd behaved itself, considering: there were some frayed nerves here and there, and more shouting than necessary and then there were those thirty-four who fainted, but, all in all, it was a first class funeral.

As it turned out, about the only person missing from all this was Melitón Burnias. As he said, days later; "I was quite busy on some personal business, and I was unable to get away to give Bruno a proper farewell. I, ah, well ... ah, you know, it ..."

Almost everyone pretended they had no idea what it was he was mumbling about, and let it go at that.

---

5.   a Latin prayer

Lionel G. García

(b. 1935)
Mexican American

Lionel G. García is a novelist who has created some of the most memorable characters in Chicano literature in a style that is well steeped in the traditions of the Texas talltale and Mexican American folk narrative. Born in San Diego, Texas, in 1935, García grew up in an environment in which Mexican Americans were the majority population in his small town and on the ranches where he worked and played. García was nurtured in a middle-class background and did so well in school that he was one of the very few Mexican Americans admitted to Texas A & M University, where he majored in biology but was also encouraged by one of his English professors to write. After graduating he attempted to become a full-time writer but was unsuccessful in getting his works published. He later returned to Texas A & M and graduated from that institution in 1969 as a doctor of veterinary medicine. Since then he has developed a successful career as a veterinarian while continuing to write in his spare time.

In 1983 Garcia won the PEN Southwest Discovery Award for his novel in progress **Leaving Home***, which was published in 1985. This and his second novel,* **A Shroud in the Family** *(1987), draw heavily on his family experiences and small-town background.* **Hardscrub** *(1989) is a departure from his former novel; it is a realistically drawn chronicle of the life of an Anglo child in an abusive family relationship. His most recent work,* **To a Widow with Children** *(1994), is a heart-warming tale of a love triangle set in rural south Texas in the early part of this century.*

The Sergeant

Manuel Laberón took off his hair-oil-stained military cap and wiped the soaked, poorly cured leather headband and then the stinging perspiration from his dirty brow with his brown Army-issue handkerchief in the steamed afternoon of the Summer of 1960 inside the dusty and crowded San Salvador International Airport as he looked through the opaque window at the big plane emitting hot waves of air as it landed from New York. Sgt. Manuel Laberón was dressed in forest green and rough-cut combat boots, with his old trusty 30 Caliber bolt action Mauser slung tightly to his shoulder, always at the ready: Sgt. Manuel Laberón of the Salvadoran army, serial number ss11122049. He was a proud, heavily starched soldier, coiling and recoiling to attention like a greased spring saluting at the immediate sight of his beloved Superior Officers who walked around the airport checking on his detail. But he was in a small Army in a small country—compared to the United States, that is. In the United States he imagined frequently, for this occupied many of his dreams, that soldiers like himself were better trained, better equipped, better fed, better housed, better taken care of in every way. But he was still proud to be a Salvadoran soldier. God willing, he intended to make it his life's work. It was better than being a neighborhood plumber as his father had been, having to beg for work and then having to put his bare hands into the diluted excrements of so many species that a lot of humans would find repulsive.

His parents, now thankfully dead, had grown to accept his career, although they had hoped for something more distinguished. They had thought, in their ignorance, that he would be the one to go beyond the stars, so much promise had he shown them.

They had admired his persistence and intellect as a young man. He was the only one of many children in his neighborhood that had grown up to read, speak and write at least basic English. He could write very well in Spanish and as a young man had won fourth place in a national contest in literature, losing out to the three men that later became literary heroes in his country. His entry had been a short story about his fictitious and adventurous grandmother and the many deathly perils she had encountered while living as a concubine among the savage indians of South America. The judges had said of the story that it was sensitive and yet not erotic, rare and strange and yet not comical.

In that poor enclave of the big city no one had ever tried to do such things.

But eventually he grew tiresome: the more he learned, the more resentful and suspicious the neighbors became of him, some even going to the unforgivable extreme of saying that he was a one-of-those, which in those days meant homosexual, just because he had briefly affected an effeminate walk, a walk he had seen used by a male star in an American movie. He could not understand the jealousy so common to the Latin mentality.

Unfortunately, his parents had unintentionally given Manuel Laberón false hopes. They had grossly miscalculated his intelligence and, when he failed the entrance examination to the University, the people turned on him and taunted him and he had to leave the neighborhood in shame. He had mistakenly thought that they were angry because he had disappointed them, but in reality they had turned against him because he had muddled once again their perfectly distilled self-image.

"A failed scholar is like a failed prostitute," the local faith healer had told him one night when he visited her for a drink of her magical Piancha tea to see if the tea could help him regain the admiration that he had lost. "They both don't get a second chance," she explained.

He had been happier in his earlier years before moving with his family into the oppressively large dry city. Those were the days when he had lived with his brothers and sisters in the central province of Piancha where then men spent most of their languid days working the fields gathering flax and herbs that they distilled into their world-famous provincial teas, the same ones that the witchcraft lady would prescribe to him on a nightly routine.

The women would take the many-hued, boiled flax and weave it into very intricate and ornate shawls that the province was also famous for. To go to El Salvador and not bring back a Piancha shawl was considered a lost trip. There was another fame, perhaps indelicate and not as well known, to acknowledge: the young men would spend their excessive leisure time chewing on a leaf of cocoa because they knew that to do so would cause their sexual members to grow and indeed it was not unusual for some of the men to have members eighteen inches long that they tied into several figure-eight knots to keep themselves from injury while they hoed the rampant weeds among the flax and herbs. Manuel Laberón had not been so fortunate. At the age of four while playing naked in the mud in the family pig-pen the sow had accidentally mistaken his little member for an emerging fat earthworm as he lay covered with mud, sucking on the cocoa leaf, and the sow had lamentably nipped his member in half, and it had grown into manhood like the vicious stump of an amputated tallow tree, gnarled and lichenified, much to the delight of his wife, who never missed the excess nine inches and the extra figure-eight because she had been born in Rio Hondo where the women were bigger than their smaller and less-endowed men.

His greatest satisfaction came when he drew airport security duty, for those were the days when he could check the inside of the planes coming from other countries. If he was extra lucky, he would get to inspect the American planes, especially the ones coming from New York. Ah! New York! he thought, loving things American. He had seen the pictures of Manhattan with the towering skyscrapers that seemed to blot the sun, buildings that were so huge and tall that he could not imagine how they had ever been built. He was also familiar with Washington, D.C.

He took a deep breath of hot air soaked with the aroma of the burnt-sugar candy as he stood by the door that led from the airport building to the outside ramp and the plane. His heart raced in excitement at the sight as he held his breath. As soon as all the passengers had cleared the door, he locked it immediately and hurried behind the immigration counter. From here he rushed behind the large group of metal cabinets heavy with incoming luggage and pushed his way inside the immigration office. On the table by the wall was the can of fumigant which he grabbed and placed in the pocket of his jacket. At the opposite side of the room was the door. He ran to it and opened it. The air was much hotter than inside and the blast of heat that surrounded the airplane that was blowing toward him made him stagger and draw heavily for his breath. In spite of the melting heat, he ran to the plane, climbed the ramp steps two at a time, and went inside. He felt the immediate relief of the coolness inside the plane. The pilot and the crew were going over their flight plan and he did not want to disturb them. They nodded at him through the tight cabin door and he felt his self-esteem rise, even as he stayed away from the cabin. They were Americans from New York. Every time he saw them he was happy. Twice a week the large blue plane came and twice a week, if he had airport duty, he would run out to the plane to inspect it. By now the crew knew him. He practiced his primitive English on them. They appreciated his being able to speak English and they were happy to see him when they landed. When they had finished checking the cabin he could hear the pilot, co-pilot, navigator and stewardesses talk about where they were going to eat on their lay-over. They greeted him more openly now that they were through with their work and they asked how things were going as he stepped into the cabin. They asked if he knew of any new places to eat. They were tired of all the other places he had suggested to them before. They asked about *El Coco Loco,* a new restaurant they had heard about, and he apologized because he had never been there. He felt badly that he had missed an opportunity to be of help.

As soon as the crew emptied, he searched the plane thoroughly and found nothing illegal. He finally was able to rest his nervous hand from the Mauser at his side. He went back to the front seat of the plane and there, where the stewardess always placed it for him, was a copy of the *New York Times.* He walked to the back of the plane and took out the large aerosol can from his forest-green jacket and began to fumigate the airplane. He worked his way to the front, slowly moving the can in a circular pattern covering all of the inside. As he reached the front he took the newspaper and stuck it under his arm and then he continued to fumigate the cabin and the front lavatory. As soon as he was finished, he got off quickly and partially closed the door. He hurried down the ramp trying to get away before the heat overtook him, running on the blistering tarmac and into the immigration office. Out of breath with the heat and excitement, he replaced the can of fumigant on the desk, rested his weapon by the can and sat down at the chair by the desk, out of sight of his superior officers. He opened the newspaper and the headlines read that Senator John F. Kennedy of Massachusetts had been nominated for the presidency of the United States by the Democratic Party.

What a beautiful thing to have happen to a person. Something like this could never happen to a man like him. This Senator Kennedy must be a good man, he thought. Senator Kennedy looked so young in the pictures. Manuel Laberón could hardly wait for six o'clock when he would go home and read the entire paper.

The stories on Kennedy were long and confusing as he had never been able to understand American idioms and euphemisms, but he read it slowly savoring every word, looking for and finding an unknown word now and then in his dictionary, the one the goat had partially eaten during her pregnancy. Why, he wondered, did they call him Jack? Was not his name John? This going back and forth between Jack and John confused him, and more so since the goat had eaten most of the J's in his dictionary. He would have to ask the flight crew what this meant. Or maybe it would be better if he didn't. He didn't want to appear ignorant, remembering what had happened to him with his neighbors when every one thought that he would go to the University. He decided that he would not ask anything. Possibly the answer would come to him in a conversation with the Americans some day. He cleared his throat as he thought, and his wife, who was busy fixing supper, asked him if he said anything. "No," he replied from the living room with a stare fixed upon the newspaper, "I was just thinking about the Americans." And he re-folded the paper to continue the story but by then supper was ready and he had to stop reading to eat with his wife and two children.

After the meal, as he sat contentedly in his chair reading the newspaper, he came upon a great and startling revelation. As he read the information before him, he shot up from the chair, rod-straight, as though he had seen the highest ranked of his beloved officers. He could hardly believe his eyes. He placed the newspaper directly under the light and he read it again and again. Could it be possible? There was no way that the great American newspaper could make such an error. It had to be true: one of Senator Kennedy's sisters was married to a sergeant! A Sergeant Shriver! Someone just like him. He could hardly contain his joy. He ran to show the story to his wife but she couldn't read. He slowly explained to her and the children what it was that he had read: the sister of one of the greatest Americans was married to a sergeant—just like him. "Only in America!" he shouted. "What a great country it must be!"

In the morning he was still as excited and animated as he had been at bedtime when he had made violent and happy love to his most appreciative wife. So preoccupied was he that he had gotten up several times during his love-making to recheck the story just to be sure he had not misinterpreted the words.

But there it was. He was right. His only concern, and one that he would not tell his family about, was that throughout the paper he could not find a single picture of this Sergeant Shriver. No matter how long or how carefully he looked, the famous sergeant's picture was not found. Was he that small innocent face in the background several rows back that was peering between the large-brimmed hats of two women? Was that a military uniform he saw a man wearing who was behind that insignificant face? What kind of sergeant was he? Army? Navy? Air Force? Marines? Shriver's wife, Eunice, appeared in several pictures, but not the good sergeant. He dismissed his concern acknowledging that his mind had always tried to keep him from having happy thoughts. What difference did it make if Shriver's picture did not appear in the newspaper? He chided himself for bringing up the doubts that now lay like whetstones in the back of his mind ready to sharpen his disappointment as they had since the days of the old neighborhood. But now things were different and he was determined that nothing would interfere with his happiness. He was prouder than ever before that he was a sergeant. He wanted his wife to be happy. After all, wasn't she the equal to the Kennedy lady, married to a sergeant also? Everyone was equal—his wife and Eunice and he and Shriver and the children, if they had any.

He made love with his large tuberous member every chance he had, and his wife, delighted with her new fortune, insisted that they start their son on the cocoa leaf and that Manuel Laberón should send some of the cocoa leaf to the American Sergeant as a token of their esteem.

"No woman should miss out on something like this," she said, spent on her back, staring at the busy spiders on the ceiling.

He was going to have to arrange to pull airport duty every Wednesday and Sunday, the days that the plane arrived from New York so that he could be sure to get the paper. It would not be hard to do. No one wanted to work on Sunday and he could use that to barter for insisting on working on Wednesday. On Sunday he would not go to church. His family could go and pray for him. Anyway the priest was repeating himself and was tiresome and always angry with the military.

He could not get his fill of the Sergeant Shriver story. Twice a week he would scour the plane for newspapers, magazines, anything that might have something about the Kennedys and Sergeant Shriver.

And since he never found a picture of the Sergeant, he decided one night that as a tribute he would write a story about the Sergeant and his life with the Kennedys, just to make him more real. If the newspapers were not going to pay any attention to Shriver, he would make him his own story. He would write it in flowery Spanish, his trade-mark, and then when he was through he would pay to have someone translate it into English and then he would send it to the good Sergeant to show him how proud he was. Late one night he had put his family to bed and began:

The great lady of American politics, Rose Kennedy, looked out the window at the expansive lawn and beyond the promontory where the lawn ended and then fell into the blue sea.

"Eunice," she said, turning to her daughter who was seated at the dresser doing her lovely auburn hair, "isn't Sergeant Shriver a wonderful man? How could you be so lucky? I am just right now at this instant watching him playing with the dogs. Such care and tenderness. Look at him run with the whippets and the danes. Such a beautiful stride ... Why was he not in the Olympics?"

"He had to work to pay for his family's education."

"If we had only known him before. He could have gone to Harvard ... Yale ... even Princeton. He could have gone with John and Bobby and Teddy ... What he could have done with a good education," Rose lamented. "It would have been unbelievable. Not that he's doing badly now, mind you. I love him so. You two make such a beautiful couple. I love to admire the both of you. It's just ... it's just that I sense what he would have done with a good university education ... like Harvard."

Eunice shook her head gently at her mother's absurdities, indeed the absurdities of all parents that feel their children could have done better. She said, "My Sergeant says that a good man does not need a formal education ... A good rooster sings in any hen-house."

"How true ... sometimes I forget. Just look at your father ... But how extraordinary your little Sergeant is. How could you be so lucky ... ?"

Eunice continued, separating her long compact strands of hair, combing each out into an abundant mass with a fine-tooth comb. "Some of us are lucky, I guess. It was just a chance meeting when I attended the ball at the fort. And then he was resplendent in his Class A uniform, dancing with everyone. How elegant he looked. Even the Colonel's wife made room for him on her dance card. He reminded me so much of John Wayne."

"Oh! Be careful, Sergeant," Rose cried, placing her thin delicate white hand to her mouth to stifle a gasp. "He tripped over one of the whippets and took a nasty fall by the promontory. He's up ... He's up and limping slightly. How the dogs love him also. Even the ones that bark and growl at your father."

Eunice smiled contentedly, her life as happy as it was possible to be, as she looked into the mirror at her classic beauty.

Rose continued to hold her sheer curtain open with her frail hand. "John and Ted are with him now ... Look! ... Your daughter is running toward her father ... How she loves to squeeze his biceps."

On Friday, November 22, 1963, he had been inspecting barracks with his fellow sergeants when the news arrived: President Kennedy had been assassinated. The news was such a shock to him that he had to sit down to keep from falling over. How could this be? Surely someone had made a mistake. They ran from the barracks to the Orderly Room and there they found a group of soldiers crowded around the small radio. It was true. The narrator was speaking in a slow monotonous voice, the voice cracking occasionally, on the verge of tears, informing them and all of Latin America that John Kennedy was dead. Manuel Laberón cried, as did all the rest of the men. But he cried louder and longer, more like a child that had lost his father and the rest of the Sergeants understood. Kennedy and Sergeant Shriver had been Manuel's idols for three years, almost all he ever spoke about. Finally Manuel wailed so much and made such a spectacle of himself outside the Orderly Room—throwing and rolling himself on the ground—that the soldiers were allowed to go home.

He wept by the radio all day and night, listening, trying to find out what had happened. Kennedy had been shot while riding in a car in Dallas. But where was Sergeant Shriver? Had he been there, perhaps this tragic affair would not have happened. Why were the Kennedys so intent on keeping the Sergeant out of the limelight when he could have possibly prevented this tragedy?

During those days when he could get to the plane from New York he read all accounts of the assassination and the funeral. He looked for Sergeant Shriver and again the good Sergeant had been obscured from all family pictures. He could read the name in print but never did he see Sergeant Shriver in uniform. Always, always, he lamented, they kept the good Sergeant behind the ladies in the big hats.

His fears were coming true. The whetstones that had been stuck to the back of his mind all this time were beginning to sharpen his disappointment. He stopped writing his story, not knowing how to proceed since he did not know exactly how the Kennedys felt about the Sergeant. Full of doubts, he could not continue so he began a time of introspection brought on by the disillusionment that had returned once again to his life.

By 1968 he had gotten over the assassination and had more or less cleared his mind of Sergeant Shriver. He had become happier, whistling while he worked, and sexually productive once more. His wife and children were happy with him, his wife especially since he was back to utilizing his colossal member every night.

He felt well enough to take his wife to the annual Heroes Ball at the Fort.

In June, however, he received another shock that would revive his passion for the good Sergeant: Robert Kennedy was assassinated in a hotel kitchen in Los Angeles.

By all accounts Sergeant Shriver, again, had not been around to protect his brother-in-law. Once again he was not to be found in the many pictures in the newspapers. Eunice, yes, but not the Sergeant. Their contempt for the man was something that they could hide no longer. Angrily, he demanded to know what had happened to the America that he loved? Were we no longer equal?

In protest, he would no longer board American planes.

Although his wife and children scolded him, he wept for the Sergeant and Eunice. His heart ached when he thought of what they must be going through. Even he and his wife, as poor as they were, were better off than the Shrivers. At least they had been loved. Even at the time that the neighborhood had turned against him, he had been loved, perhaps even more then that at any time in his life. He was inconsolable and he lost the use of his superlative member. His wife threatened to kick him out of the house if he did not forget this crazy dream. She screamed to him one night: "The sow should have bitten it all off for all the good it is doing us!"

But by now he knew everything about the Kennedys from reading the American press. In fact, he thought he knew everything about America from reading the American press. He would rewrite his story:

The great lady of American politics, Rose Kennedy, looked out the window at the expansive lawn and beyond the promontory where the lawn ended and then the sea below, the beautiful Atlantic where she and her husband Joseph and the children had had such wonderful times: the shores, the water, sailing, rowing, sculling, swimming—everything was a blur awash with memories. But that had been such a long time ago, the completely happy days before Eunice had soiled the family. She looked down closer to the house and on the lawn she could see her children, now grown, playing a game of touch football. There were John and Robert and Teddy all on the same team, Jack running with the ball under his arm. E.F. Hutton was running after him and Bobby was shoving him away from Jack. Cabot-Lodge was chasing from behind and gaining. Teddy was trying to block him but was laughing so much that he could not be very effective, presently falling exhausted into the sideline ditch. Smith Barney was taking an angle on Jack and appeared to be heading him off. It would be a tight race to the goal unless the deceptively fast Pierre Salinger got to Jack first. Jack made it to the goal line just as Salinger and Smith Barney caught up with him. E.F. Hutton had stumbled over Teddy's feet. Jack threw the ball in the air and everyone fell to the green plush lawn and laughed. One of the Rockefeller girls, she didn't know which one, there were so many, ran to the bunch and dove on top of them showing her white-with-rose embroidered underwear.

Rose grinned as a sign of contentment.

Her gaze automatically went to the area beyond the playing field. And there under the trees, in the shadows of the towering salt-cedars, she saw this sight: Sergeant Shriver standing in the dark wondering if he should or should not run out to the group to join in their felicity. In his indecisiveness he appeared to take one step forward and two backwards, receding deeper and deeper into the shadows of the woods. The dogs were surrounding him as though they knew that he needed protection from the happy crowd in the playing field.

All of the players and the Rockefeller girls ran off the field and into the club-house for refreshments.

The Sergeant gathered the danes and the whippets around him and walked further into the eternal solitude of the lightless forest. "What is it about me that they don't like?" he asked the canine group and they happily wagged their tails and salivated on his pressed fatigues not caring, in their bestial innocence, whether he was a Sergeant or a General. "Is it the tattoo? ... What have I done? Pray tell me?" The dogs barked excessively in defense of their beloved Sergeant. He looked toward the house and he could see his mother-in-law standing at the large upstairs window.

"How could you, Eunice? How could you do this to the family?" Rose Kennedy asked, not really expecting Eunice to answer. What was the use after all these years? She had asked her until she blue in the face.

She and Eunice were alone in the room. Eunice acted nonchalantly. She was sitting in the chaise doing her nails even though she had been told not to do her nails where she could spill the polish and ruin the carpets. If she had regretted marrying the Sergeant, she had never admitted it. She was not the type. She was a Kennedy. Rose looked at her and wished for once that she and Joseph had not raised such head-strong children. No one ever admitted a mistake, not Joe, or Jack or ... What was the use?

"Did I tell you," Eunice proclaimed, happily, "that we're being stationed in Yokohama?"

Rose gasped as she grabbed the curtain to keep from falling, and murmured, "Heaven forbid. Of all places. Where is that?"

"Oh, it's not bad. It's in the Orient and we can get good bargains on stuff. I'll send you pieces of china every month until you complete the set and maybe some pillow covers for the couches. Shriver says that the housing is great. Better than El Salvador, anyway."

Rose gasped again, a double recoil. When had they been in an awful, dirty, Latin American country controlled by dictators? What a ghastly thought.

"And the children can learn some Japanese."

Rose clutched her throat as though she was about to collapse again from the strain of seeing her son-in-law among the dogs hiding behind the trees. "Heaven Forbid!" she exclaimed. "Don't let them learn such foolishness."

"At least," Eunice said, blowing on her nails, "we won't have the crime and racial discrimination that we have in the United States. All the murder ... Murder ... Murder everywhere. That's all we see in the papers. Graft ... Corruption ... Rape ... Swindle ... Corrupt politicians ... Hunger ... Poverty ... Riots. Blacks against whites ... Oh, we'll be glad to get a rest from all that in Yokohama. You can be sure of that."

Rose walked defiantly toward Eunice and said with an air charged with resentment: "Eunice dear, you know that Jack and Bobby and Teddy are trying very very hard to get rid of all those problems."

"Yes, but are they? It seems worse now than ever."

"Hush ... don't say that. What if the press would hear you? Think of what the conservatives would do with ammunition like that?"

"It's true though," Eunice offered, "it's getting worse. When was the last time you had a black for lunch?"

"Hush your mouth. Maybe it's better that you do leave for that God-forsaken place."

"Maybe," she answered, defiantly. "Maybe you want to get rid of me and the Sergeant?"

"Don't be absurd ... And still ... " There was a wishful-like quality in her eyes.

"You see. I told you. You want to get rid of him."

"What would please me would be if he got rid of his tattoo. That's all. It's the talk of Hyannis this summer."

"But mother, everyone in the outfit got the same tattoo. It's camaraderie."

"Camaraderie, shamaraderie, a snake wrapped around a naked lady showing frontal nudity with electrified pubic hairs and all that junk is not my idea or the boys' idea or your father's idea of camaraderie."

"It's symbolic, mother. Open up your mind. The electrically charged hairs, the little thin lightnings around the pubis symbolize how fast their outfit can attack the enemy. You know that he keeps telling us that his outfit can be defending us anywhere in the world in just eight hours. It's just that all of you refuse to listen."

"I just wish he had a more pleasant way of expressing himself. And to have it done on his forearm! Is he going to have the tattoo removed? That's what I want to know."

"I don't pay attention to those things," Eunice replied. She knew that he wouldn't. He was too proud to use the Kennedy money.

"What did he do with the money for the surgery? The money that your father gave him?"

"Mother," Eunice said, scolding Rose. "Why be so petty about money? He didn't take it. He would never take money from father."

"I saw your father give him the money, Eunice. Now what happened to it?"

"If you must know ... I spent it," she said. "I needed it for the children. Shoes ... clothes ... The car needed a tune-up ... Oh, mother, why must we keep on. Shriver gave it to me. He felt it was mine anyway. Why must we be so conscious of money."

"Because that's all we have, sweetie," she said. "And everyone is trying to take it away from us, including your Sergeant."

One Sunday when he couldn't take the ache anymore, Manuel broke down and boarded the American plane and looked for his beloved newspaper. He searched the whole plane and could not find it. The crew had become accustomed to not leaving one behind. What he found, however, was a smaller paper that he had never been given before. He noticed that it was mysteriously hidden very well under the pilot's seat. He was curious, of course. He bent down and reached under the seat, took the paper and unfolded it. The *New York Times Book Review* it read at the top as he opened it. Many people were writing stories as he was, he thought, perhaps the other famous native authors that had won the awards along with him. Realizing that he could not take the paper with him, he sat down on one of the seats and began to read. As he paged his way through the *Review* he found, as if by divine intercession, what he had been looking for all this time but didn't know existed—"The Query Letter." Acting as if his wildest dreams had been answered, he excitedly studied the form used for writing such a letter and committed it to memory. It was simple enough and he would compose a letter in English. He would find his friend, the Sergeant, after all.

He wrote and mailed:

> For a story on Sergeant Shriver, the Kennedy brother-in-law married to Eunice, I would appreciate hearing from anyone of his whereabouts, anecdotes, reminiscences, military outfits, medals, posts, pictures of him especially and of Eunice and the children.

Sgt. Manuel Laberón
Apartado 3427 Avenida P
San Salvador
El Salvador

He felt better than he had in a long time as he waited for a reply and had begun to reuse his sledge-like member with the consistency of his early years when most of his time was spent chewing on the cocoa leaves, the re-awakening of his tool even causing pain to his wife as it had appeared to have gotten bigger through disuse. He was awakened in the middle of the night after making love by someone striking the front door with such force that he thought that each blow would knock the door down. He told his wife, who was now pleasantly awake in the warm afterglow, to cover up and stay in bed. He got up hurriedly, put on his shorts and arranged his still partially tumescent piece to the side by his leg and held it there under the shorts with his hand. He lit the candle with the other and as fast as he could got to the door fearing that if he did not hurry that someone outside would surely break his door down. He saw the door shudder in fright with every blow being struck. He placed the candle on the table by the front wall. As he unlocked the door the soldier struck the door again with the rifle butt and the door flew open violently and hit him in the face. That one act softened his member.

The Lieutenant with the men asked, "Are you Sgt. Manuel Laberón?" ignoring the blow that they had delivered to him.

Manuel was kneeling on the floor holding his nose and then he looked at his hand. He was not bleeding, thank God. His face was numb.

"Yes, sir," he replied, acknowledging his name when he had recovered his senses and as he tried to get up to salute.

"Then come with us," the Lieutenant informed him, returning the salute with a gesture of disgust.

Manuel, thinking that he was being needed at the military fort started to go back to his room. "Come in and wait a minute, Lieutenant," he said. "I'll be in uniform in a few minutes." He wondered in his stupor from the sleep and the blow what it was that he was needed for at this time of night.

Two soldiers, corporals, upon a silent command, a nod of the head from the Lieutenant, grabbed him as he walked away and forced his arms behind his back. The Lieutenant entered swinging his swagger stick, whipping his own leg and said, "I'm afraid that you don't have time to dress. You go with us just as you stand there."

How could he travel in his underwear? Could the good Lieutenant give him a few minutes to dress?

"You are Sergeant Laberón, aren't you?" he asked again.

"Yes, my Lieutenant."

"Do you own any rifles, pistols, explosives, anything that might be used for the overthrow of a government, or the assassination of any person?"

The only weapon he had at home was an old army issue forty-five. The trusty Mauser stayed in the Orderly Room upon orders from the President himself who was afraid of a revolution if all the arms were being carried back and forth to work.

"Where is it?" the Lieutenant wanted to know.

He replied that he would go get it but the Lieutenant refused. "Just tell us where it is and one of the men will get it for me."

It was on top of the dresser in the bedroom where his wife was in bed. Another corporal rushed into the bedroom and Manuel's wife screamed. He heard his children cry. His wife, hearing all the commotion, had put them in bed with her. Manuel felt rage as he heard his wife. If he had not been held by two large men he would have beaten the corporal *and* the Lieutenant, even if it had meant his army career. The corporal ran out with the pistol in his hand and handed it to the Lieutenant. "Is this it?" the Lieutenant asked.

That was it. Manuel nodded. He could not move. He was being held very tightly and for no reason. What had he done? He started to speak and the Lieutenant signaled the men to twist his arms so that the pain would silence him.

The Lieutenant walked through the house and very carefully went through all of Manuel's belongings. When he found the old newspapers and Manuel's stories, he scanned them with interest. He grinned and shook his head as he gathered all the papers into one pile. He ordered the soldiers to take Manuel out and put him in the car while he stayed behind. He wanted to interrogate the wife and children without Manuel being present. Manuel tried to object but the Lieutenant had the men re-twist his arms to quiet him.

Manual, wearing only his shorts, was thrown into the back seat of the car. The corporals stood outside leaning against the car, smoking, waiting for the Lieutenant. When the Lieutenant rushed out of Manuel's house, the corporals quickly threw away their cigarettes and opened the door for him. He had in his hands the large bulk of newspapers and pages with Manuel's writings.

At the headquarters for the *Policía Nacional Salvadoreña,* he was taken to the Interrogation Office for Domestic Subversion.

The Lieutenant and the three corporals left the room at the same time that a large man, a Colonel, came in and sat at the desk in front of Manuel Laberón. He was the only officer he had ever seen that did not have a moustache. He glared at Manuel with an unblinking hatred that made Manuel nervous.

"Did you write this?" he demanded, showing Manuel Laberón the query letter in the *New York Times.*

Manuel answered that he had. He couldn't help but be fascinated. That was the second time he had ever seen his name in print. And to think it was in the *Times.*

"You are either very stupid or you are up to something that could create an international embarrassment," the Colonel said. The Colonel stood up and pulled on his crotch. Manuel looked the other way, disturbed and confused, "and we are here to find out which of the two possibilities is the truth. We are prepared to keep you here until hell freezes over. Until we find out the truth!" he shouted, shaking his swagger stick in front of Manuel's face. The Colonel paced behind his desk, the profile of his long flat buttocks offensive to Manuel.

The Colonel knew that, if Sgt. Manuel Laberón was an assassin, it would be a black mark on his country. The last thing El Salvador needed was for a member of the Kennedy family to be assassinated while visiting his country.

Being the good soldier that he was, Manuel Laberón agreed to cooperate but still he had to confess that he knew nothing about any assassination. He admitted that he had a fondness for Sergeant Shriver, perhaps something more than would be considered normal, since they were both sergeants.

The Colonel looked at him as if he didn't know whether to believe him or not. "Suppose you tell me from the beginning all about your obsession with the Honorable Sargent Shriver."

"Honorable?" Manuel thought. He was now called Honorable?

In his confused and ignorant way, Manuel Laberón began to tell the Colonel his story as the Colonel coaxed him. By morning the Americans had arrived and were listening to him as he repeated his story. Each time after he finished, the Americans and the Salvadorans met in the glass partitioned office next door and they reviewed what he had said. For two days he sat in his shorts, his nose broken, as they made him tell the story over and over again.

As he sat there, he thought of his wife and family and wondered how they were holding up. At first he wept silently for them, not wanting to disturb his beloved officers and the Americans. Later on, when he realized that he was not loved, he cried for his family like he had cried for President Kennedy. He felt that he had gotten them unjustly involved in his troubles and yet he still did not know why everyone had made it appear so important. After all, he had said nothing to anyone about how poorly he thought the Kennedys were treating Sargent Shriver. Could not a man think anything anymore without someone finding out? Who could have turned him in? The crew of the airplane? His family? His neighbors? Why were the Kennedys so vindictive?

No matter how many times he told his story it was always the same. His wife and children had separately verified his story. In the end the investigators conceded that it was possible for someone to confuse the name of Sargent Shriver. Who knows how many Americans themselves felt sorry for the Kennedy lady that had married a sergeant while everyone else had married politicians and royalty and photo-journalists and lawyers and movie stars? Nonetheless, there was the official visit that was coming in the next days and they could not take a chance. It was decided that Manuel Laberón should stay in prison until the trip was over, until the Honorable Sargent Shriver was safely in his plane and on his way home.

Manuel Laberón was placed in solitary confinement at the Prisión Federal. Furthermore, it was decided by the authorities to set Manuel Laberón straight, to tell him who Sargent Shriver was, and to tell him that Sargent Shriver would be visiting San Salvador. At first he did not believe the story. He believed that it was a conspiracy to quiet him so that no one would know about his beloved Sergeant Shriver and the Kennedys.

The events that followed forced him to change his mind. He had been watching as best he could on tip-toes from his small high window at the daily progress being made by the workmen erecting a large platform across the street from the prison. Slowly, day by day, like ants they added to it, the work crews coming very early in the morning and leaving very late. By the time they were through, they had built an enormous platform and had set up chairs and had decorated the platform with beautiful red, white and blue bunting. Manuel Laberón waited anxiously for the parade and reception. Would he get to see his Sergeant Shriver or Sargent Shriver? Would he be proven wrong? Had he been that ignorant? The next day, in the middle of the morning, he heard the bands and the bugle corps and the marching men striking their feet in unison as the parade marched by. The dignitaries had already been seated quietly on the platform. The President of his country was there. Sitting next to the President was a very well dressed and distinguished gentleman. Could this be his Sergeant Shriver, he thought, as he stood on his bed on tip-toes trying to see the ceremony going on outside. The band grew quiet. The sounds of marching boots slowly faded into the distant side streets. By now a huge crowd had gathered in front of the platform. Suddenly the crowd was held in the grip of an anticipatory quiet. The bugler standing erect to the right of the platform sounded a prolonged call that Manuel Laberón recognized as the Call to Dignitaries of the Highest Rank and the President arose and approached the rostrum waiting for the bugler to end his piece.

"People of this great sovereign nation of ours," he began. "It is with a heart warm with pleasure that we welcome to our great nation the Honorable Ambassador and dear friend, the Honorable Sargent Shriver."

Manuel Laberón had not heard so much applause in his life. At the same time he felt devastated as the weight of the truth of the world fell on his shoulders. From the prison window he saw the Honorable Sargent Shriver get up from his chair and wave at the crowd. He was handsome and well bred. He was truly not a sergeant. One could tell, he had to admit. This man would never wear a tattoo of a snake wrapped around a naked lady showing electrified pubic hairs. He would not be running with the dogs like a common man beneath the shadows of the salt cedars at the edge of the promontory. He could have easily taken the ball and run with it himself.

Manuel Laberón had been wrong, not only this time but for all his life. What an illusion his life had been! He cursed himself for putting himself and his wife and children through such an embarrassment. He was crying and striking his head on the iron bars. He could taste the saltiness of his tears as they moistened his thick, black moustache. Sargent Shriver was a very important man. There was no hope then for people like him. He slid down the wall and sat on his bed weeping, rubbing his hands violently, unconsciously. He was brought back to reality when he heard the President say: "When we were both going through law school at Yale, we were the best of friends. His gracious parents would invite my parents to stay with them at their house. We were like one big family and he and I like brothers ..."

Manuel, crazed, suddenly jumped up from his bed and grabbed the iron bars of his window and in his disoriented state yelled at the top of his voice to the huge crowd below, disturbing the whole ceremony: "Forgive me for I am a common man. Give me my freedom! Help me, Mr. Shriver!"

Manuel Laberón was court-martialed, found guilty of misconduct and discharged from the Army he loved. He was removed without severance pay and without pension benefits. Daily he thanked God that his parents were dead and had not witnessed his ill fate. He moved his family to the old neighborhood and became the neighborhood plumber, just as his father had been, walking the streets with his tools on his back in a yellow burlap pouch caked with mud, yelling self-consciously, "Plumbing! Plumbing! Plumber works cheap! Whatever you want to offer the plumber! The plumber needs work!" hoping that no one would recognize him. And he had to work with his bare hands in the diluted excrement of so many species that after a while it became unimportant as the smell became a part of him as it had of his father. And since he could no longer stand to chew the cocoa leaf, in time his large stump-like member became as small and gentle as a green twig of the flax that he had dyed as a child.

Everyone in the neighborhood loved him as he spent his time trying to please everyone.

One day, while he was walking the street in search of work, a letter from New York arrived, originally addressed to his former home. Fearing that Manuel Laberón would return at an unexpected moment, his wife opened it immediately. It read:

> In response to query letter, knew Sergeant Shriver well and Eunice too. Kennedys too. Have many photos, anecdotes, reminiscences. Was stationed in Yokohama with him. Reply if interested. Please send one-hundred dollars as deposit.

> J. Jones
> Gotham Literary Services
> Box 1034
> Grand Central Station
> New York, NY 10004

She never showed him the letter. She burned it with the kindling in her stove, hoping to put the matter to rest for good.

But that night, Manuel Laberón dreamed of the letter that never came, and the Kennedys and the Shrivers, and all the important people that had once been his friends, and it was he who was running with the whippets and the danes in that marvelously expansive lawn.

Nicholasa Mohr

(b. 1935)
Puerto Rican

To date, Nicholasa Mohr is the only Hispanic woman in the United States to have developed a long career as a creative writer for the major publishing houses. Since 1973 her books for such publishers as Dell/Dial, Harper & Row, and Bantam in both the adult and children's literature categories have won numerous awards and received outstanding reviews. Part and parcel of her work is the experience of growing up as a female, Hispanic, and member of a minority group in New York City.

Born on November 1, 1935, in New York City, Nicholasa Mohr was raised in Spanish Harlem. Educated in New York City schools, she finally escaped poverty after graduating from the Pratt Center for Contemporary Printmaking in 1969. From that date until the publication of her first book, **Nilda** (1973), Mohr developed a successful career as a graphic artist. **Nilda** traces the life of a young Puerto Rican girl confronting prejudice and coming of age during World War II; it won the Jane Addams Children's Book Award and was selected by School Library Journal as a Best Book of the Year. After **Nilda's** success, Mohr was able to produce numerous stories, scripts, and the following titles: **El Bronx Remembered** (1975), **In Nueva York** (1977), **Felita** (1979), **Rituals of Survival: A Woman's Portfolio** (1985), and **Going Home** (1986). Selections from all of these story collections have been reprinted widely in anthologies and textbooks.

Mohr's works have been praised for depicting the life of Puerto Ricans in New York City with empathy, realism, and humor. In her stories for children, Mohr has been able to deal with the most serious and tragic of subjects, from the death of a loved one to incest, in a sensitive and humane way. Mohr has contributed to the world of commercial publishing—where stereotypes have reigned supreme—some of the most honest and memorable depictions of Puerto Ricans in the United States.

Aunt Rosana's Rocker

Casto paced nervously, but softly, the full length of the small kitchen, then quietly, he tiptoed across the kitchen threshold into the living room. After going a few feet, he stopped to listen. The sounds were getting louder. Casto returned to the kitchen, switched on the light, and sat down trying to ignore what he heard. But the familiar sounds were coming directly from their bedroom where Zoraida was. They grew louder as they traveled past the tiny foyer, the living room and into the kitchen, which was the room furthest away from her.

Leaning forward, Casto stretched his hands out palms down on the kitchen table. Slowly he made two fists, squeezing tightly, and watched as his knuckles popped out tensely under his skin. He could almost feel her presence there, next to him, panting and breathing heavily. The panting developed into moans of sensual pleasure, disrupting the silence of the apartment.

panting and breathing heavily. The panting developed into moans of sensual pleasure, disrupting the silence of the apartment.

"If only I could beat someone!" Casto whispered hoarsely, banging his fists against the table and upsetting the sugar bowl. The cover slipped off the bowl, landed on its side and rolled toward the edge of the table. Casto waited for it to drop to the floor, anticipating a loud crash, but the cover stopped right at the very edge and fell quietly and flatly on the table, barely making a sound.

He looked up at the electric clock on the wall over the refrigerator; it was two-thirty in the morning.

Again, Casto tried not to listen and concentrated instead on the noises outside in the street. Traffic on the avenue had almost completely disappeared. Occasionally, a car sped by; someone's footsteps echoed against the pavement; and off at a distance, he heard a popular tune being whistled. Casto instinctively hummed along until the sound slipped away, and he then realized he was shivering. The old radiators had stopped clanking and hissing earlier; they were now ice cold. He remembered that the landlord never sent up heat after ten at night. He wished he had thought to bring a sweater or blanket with him; he was afraid of catching a cold. But he would not go back inside; instead, he opened his special section of the cupboard and searched among his countless bottles of vitamins and nutrient supplements until he found the jar of natural vitamin C tablets. He popped several tablets into his mouth and sat down, resigned to the fact that he would rather stay here, where he felt safe, even at the risk of getting a chill. This was as far away as he could get from her, without leaving the apartment.

The sounds had now become louder and more intense. Casto raised his hands and covered his ears. He shut his eyes trying not to imagine what she was doing now. But with each sound, he could clearly see her in her ecstasy. Casto recalled how he had jumped out of bed in a fright the first time it had happened. Positive that she had gone into convulsions, he had stood almost paralyzed at a safe distance looking down at her. He didn't know what to do. And, as he helplessly watched her, his stomach had suddenly turned ice-cold with fear. Zoraida seemed to be another person. She was stretched out on the bed pulling at the covers; turning, twisting her body and rocking her buttocks sensually. Her knees had been bent upward with her legs far apart and she had thrust her pelvis forward forcefully and rhythmically. Zoraida's head was pushed back and her mouth open, as she licked her lips, moaning and gasping with excitement. Casto remembered Zoraida's eyes when she had opened them for brief moments. They had been fixed on someone or something, as if beckoning; but there was no one and certainly nothing he could see in the darkness of the room. She had rolled back the pupils and only the whites of her eyes were visible. She had blinked rapidly, shutting her eyes and twitching her nose and mouth. Then, a smile had passed her lips and a stream of saliva had run down her chin, neck and chest.

Now, as he heard low moans filled with pleasure, interrupted by short painful yelps that pierced right through him, Casto could also imagine her every gesture.

Putting down his hands, Casto opened his eyes. All he could do was wait patiently, as he always did, wait for her to finish. Maybe tonight won't be a long one; Casto swallowed anxiously.

He remembered about the meeting he had arranged earlier in the evening without Zoraida's knowledge, and felt better. After work, he had gone to see his mother; then they had both gone to see Zoraida's parents. It had been difficult for him to speak about it, but he had managed somehow to tell them everything. At first they had reacted with disbelief, but after he had explained carefully and in detail what was happening, they had understood his embarrassment and his reluctance to discuss this with anyone. He told them that when it all had begun, he was positive Zoraida was reacting to a high fever and was simply dreaming, perhaps even hallucinating. But, it kept happening, and it soon developed into something that occurred frequently, almost every night.

He finally realized something or someone had taken a hold of her. He was sure she was not alone in that room and in that bed!

It was all bizarre and, unless one actually saw her, he explained, it was truly beyond belief. Why, her actions were lewd and vulgar, and if they were sexual, as it seemed, then this was not the kind of sex a decent husband and wife engage in. What was even harder for him to bear was her enjoyment. Yes, this was difficult, watching her total enjoyment of this whole disgusting business! And, to make matters more complicated, the next day, Zoraida seemed to remember nothing. In fact, during the day, she was normal again. Perhaps a bit more tired than usual, but then, who wouldn't be after such an exhausting ordeal? And, lately she had become even less talkative with him, almost silent. But, make no mistake, Casto assured them, Zoraida remained a wonderful housekeeper and devoted mother. Supper was served on time, chores were done without fuss, the apartment was immaculate, and the kids were attended to without any problems. This happened only at night or rather early in the morning, at about two or two-thirty. He had not slept properly since this whole affair started. After all, he had to drive out to New Jersey to earn his living and his strength and sleep were being sapped away. He had even considered sleeping on the living room couch, but he would not be driven out of his own bed. He was still a man after all, a macho, master of his home, someone to be reckoned with, not be pushed out.

reminded them that he, as a man, had his needs, and this would surely make him ill, if continued. Of course, he would not touch her ... not as she was right now. After all, he reasoned, who knows what he could catch from her? As long as she was under the control of something—whatever it might be—he would keep his distance. No, Casto told them, he wanted no part of their daughter as a woman, not as long as she remained in this condition.

When her parents had asked him what Zoraida had to say about all of this, Casto had laughed, answering that she knew even less about it than he did. In fact, at one point she did not believe him and had sworn on the children's souls, claiming her innocence. But Casto had persisted and now Zoraida had finally believed him. She felt that she might be the victim of something, perhaps a phenomenon. Who knows? When Zoraida's parents and his mother suggested a consultation with Doña Digna, the spiritualist, he had quickly agreed.

Casto jumped slightly in his chair as he heard loud passionate moans and deep groans emanate from the bedroom and fill the kitchen.

"Stop it ... stop, you bitch!" Casto clenched his teeth, spitting out the words. But he took care not to raise his voice. "Stop it! What a happy victim you are! *Puta!* Whore! Some phenomenon ... I don't believe you and your story." But, even as he said these words, Casto knew he was not quite sure what to believe.

The first loud thump startled Casto and he braced himself and waited, anticipating what was to come. He heard the legs on their large double bed pounding the floor as the thumping became louder and faster.

Casto shuddered and folded his arms, digging his fingers into the flesh of his forearms. After a few moments, he finally heard her release, one long cry followed by several grunts, and then silence. He relaxed and sighed deeply with relief; it was all over.

"Animal ... she's just like an animal, no better than an alley cat in heat." Casto was wet with cold perspiration. He was most frightened of this last part. "Little hypocrite!"

Casto remembered how she always urged him to hurry, be quiet, and get it over with, on account of the children. A lot she cares about him tonight! Never in all their years of marriage had she ever uttered such sounds—he shook his head—or shown any passion or much interest in doing it.

Casto looked up at the clock; it was two minutes to three. He thought about the noise, almost afraid to move, fearful that his downstairs neighbor Roberto might knock on the door any moment. He recalled how Roberto had called him aside one morning and spoken to him, "Two and three in the morning, my friend; can't you and your wife control your passions at such an ungodly hour? My God ... such goings on! Man, and to tell you the truth, you people up there get me all worked up and horny.

Then, when I touch my old lady, she won't cooperate at that time, eh?" He had poked Casto playfully and winked, "Hey, what am I gonna do? Have a heart, friend." Casto shook his head, how humiliating and so damned condescending. They were behaving like the most common, vulgar people. Soon the whole fucking building would know! Roberto Thomas and his big mouth! Yes, and what will that sucker say to me next time? Casto trembled with anger. He wanted to rush in and shake Zoraida, wake her, beat her; he wanted to demand an explanation or else! But, he knew it wouldn't do any good. Twice he had tried. The first time, he had spoken to her the following day. The second time, he had tried to wake her up and she had only become wilder with him, almost violent, scaring him out of the bedroom. Afterwards, things had only become worse. During the day she withdrew, practically not speaking one word to him. The next few nights she had become wilder and the ordeal lasted even longer. No, he could not confront her.

Casto realized all was quiet again. He shut off the light, then stood and slowly, with trepidation, walked through the living room and entered the small foyer leading to their bedroom. He stopped before the children's bedroom, and carefully turned the knob, partially opening the door. All three were fast asleep. He was grateful they never woke up. What could he say to them. That their mother was sick? But sick with what?

As he stood at the entrance of their bedroom, Casto squinted scrutinizing every corner of the room before entering. The street lights seeping through the venetian blinds dimly illuminated the overcrowded bedroom. All was peaceful and quiet; nothing was disturbed or changed in any visible way. Satisfied, he walked in and looked down at Zoraida. She was fast asleep, breathing deeply and evenly, a look of serene contentment covered her face. Her long dark hair was spread over the pillow and spilled out onto the covers. Casto was struck by her radiant appearance each time it was all over. She had an air of glamour, so strange in a woman as plain as Zoraida. He realized, as he continued to stare at her, that he was frightened of Zoraida. He wanted to laugh at himself, but when Zoraida turned her head slightly Casto found himself backing out of the room.

Casto stood at the entrance and whispered, "Zoraida *nena* ... are ... are you awake?" She did not stir. Casto waited perfectly still and kept his eyes on her. After a few moments, Casto composed himself. He was sure she would remain sleeping; she had never woken up after it was all over. Slowly, he entered the room and inched his way past the bulky bureau, the triple dresser and the rocking chair near the window, finally reaching his side of the bed.

Casto rapidly made the sign of the cross before he lay down beside Zoraida. He was not very religious, he could take it or leave it; but, now, he reasoned that by crossing himself he was on God's side.

Casto glanced at the alarm clock; there were only two-and-a-half hours of sleep left before starting the long trip out to the docks of Bayonne, New Jersey. God, he was damned tired; he hardly ever got enough sleep anymore. This shit had to stop! Never mind, wait until the meeting. He remembered that they were all going to see Doña Digna, the spiritualist. That ought to change things. He smiled and felt some comfort knowing that this burden would soon be lifted. Seconds later he shut his eyes and fell fast asleep.

Everyone finished supper. Except for the children's chatter and Junior's protests about finishing his food, it had been a silent meal.

Casto got up and opened his special section of the cupboard. The children watched the familiar ritual without much interest as their father set out several jars of vitamins, two bottles of iron and liver tonic and a small plastic box containing therapeutic tablets. Casto carefully counted out and popped an assortment of twenty-four vitamin tablets into his mouth and then took several spoonfuls of tonic. He carefully examined the contents of the plastic box and decided not to take any of those tablets.

"Okay, Clarita, today you take vitamin C ... and two multi-vitamin supplements. You, too, Eddie and Junior, you might as well ..."

The children accepted the vitamins he gave them without resistance or fuss. They knew by now that no one could be excused from the table until Casto had finished taking and dispensing vitamins and tonic.

"Okay, kids, that's it. You can all have dessert later when your grandparents get here."

Quickly the children left.

Although Casto often suggested that Zoraida should eat properly, he had never asked her to take any of his vitamins or tonic, and she had never expressed either a desire or interest to do so.

He looked at Zoraida as she worked clearing the table and putting things away. Zoraida felt her heart pounding fiercely and she found it difficult to breathe. She wanted him to stop staring at her like that. Lately she found his staring unbearable. Zoraida's shyness had always determined her behavior in life. Ever since she could remember, any attempt that others made at intimate conversations or long discussions created feelings of constraint, developing into such anxiety that when she spoke, her voice had a tendency to fade. This was a constant problem for her; people often asked, "What was that?" or "Did you say something?" These feelings extended even into her family life. When her children asked impertinent questions, she would blush, unable to answer. Zoraida was ashamed of her own nakedness with Casto and would only undress when he was not present. When her children chanced to see her undressed at an unguarded moment, she would be distraught for several days.

It had been Casto's self assurance and his ability to be aggressive and determined with others that had attracted her to him.

Casto looked at Zoraida as she worked. "I'll put my things back and get the coffee started for when they get here," he said. She nodded and continued swiftly and silently with her chores.

Zoraida was twenty-eight, and although she had borne four children (three living, one stillborn) and had suffered several miscarriages, she was of slight build and thin, with narrow hips. She had a broad face and her smile revealed a wide space between her two front teeth. As a result, she appeared frail and childlike, much younger than her years. Whenever she was tired, dark circles formed under her eyes, contrasting against the paleness of her skin. This evening, she seemed to look even paler than ever to Casto; almost ghostlike.

Casto was, by nature, hypochondriacal and preoccupied with avoiding all sorts of diseases. He was tall and robust, with a broad frame; in fact, he was the picture of good health. He became furious when others laughed at him for taking so many vitamins and health foods. Most people ignored his pronouncements of ill health and even commented behind his back. "Casto'll live to be one hundred if he lives a day ... why, he's as fit as an ox! It's Zoraida who should take all them vitamins and then complain some. She looks like a toothpick, una flaca! That woman has nothing to show. I wonder what Casto ever saw in her, eh?"

Yet, it was her frail and sickly appearance that had attracted him the first time he saw her. He was visiting his married sister, Purencia, when Zoraida had walked in with her friend, Anna. Anna was a beautiful, voluptuous young woman with an olive tone to her skin that glowed; and when she smiled, her white teeth and full lips made her appear radiant. Zoraida, thin and pale by contrast, looked ill. In Casto's presence, she had smiled sheepishly, blushing from time to time. Anna had flirted openly, and commented on Purencia's brother, "You didn't tell me you had such a gorgeous macho in your family. Trying to keep him a secret, girl?" But it had been Zoraida that he was immediately drawn to. Casto had been so taken with her that he had confided in a friend that very day, "She really got to me, you know? Not loud or vulgar like that other girl, who was acting like a man, making remarks about me and all. No, she was a real lady. And, she's like, well, like a little sick sparrow flirting with death and having the upper hand. Quietly stubborn, you know? Not at all submissive like it might seem to just anybody looking at Zoraida. It's more as if nobody's gonna make the sparrow healthy, but it ain't gonna die either ... like it's got the best of both worlds, see?"

Yet, in all their nine years of marriage, Zoraida had never become seriously ill. Her pregnancies and miscarriages were the only time that she had been unable to attend to her family. After the last pregnancy, in an attempt to prevent children, Casto had decided on the rhythm system, where abstention is practiced during certain days of the month. It was, he reasoned, not only sanctioned by the Catholic Church, but there were no drugs or foreign objects put into one's body, and he did not have to be afraid of catching something nor getting sick.

Even after this recent miscarriage, Zoraida appeared to recover quickly, and with her usual amazing resiliency, managed the household chores and the children all by herself. She even found time to assuage Casto's fears of sickness and prepare special foods for him.

Casto could feel his frustration building inside as he watched her. What the hell was the matter with this wife of his? Quickly he reached into his cupboard and took out some Maalox; God, the last thing he wanted was an ulcer on account of all of this.

"I think I'll coat my stomach." Casto chewed several Maalox tablets vigorously, then swallowed. "This way, I can have coffee later and it won't affect me badly." He waited for a response, but she remained silent. Casto sighed, she don't even talk to me no more .... well, that's why I invited everybody here tonight, so they could see for themselves! He waited, staring at her, and then asked, "You got the cakes ready? I mean, you got them out of the boxes and everything?"

Zoraida nodded, not looking in his direction.

"Hey! Coño, I'm talking to you! Answer!"

"Yes," Zoraida whispered.

"And the cups and plates, you got them for the coffee and cake?"

"Yes," Zoraida repeated.

"I don't know, you know? It's been almost three months since Doña Digna did her job and cured you. I didn't figure you were gonna get so .... so depressed." Zoraida continued to work silently. "Wait. Stop a minute. Why don't you answer me, eh? Will you look at me, for God's sake!"

Zoraida stopped and faced Casto with her eyes lowered.

"Look, I'm trying to talk to you, understand? Can't you talk to me?" Zoraida kept perfectly still. "Say something, will you?"

"What do you want me to say?" Zoraida spoke softly, without looking at him.

"Can't you look at me when you talk?"

Swiftly and furtively, Zoraida glanced at Casto, then lowered her eyes once more.

"Coño, man, what do you think I do all day out there to make a living? Play? Working my butt off in those docks in all kinds of weather ... yeah. And for what? To come home to a woman that won't even look at me?" Casto's voice was loud and angry. He stopped, controlled himself, then continued, lowering his voice. "I get up every morning before six. Every freaking morning! I risk pneumonia, rheumatism, arthritis, all kinds of sickness. Working that fork lift, eight, ten hours a day, until my kidneys feel like they're gonna split out of my sides. And then, to make it worse, I gotta take orders from that stupid foreman who hates Puerto Ricans. Calling me a spic. In fact, they all hate Puerto Ricans out there. They call me spic, and they get away with it because I'm the only P.R. there, you know? Lousy Micks and Dagos! Listen, you know what they … ah, what's the use, I can't talk to you. Sure, why should you care? All you do is stay in a nice apartment, all warm and cozy. Damn it! I can't even have my woman like a normal man. First you had a phantom lover, right? Then, ever since Doña Digna took him away, you have that lousy chair you sit in and do your disappearing act. That's all you're good for lately. I can't even come near you. The minute I approach you like a human being for normal sex, you go and sit in that … that chair! I seen you fade out. Don't think I'm blind. You sit in that freaking thing, rocking away. You look … you … I don't even think you're breathing when you sit there! You should see yourself. What you look like is enough to scare anybody. Staring into space like some God damned zombie! You know what I should do with it? Throw it out, or better yet, bust that piece of crap into a thousand splinters! Yeah, that's what I ought to do. Only thing is, you'll find something else, right? Another lover, is that what you want, so you can become an animal? Because with me, let me tell you, you ain't no animal. With me you're nothing. Mira, you know something, I'm not taking no more of this. Never mind, when they get here they can see your whole bullshit act for themselves. Especially after I tell them … "

Zoraida barely heard him. The steady sound of the television program and the children's voices coming from their bedroom filled her with a pleasant feeling. How nice, she thought, all the children playing and happy. All fed and clean; yes, it's nice and peaceful.

The front doorbell rang.

"There they are." Casto had finished preparing the coffee. "I'll answer the door, you go on and get things ready."

Zoraida heard voices and trembled as she remembered Casto's threats and the fury he directed at her. Now he was going to tell them all sorts of things about her … untruths.

"Zoraida, where are you?" She heard her mother's voice, and then the voices of her father, mother-in-law and sister-in-law.

"Mommy, Mommy," Clarita ran into the kitchen, "Nana and Granpa, and Abuelita and Titi Purencia are here. Can we have the cake now?"

"In a little while, Clarita." Zoraida followed her daughter out into the living room and greeted everybody.

"Mommy, Mommy!" Junior shouted, "Tell Eddie to stop it, he's hitting me!"

"I was not, it was Clarita!" Eddie walked over to his little brother and pushed him. Junior began to cry and Clarita ran over and smacked Eddie.

"See?" Casto shouted, "Stop it! Clarita, you get back inside." He jumped up, grabbing his daughter by an elbow and lifting her off the ground. "Demonia, why are you hitting him? Zoraida, can't you control these kids?" He shook Clarita forcefully and she began to whine.

"Casto," Zoraida's thin shriek whistled through the room. "Don't be rough with her, please!"

"See that, Doña Clara, your daughter can't even control her own kids no more." He turned to the children, "Now, all of you, get back inside your room and watch television; and be quiet or you go right to bed and nobody gets any cake. You hear? That means all three, Clarita, Eddie and you too Junior."

"Can we have the cake now?" Eddie asked.

"I'll call you when it's time. Now go on, go on, all of you." Quickly, the children left.

"Calm yourself, son." Doña Elvira, Casto's mother, walked over to him. "You know how children are, they don't know about patience or waiting; you were no angel yourself, you and your sister."

"Let's go inside and have coffee, everybody." Casto led them into the kitchen. There were six chairs set around the kitchen table. Doña Clara and her husband, Don Isidro, Doña Elvira and her daughter, Purencia, squeezed in and sat down.

"Cut some cake for the kids and I'll bring it in to them," Casto spoke to Zoraida, who quickly began to cut up the chocolate cake and place the pieces on a plate. Everyone watched in silence. "Milk," snapped Casto. Zoraida set out three glasses of milk. Casto put everything on a tray and left.

"So, mi hijita,[1] how are you?" Doña Clara asked her daughter.

"I'm okay." Zoraida sat down.

"You look pale to me, very pale. Don't she, Papa?" Doña Clara turned for a moment to Don Isidro, then continued without waiting for an answer. "You're probably not eating right. Zoraida, you have to take better care of yourself."

"All right." Casto returned and sat down with the others. "They're happy now."

"Son," Doña Elvira spoke to Casto. "You look tired, aren't you getting enough rest?"

"I'm all right, Ma. Here, everybody, have some cake and coffee."

Everyone began to help themselves.

"It's that job of his. He works so hard," Doña Elvira reached over and placed an extra large piece of chocolate cake on Casto's plate before continuing, "He should have stayed in school and become an accountant, like I wanted. Casto was so good at math but ... instead, he ... "

---

1. my daughter

"Pass the sugar, please," Doña Clara interrupted, "and a little bit of that rum cake, yes. Thank you."

They all ate in silence.

Doña Elvira looked at Zoraida and sighed, trying to hide her annoyance. What a sickly looking woman, bendito. She looks like a mouse. To think my handsome, healthy son, who could have had any girl he wanted, picked this one. Doña Elvira could hardly swallow her cake. Duped by her phony innocence is what it was! And how could he be happy and satisfied with such a woman? Look at her, she's pathetic. Now, oh yes, now, he's finding out who she really is: not the sweet innocent one, after all. Ha! First a phantom lover and now … who knows what! Well we'll see how far she can go on with this, because now he's getting wise. With a sense of smug satisfaction, Doña Elvira half smiled as she looked at her daughter-in-law, then ate her cake and drank her coffee.

Purencia saw her mother's look of contempt directed at Zoraida. She's jealous of Zoraida, Purencia smiled. Nobody was ever good enough for Casto. For her precious baby boy well, and there you have it! Casto finally wanted Zoraida. Purencia smiled, serves Ma right. She looked at her sister-in-law who sat with her head bowed. God, she looks sicker than ever, but she never complains. She won't say nothing, even now, when he's putting her through this whole number. Poor goody-two-shoes Zoraida, she's not gonna get on Casto's case for nothing; like, why is he jiving her? I wonder what it is she's doing now? After that whole scene with Doña Digna, I thought she cured her of whatever that was. Purencia shrugged, who knows how it is with these quiet ones. They're the kind that hide the action. Maybe she's doing something nobody knows about … well, let's just see.

Doña Clara looked at her son-in-law, Casto, with anger and a scowl on her face. Bestia … brute of a man! He doesn't deserve anyone as delicate as Zoraida. She has to wait on that huge monster hand and foot. With all his stupid medicines and vitamins when he's as fit as a horse! Ungrateful man. He got an innocent girl, pure as the day she was born, that's what. Protected and brought up right by us. Never went out by herself. We always watched out who her friends were. She was guarded by us practically up until the moment she took her vows. Any man would have been proud to have her. Canalla! Sinvergüenza![2] She's clean, hardworking and obedient. Never complains. All he wants to do is humiliate her. We already went to Doña Digna, and Casto said Zoraida was cured. What now, for pity's sake? Doña Clara forced herself to turn away from Casto because the anger fomenting within her was beginning to upset her nerves.

Don Isidro sat uneasily. He wished his wife would not drag him into these things. Domestic disputes should be a private matter, he maintained emphatically,

---

2. cur/mongrel

between man and wife. But, his wife's nerves were not always what they should be, and so he had to be here. He looked at his daughter and was struck by her girlish appearance. Don Isidro sighed, the mother of three children and she hasn't filled out ... she still has the body of a twelve-year old. Well, after all, she was born premature, weighing only two pounds at birth. Don Isidro smiled, remembering what the doctors had called her. "The miracle baby," they had said, "Mr. Cuesta, your daughter is a miracle. She should not be alive." That's when he and Clara had decided to give her the middle name of Milagros. He had wanted a son, but after Zoraida's birth, his wife could bear no children, and so he had to be satisfied with what he had. Of course, he had two grandsons but they wouldn't carry on his last name, so, in a way it was not the same. Well, she's lucky to be married at all. Don Isidro nodded slightly, and Casto is a good, honest, hardworking man, totally devoted. Don't drink or gamble; he don't even look at other women. But, he too was lucky to get our Zoraida. After all, we brung her up proper and right. Catholic schools. Decent friends. Don Isidro looked around him at the silent table and felt a stiffness in his chest. He took a deep breath; what had she done? This whole business confused him. He thought Doña Digna had made the situation right once more.

"So, Casto, how are you? How's work?" Don Isidro asked.

"Pretty good. The weather gets to me, though. I have to guard against colds and sitting in that forklift gives me a sore back. But, I'm lucky to have work, the way things are going."

"You're right, they're laying off people everywhere. You read about it in the news everyday."

"Zoraida, eat something," Doña Clara spoke to her daughter.

"I'm not hungry, Mami," Zoraida's voice was just above a whisper.

"Casto, you should see to it that she eats!" Doña Clara looked at her son-in-law, trying to control her annoyance. "Whatever this problem is, I'm sure part of it is that you wife never eats."

"Why should he see that she eats or not?" Doña Elvira interjected, "He has to go to work everyday to support his family ... he hasn't got time to ... "

"Wait a minute, Ma," Casto interrupted, "the problem here ain't food. That's not gonna solve what's going on."

"It seems to solve all your problems, eh?" Doña Clara looked at Casto with anger.

"Just hold on now... wait," Don Isidro raised his hand. Now, we are all arguing here with each other and we don't even know what the problem is. Why don't we find out what's going on?" Don Isidro turned to Casto and waited.

Everyone fell silent. Don Isidro continued, "I thought that Doña Digna's treatment worked. After all, you told us that yourself."

"It's not that no more," Casto looked around him, "it's something else now."

"What?" Doña Elvira asked.

Casto looked at Zoraida who sat with her hands folded on her lap and her eyes downcast.

"Weren't things going good for you two?" Don Isidro asked. "I mean, things were back to normal relations between you, yes?"

"Yes and no," Casto said. "Yes for a while and then ..."

"Then what?" Doña Elvira asked. "What?"

Casto looked at Zoraida. "You want to say something, Zoraida?" She shook her head without looking at anyone.

"All right, then like usual, I gotta speak. You know that rocking chair Zoraida has? The one she brought with her when we got married?"

"You mean the one she's had ever since she was little? Why, we had that since Puerto Rico, it belonged to my titi Rosana." Doña Clara looked perplexed. "What about the rocker?"

"Well, she just sits in it, when... when she shouldn't." Casto could feel the blood rushing to his face.

"What do you mean she sits in it?" Doña Clara asked. "What is she supposed to do? Stand in it?"

"I said *when she shouldn't.*"

"Shouldn't what?" Doña Clara turned to Don Isidro, "Papa, what is this man talking about?"

"Look," Casto continued, "this here chair is in the bedroom. That's where she keeps it. All right? Now when, when I ... when we ..." Casto hesitated, "you know what I mean. Then, instead of acting like a wife, she leaves the bed and sits in the chair. She sits and she rocks back and forth."

"Does she stay there all night?" Doña Elvira asked.

"Pretty much."

Everyone looked at Zoraida, who remained motionless without lifting her eyes. A few moments passed before Don Isidro broke the silence.

"This is a delicate subject, I don't know if it's a good thing to have this kind of discussion here, like this."

"What do you want me to do, Isidro? First she had those fits in bed driving me nuts. Then we call in Doña Digna, who decides she knows what's wrong, and puts me through a whole freakin rigamarole of prayers and buying all kinds of crap. After all of that pendejá,[3] which costs me money that I frankly don't have, then she tells me my wife is cured. Now it starts again, except in another way. Look, I'm only human, you know? And she," Casto pointed to Zoraida, "is denying me what is my right as a man

---

3.   stupid mess

and as her husband. And I don't know why she's doing this. But I do know this time you're gonna be here to know what's going on. I ain't going through this alone. No way. And get myself sick? No!"

"Just a moment, now," Doña Clara said, "you say Zoraida sits in the rocker when you … approach her. Does she ever sit there at other times? Or only at that time?"

"Once in a while, at other times, but always … always, you know, at that time!"

"Ay … Dios mio!"[4] Doña Elvira stood up. "I don't know how my son puts up with this, if you ask me." She put her hands to her head. "Casto has the patience of a saint, any other man would do … do worse!"

"What do you mean, the patience of a saint?" Doña Clara glared at Doña Elvira. "And do worse what? Your son might be the whole cause of this, for all I know …"

"Now, wait." Don Isidro stood up. "Again, we are fighting and blaming this one or that one. This will get us nowhere. Doña Elvira, please sit down." Doña Elvira sat, and then Don Isidro sat down also. "Between a man and wife, it's best not to interfere."

"Okay then, Papa, what are we here for?" Doña Clara asked.

"To help, if we can," Purencia spoke. Everyone listened; she had not spoken a word before this. "I think that's what my brother wants. Right, Casto?" Casto nodded, and then shrugged. "Let Zoraida say something," Purencia continued. "She never gets a chance to say one word."

"Nobody's stopping her." Casto looked at Zoraida. "Didn't I ask her to say something? In fact, maybe she can tell us what's going on. Like, I would like to know too, you know."

"Zoraida," Doña Clara spoke firmly to her daughter, "mira, you better tell us what all of this is about."

Zoraida looked up, meeting her mother's angry stare. "I don't know what Casto means about the chair."

"Do you sit in the rocker or do you not sit there, like he says?" Her mother asked.

"Sometimes."

"Sometimes? What times? Is it like the way he says it is? Because, if this is so, we want to know why. Doña Digna told me, you and all of us, that there was an evil spirit in you that was turning your thoughts away from your husband, so that you could not be a wife to him. After she finished her treatment, she said the evil spirit or force was gone, and that you would go back to a normal husband-and-wife relationship. We have to accept that. She is a woman of honor that has been doing this work for many years, and that she is telling us the truth, yes?" Doña Clara took a deep breath. "But, if you feel anything is wrong, then it could be that Doña Digna did not succeed." She turned to Casto. "That's possible too, you know. These things sometimes get very

---

4.   Oh … my God!

complicated. I remember when the Alvarez household was having the worst kind of luck. Don Pablo had lost his job, his wife was sick, and one of their boys had an accident; all kinds of problems, remember? You remember, Papa? Well, Doña Digna had to go back, and it took her a long time to discover the exact cause and then to make things straight again." She turned to Zoraida, "Bueno, mi hija, you have to tell us what you feel, and if you are doing this to your husband, why." Doña Clara waited for her daughter's response. "Go ahead. Answer, por Dios!"

"I . . . " Zoraida cleared her throat in an effort to speak louder. "I just sit in the rocker sometimes. Because I feel relaxed there."

"Yeah!" Casto said, "Every time I go near her at night, or at two or three in the morning, she relaxes." He raised his hand and slammed the table, "God damned chair!"

"Calmate, mi hijito, calm yourself." Doña Elvira put her hand over her eyes. "I don't know how long my son can put up with all of this. Now she's got an obsession with a chair. Virgen purisima! Somebody has to tell me what is going on here!"

"Listen to me," Don Isidro spoke in a firm voice, "if it's the chair that bothers you, then we'll take it back home with us. Right, Mama?" He turned to Doña Clara who nodded emphatically. "There should be no objection to that, eh?"

Everyone looked at Casto who shrugged, and then at Zoraida who opened her mouth and shook her head, but was unable to speak.

"Very good." Don Isidro clasped his hands and smiled. "There, that ought to take care of the problems pretty much."

"Except, she might find something else." Casto said, "Who knows with her."

"Well, but we don't know that for sure, do we?" Don Isidro replied "and in the meantime, we gotta start somewhere."

"I feel we can always call Doña Digna in again if we have to," Doña Clara poured herself a cup of coffee. "After all, she was the one that told us Zoraida was cured."

"I agree," Doña Elvira said, "and even though she don't ask for money, I know my Casto was very generous with her."

"That's right, they don't charge, but after all, one has to give these people something, or else how can they live?" agreed Doña Clara.

"Isn't the weather funny this Spring?" Doña Elvira spoke amiably. "One minute it's cold and the next it's like summer. One never knows how to dress these . . . "

They continued speaking about the weather and about television programs. Purencia spoke about her favorite movie.

"That one about the professional hit-man, who has a contract out to kill the President of England . . . no, France, I think. Anyway, remember when he goes into that woman's house and kills her? I was so scared, I loved that movie."

Everyone agreed, the best kinds of movies were mysteries and thrillers.

Zoraida half-listened to them. They were going to take away the rocker. She had always had it, ever since she could remember. When she was a little girl, her parents told her it was a part of their history. Part of Puerto Rico and her great Aunt Rosana who was very beautiful and had countless suitors. The chair was made of oak with intricate carving and delicate caning. As a little girl, Zoraida used to rub her hands against the caning and woodwork admiringly, while she rocked, dreamed and pretended to her heart's content. Lately it had become the one place where she felt she could be herself, where she could really be free.

"Bueno, we have to go. It's late."

"That's right, me too."

"Wait," Casto told them, "I'll drive you people home."

"You don't have to ... " Don Isidro protested. "We know you are tired."

"No, I'm not. Besides, I gotta drive ma and Purencia home anyway."

"That's right," Purencia said, "my old man doesn't like me going out at night. It's only because of Mami that he let me. So, Casto has to take me home."

"I gotta get you the chair, wait," Casto said. "And, you don't wanna carry that all the way home. It's not very big, but still, it's a lot to lug around."

"All right then, very good."

Everyone got up and Zoraida began to clear away the dishes.

"Let me help you," Doña Clara said as she stood up.

"Me too," Doña Elvira said, without rising.

"No, no thanks. That's all right. I can do it myself," Zoraida said. "Besides, I have to put the kids to bed and give them their milk and all."

"I don't know how she does it. Three little ones and this place is always immaculate." Doña Clara turned to Doña Elvira. "It's really too much for her, and she has no help at all."

Doña Elvira stood. "She keeps a very clean house," she said and walked out with Purencia following after Casto and Don Isidro.

Doña Clara looked at her daughter, who worked silently and efficiently. "Mira, mi hija, I better talk to you." She stood close to Zoraida and began to speak in a friendly manner keeping her voice low. "You have to humor men; you must know that by now. After all, you are no longer a little girl. All women go through this difficulty, eh? You are not the only one. Why, do you know how many times your father wants ... well, you know, wants it? But I, that is, if I don't want to do it, well I find a way not to. But diplomatically, you know? All right, he's older now and bothers me less; still, what I mean is, you have to learn that men are like babies and they feel rejected unless you handle the situation just right. Now, we'll take the rocker back home with us because it will make him feel better. But you must do your part too.

Tell him you have a headache, or a backache, or you can even pretend to be asleep. However, once in a while you have to please him, you know. After all, he does support you and the children and he needs it to relax. What's the harm in it? It's a small sacrifice. Listen, I'll give you some good advice; make believe you are enjoying it and then get it over with real quick, eh? So, once in a while you have to, whether you like it or not, that's just the way it is for us. Okay? Do you understand? Zoraida turned away and, without responding, continued with her work. "Did you hear what I just told you?" Doña Clara grabbed Zoraida's shoulder firmly, squeezing her finger against the flesh. "You didn't even hear what I said to you!"

Zoraida pulled away and turned quickly facing her mother. She looked directly at Doña Clara, "I heard you … " Zoraida stopped and a smile passed her lips. "I heard every word you said, Mami."

"Oh, all right then … " Doña Clara said, somewhat startled by her daughter's smile. "I only wanted to … "

"Mama! Come on, it's time to go," Don Isidro's voice interrupted her.

Doña Clara and Zoraida went into the living room. Casto carried the rocking chair and waited by the door. The children had come out of their room and were happily jumping about.

"Look, Mommy, Granpa gave me a quarter." Clarita said.

"Me too," said Eddie. "He even gave Junior one."

"All right, get to bed!" Casto shouted. "Zoraida, put them down, will you?"

Everybody said goodbye and, in a moment, Casto and the others left.

"Mommy, where is Daddy taking your chair?" Clarita asked.

"To Nana's."

"Why?"

"Because they want it now?"

"Don't you want it no more?"

"I already had it for a long time, now they need to have it for a while."

Zoraida gave the children their milk, bathed them and put them to bed. Then, she finished rapidly in the kitchen and went to bed herself. She looked over at the empty space near the window. It was gone. She wouldn't be able to sit there anymore and meet all her suitors and be beautiful. The last time … the last time she was dancing to a very slow number, a ballad. But she couldn't remember the words. And she was with, with … which one? She just couldn't remember him anymore. If she had the rocker, she could remember; it would all come back to her as soon as she sat down. In fact, she was always able to pick up exactly where she had left off the time before. She shut her eyes, deciding not to think about the rocker, about Casto, Doña Digna or her mother. Instead, Zoraida remembered her children who were safe and asleep in their own beds. In a short while, she heard the front door open and recognized Casto's footsteps. She shut her eyes, turned over, facing away from his side of the bed. Casto found the apartment silent and dark, except for the night light.

In the bedroom, Casto looked at Zoraida, who seemed fast asleep, then at the empty space near the window where the rocker usually stood. Their bedroom seemed larger and his burden lighter. Casto sighed, feeling better. He reached over and lightly touched Zoraida; this was a safe time of the month, maybe she would wake up. He waited and, after a moment decided to go to sleep. After all, he could always try again tomorrow.

Tomás Rivera

(1935–1984)
Mexican American

Tomás Rivera is one of the most beloved figures in Chicano literature. Besides authoring a pioneering novel, ... **y no se lo tragó la tierra/And the Earth Did Not Devour Him**, *and other important shorter works, Rivera was a tireless organizer and popularizer of the Chicano literary movement. Through numerous speeches, essays, and formal presentations as well as through collaborations in small magazines and correspondence with writers around the country, he proclaimed the need for a literature of the Chicano people, he outlined the parameters of such a literature, and he offered encouragement and publishing opportunities to younger writers. He also created stories and a novel that would help to establish a canon for Chicano literature.*

Rivera was born and raised in Crystal City, Texas, as the son of Mexican immigrants who became seasonal farmworkers in the migrant stream to the Midwest. Despite the disruptions of migrant labor, Rivera was able to finish high school and, with his parents' encouragement, only work the fields in the summer months in order to attend college. After continuing his education and earning his doctorate in Romance languages and literature at the University of Oklahoma in 1969, his rise in academia was meteoric: just ten years later he was appointed chancellor of the University of California at Riverside. He had held this position for five years when he died of a sudden heart attack in 1984.

Rivera's most important contribution as a writer has been his novel ... **y no se lo tragó la tierra**. *The interrelated stories that make up the novel are tied together by the central character, who is trying to remember and understand his experiences and those of his family. As such, the novel takes on two levels: in the first, the adolescent searches for his identity in society and the universe and, in the second, he seeks to order the Chicano experience and the social and psychological forces that condition that experience.*

First Communion *is one of the central triad of narratives in* ... **y no se lo tragó la tierra**. *After the adolescent protagonist has confronted God, the devil, and fatalism from within the context of folklore, family, and religion, the adolescent remembers in* **First Communion** *the events leading up to his initiation into the body of the Catholic faithful and into adult society.*

First Communion

The priest always held First Communion during mid-spring. I'll always remember that day in my life. I remember what I was wearing and I remember my godfather and the pastries and chocolate that we had after mass, but I also remember what I saw at the cleaners that was next to the church. I think it all happened because I left so early for church. It's that I hadn't been able to sleep the night before, trying to remember all of my sins, and worse yet, trying to arrive at an exact number. Furthermore since Mother had placed a picture of hell at the head of the bed and since the walls of the room were papered with images of the devil and since I wanted salvation from all evil, that was all I could think of.

"Remember, children, very quiet, very very quiet. You have learned your prayers well, and now you know which are the mortal sins and which are the venial sins, now you know what sacrilege is, now you know that you are God's children, but you can also be children of the devil. When you go to confession you must tell all of your sins, you must try to remember all of the sins you have committed. Because if you forget one and receive Holy Communion then that would be a sacrilege and if you commit sacrilege you will go to hell. God knows all. You cannot lie to God. You can lie to me and to the priest, but God knows everything; so if your soul is not pure of sin, then you should not receive Holy Communion. That would be a sacrilege. So everyone confess all of your sins. Recall all of your sins. Wouldn't you be ashamed if you received Holy Communion and then later remembered a sin that you had forgotten to confess? Now, let's see, let us practice confessing our sins. Who would like to start off? Let us begin with the sins that we commit with our hands when we touch our bodies. Who would like to start?"

The nun liked for us to talk about the sins of the flesh. The real truth was that we practiced a lot telling our sins, but the real truth was that I didn't understand a lot of things. What did scare me was the idea of going to hell because some months earlier I had fallen against a small basin filled with hot coals which we used as a heater in the little room where we slept. I had burned my calf. I could well imagine how it might be to burn in hell forever. That was all that I understood. So I spent that night, the eve of my First Communion, going over all the sins I had committed. But what was real hard was coming up with the exact number like the nun wanted us to. It must have been dawn by the time I finally satisfied my conscience. I had committed one hundred and fifty sins, but I was going to admit to two hundred.

"If I say one hundred and fifty and I've forgotten some, that would be bad. I'll just say two hundred and that way even if I forget lots of them I won't commit any kind of sacrilege. Yes, I have committed two hundred sins ... Father, I have come to confess my sins ... How many? ... Two hundred ... of all kinds ... The Commandments? Against all of the Ten Commandments ... This way there will be no sacrilege. It's better this way. By confessing more sins you'll be purer."

I remember I got up much earlier that morning than Mother had expected. My godfather would be waiting for me at the church and I didn't want to be even one second late.

"Hurry, Mother, get my pants ready, I thought you already ironed them last night."

"It's just that I couldn't see anymore last night. My eyesight is failing me now and that's why I had to leave them for this morning. But tell me, what's your hurry now? It's still very early. Confession isn't until eight o'clock and it's only six. Your padrino[1] won't be there until eight."

"I know, but I couldn't sleep. Hurry, Mother, I want to leave now."

"And what are you going to do there so early?"

"Well, I want to leave because I'm afraid I'll forget the sins I have to confess to the priest. I can think better at the church."

"All right, I'll be through in just a minute. Believe me, as long as I can see I'm able to do a lot."

I headed for church repeating my sins and reciting the Holy Sacraments. The morning was already bright and clear but there weren't many people out in the street yet. The morning was cool. When I got to the church I found that it was closed. I think the priest might have overslept or was very busy. That was why I walked around the church and passed by the cleaners that was next to the church. The sound of loud laughter and moans surprised me because I didn't expect anybody to be in there. I thought it might be a dog but then it sounded like people again and that's why I peeked in through the little window in the door. They didn't see me but I saw them. They were naked and embracing each other, lying on some shirts and dresses on the floor. I don't know why but I couldn't move away from the window. Then they saw me and tried to cover themselves, and they yelled at me to get out of there. The woman's hair looked all messed up and she looked like she was sick. And me, to tell the truth, I got scared and ran to the church but I couldn't get my mind off of what I had seen. I realized then that maybe those were the sins that we committed with our hands. But I couldn't forget the sight of that woman and that man lying on the floor. When my friends started arriving I was going to tell them but then I thought it would be better to tell them after communion. More and more I was feeling like I was the one who had committed a sin of the flesh.

"There's nothing I can do now. But I can't tell the others 'cause they'll sin like me. I better not go to communion. Better that I don't go to confession. I can't, now that I know, I can't. But what will Mom and Dad say if I don't go to communion? And my padrino, can't leave him there waiting. I have to confess what I saw. I feel like going back. Maybe they're still there on the floor. No choice, I'm gonna have to lie. What if I forget it between now and confession? Maybe I didn't see anything? And if I hadn't seen anything?"

I remember that when I went in to confess and the priest asked for my sins, all I told him was two hundred and of all kinds. I did not confess the sin of the flesh. On returning to the house with my godfather, everything seemed changed, like I was and yet wasn't in the same place. Everything seemed smaller and less important. When I

---

1.   godfather

saw my Dad and my Mother I imagined them on the floor. I started seeing all of the grown-ups naked and their faces even looked distorted, and I could even hear them laughing and moaning, even though they weren't even laughing. Then I started imagining the priest and the nun on the floor. I couldn't hardly eat all of the sweet bread or drink the chocolate. As soon as I finished, I recall running out of the house. It felt like I couldn't breath.

"So, what's the matter with him? Such manners!"

"Ah, compadre,[2] let him be. You don't have to be concerned on my account. I have my own. These young ones, all they can think about is playing. Let him have a good time, it's the day of his First Communion."

"Sure, compadre, I'm not saying they shouldn't play. But they have to learn to be more courteous. They have to show more respect toward adults, their elders, and all the more for their padrino."

"No, well that's true."

I remember I headed toward the thicket. I picked up some rocks and threw them at the cactus. Then I broke some bottles. I climbed a tree and stayed there for a long time until I got tired of thinking. I kept remembering the scene at the cleaners, and there, alone, I even liked recalling it. I even forgot that I had lied to the priest. And then I felt the same as I once had when I had heard a missionary speak about the grace of God. I felt like knowing more about everything. And then it occurred to me that maybe everything was the same.

---

2.   co-parent (the godfather of the parent's child)

Ed Vega

(b. 1936)
Puerto Rican

Ed Vega is a Puerto Rican fiction writer who bases many of his works on life in New York City's Spanish Harlem. Edgardo Vega Yunqué was born in Ponce, Puerto Rico, on May 20, 1936, where he lived with his family until they moved to the Bronx, New York, in 1949. He was raised in a devout Baptist home, his father having been a minister of that faith; today, Vega and his wife and children have adopted the Buddhist faith. As a child, books were very accessible at home and he began both his education and writing at an early age in Spanish in Puerto Rico. After moving to New York and going through the public education system of the city he graduated in 1969 Phi Beta Kappa from New York University. From 1982 to the present he has been a full-time writer.

Vega is one of the most prolific Hispanic prose writers, although much of his work remains unpublished. In 1977 he began actively publishing short stories in Hispanic magazines, and in 1985 he published his first novel, **The Comeback,** *a rollicking satire of ethnic autobiography and the identity crisis as personified by a half–Puerto Rican and half–Eskimo ice hockey player who becomes involved in an underground revolutionary movement for Puerto Rican independence. In 1987 he published a collection of inter-connected short stories,* **Mendoza's Dreams,** *narrated by a warm-hearted observer of the human comedy, Alberto Mendoza. Vega's third book,* **Casualty Report** *(1991), is a collection of stories that chronicle the death of dreams, as characters faced with racism, poverty, and crime succumb to despair in many forms: violence, alcohol and drug abuse, withdrawal and resignation.*

The Kite

As if his office were a giant magnet which attracted neighborhood hysteria, his day invariably began with a frantic call from one of his clients. There was no translator at the Welfare Department; the nurse at the Public Health Clinic had made them return home for their clinic card even though she knew them by name; and crime of crimes, the building inspector had arrived too early, and naturally, he didn't expect to get in, with the apartment still in that condition. It never stopped. Like waves upon a shore, they buffeted his conscience with their helpless demands. Their voices heavy, they clung desperately to him.

This time the phone call was not from a client but from his own mother, concerned again about his father's health. "It's his heart, Ricky," she said, tremulously, adding that his father had complained of chest pains the previous week, and she'd made him go to Kings County Hospital for a checkup. She paused and, holding back her tears, told him the doctors had suggested he take it easy for a few months. "He can't go lifting heavy things in the job," she said. "They laid him off yesterday, Ricky.

Le dieron leiof." His mother pronounced the word *issy*, and compulsively he corrected her. "Easy, Ma," he said. "And on the job. Not in the job."

"*Si, m'ijito,*[1] she replied, becoming self-conscious and lapsing totally into Spanish.

"Did you tell Becky?" he asked.

"*No, todavia no.*"[2]

"Why not, Ma?"

"*No quiero que tenga problemas con la criatura,*" she explained she hoped Becky would not have problems with the baby. He said he understood but silently wished she hadn't reminded him of his clients. The following day Mrs. Ramos and her daughter, Amy, were due in his office to plan a strategy for letting Mr. Ramos know that his daughter, at age fifteen, was pregnant and had no way of determining who had "given her the baby." That's what Amy had said, as if babies were acquired in much the same manner as the common cold. From the sublime to the ridiculous with something lost in translation.

His sister Rebecca was due to have her second child and his mother didn't want her to have problems with the creature. He wanted to be sympathetic but felt only annoyance and consequently guilt. As he listened to his mother, his temples began throbbing, a sure sign of an upcoming tension headache. In a nightmarish fantasy which he recognized as a Kafkaesque indulgence on his part, it seemed as if the green-gray institutional walls of his small office, decorated with posters in English and Spanish, warning and exhorting on the perils of venereal disease, unwanted pregnancy, tooth decay, drugs, and a poor diet, were closing in on him, rendering him a felon condemned to spend the rest of his life doling out advice on how people could work themselves up from the morass of their lives. He didn't want to think about it. His mother was going on about the difficulty of his sister's last pregnancy.

"That's okay, Ma," he said, a bit shrilly. "I'll call Becky if you want."

"No, no," she answered. "Don't worry. It's all right. Just come tonight, Ricky. Come and visit. Sit down and have supper with your father. I'll make *chuletas*[3] and *tostones*[4] the way you both like them."

"Okay, Ma. I'll be there after work," he said, and held back from saying that the fried food was killing his father.

"What time?" she asked.

"About seven, Ma."

"No school tonight?"

---

1. Yes, my son
2. No, not yet
3. pork chops
4. fried plantains

"No, no school, Ma," he said. *"Bendicion."*

"Qué Dios te bendiga, m'ijito," she said, blessing him. Rick Sánchez hung up the phone and for the rest of the day, as he attempted to bring some order to other people's lives, at times vacillating between despair and anger, he thought about his father: busting himself up year after year, handling heavy scrap metal in winter and summer so that his hands were cracked, the fingers twisted, the fingernails crushed and grown over. And when he picked up his guitar to play his *decimas,* he looked like a trained brown bear, except that his face took on a look of such kindness that Rick felt like he was ten again, walking hand in hand with him on the boardwalk in Coney Island, never afraid because his Papi was there with his big muscles, holding him tight on the roller coaster rising and falling so that the ocean looked tilted and the sky so close he could almost touch it. Papi, make a muscle. Show Juanny and Pito. Show 'em, Papi. Busting himself up inside all those years so his kids could go to college, foregoing that psychically ubiquitous dream house on the island to pay for books and clothes and later a few bucks for him, his only son, *sangre de mi sangre y alma de mi alma,* bloodofmyblood and soulofmysoul. Extra *cocos* for him to entertain the ladies, like he said, winking knowingly, or seemingly so, as he put on his air of macho around town, but not fooling anyone, because there had never been another woman since he'd met Rick's mother in Cacimar, up there in the mountains, and had serenaded her until, hat in hand, twisting and sweating, he had asked for her hand in marriage and then had promised to love her and keep her in sickness and in health and all the other hallowed garbage, Rick thought.

Thinking and wishing, as he traveled the maze of other people's pain, that his father could finally understand that they were not the same men and that too much had happened in the passage from one culture into the other. He wanted desperately to convey his respect but the words always came out short and angry, so full of the New York wise guy that even after Psychology and Sociology, and Freud and Jung, and Sartre and Camus, and the rest of the booknames, the distance was still there between them. And now his father was ready to check out forever without a resolution to their differences.

Numbed by the knowledge that he might soon be faced with the paradox of freedom brought on by grief, Rick Sánchez, as if in sleep, listened mechanically to the faceless voices and called, and referred, and counseled until he finished his daily penance. He left work aching. Not only his head, but his entire body felt as if it had absorbed each single pain brought to him. Out in the street he walked in a daze, the gray tenements echoing his own helpless cry for release from the daily agony of existing among tortured souls.

Once on the subway he tried amusing himself by wondering why "Only the Dead Know Brooklyn," a favorite short story by Thomas Wolfe. Deeper and deeper into Brooklyn and into himself he went, listening, watching, as he grew closer to home, the waters of the Atlantic, winter dark, the sky too gray to describe at day's end, identifying the responsibilities of impending death, categorizing major and minor anxieties, minimizing guilt while doors opened and closed and opened and the train click-clacked over the rails, click-clacking to keep the beat for swarms of pushing, squirming, dying people, until exhausted, more by not knowing what awaited him than from the hour-long ride, he bolted upright and rode the last few stops standing, anticipating the hatred he now felt towards the crass amusement park of his childhood, so desolate in winter, his memories like shadows thrown upon the wall of time.

He walked quickly down the stairs of the elevated train platform, despising the street, the shuttered game booths and smells of warmed-over quick food. The voices of his innocence were calling him, beckoning him to his childhood, lulling him so he felt as if he'd drown in anxiety before he arrived. He knew there was to be no respite once he reached his father's home and yet he felt not as harried and therefore more conscious that he was trapped and was being asked to return to a kind of amusement park called Spicland, where one took rides and played games of chance in Spanish.

In the elevator of the massive housing project, he thought about the Ramos' case, wondering if his father would've understood Rebecca becoming pregnant at fifteen. When he rang the doorbell his mother immediately opened the door. This confirmed his suspicion that she was watching the street and had timed his arrival. He asked her for her blessing, received it, and kissed her dutifully. "Where's Pop?" he asked, expecting to be informed that he was in the bedroom, resting.

"He's in the kitchen peeling the *platanos* for the *tostones*," his mother said, wiping her hands on her apron and closing the door. She was thin and small and finally, in the last year, she was beginning to look old, her dark skin a little wrinkled and her fine, Indian hair, once so black, beginning to gray. "You know how he is," she added in Spanish, excusing his presence in the kitchen. "He's got to be moving his hands all the time." Rick laughed self-consciously and let out a big breath. When he had taken off his overcoat and loosened his tie, he called out, "How you doing, Pop?" wanting his father's voice to reassure him before he saw the man and had to take in any change in him.

"I'm all right, Rick," his father answered. "C'mon in and have a beer."

Rick crossed the neat, linoleum-covered living room, the furniture like that inside a showcase: lamps, tables, shelves, figurines, plaster bullfighters and ballerinas on the walls, sofa and chairs, straight out of some unpublished Latin *House Beautiful* or *Better Homes and Fire Escapes* magazine; cheap, expensive-looking furniture which offered some semblance of unconscious upward mobility, a concept which his parents would never understand, just like they did not understand middle class or ethnic. New Yorkers were either Irish, Jewish, Italian, Chinese or Negro. The rest were Puerto Ricans, acknowledging other Latins as mere extensions, latecomers who spoke the language, albeit oddly, and therefore fell into that all encompassing category of *hispanos*. Kathy, the corn-fed blonde VISTA volunteer from Iowa, whom he had brought to dinner to satisfy their curiosity and hers, had baffled his mother. When asked if Bauer were an Irish name, Kathy had responded that it was German. His mother had nodded politely but with undisguised incredulity—as if to point out that Kathy need not be ashamed of her background, at least not in her house—commented that it was funny but that Kathy looked Irish. In her scheme of things, blondes and redheads were Irish, brunettes Italians, and the ones who weren't black and obviously not Latin, were Jewish. So much for the melting pot theory, a concept which his mother had never encountered, but had nonetheless mastered.

"How you making out, Pop?" Rick said, as he took a seat at the other end of the table, opposite his father.

"You know. Working," his father said. Then he laughed, embarrassed by his choice of words. "Well, not right now. But I keep busy talking to your mother. She likes to hear me talk about the old country."

Having worked on the Brooklyn docks and for the last ten years with the metal company, his father used the phrase as if he were a European immigrant. And when he said "the old country," his eyes took on the same wistful look of the man who has admitted he has been seduced by America, not resenting his folly because life had been good in some respects, and this was all a man could ask for, but wishing once more for youth and therefore connecting the desire to the homeland. But he hadn't changed. There was not a trace of whatever the doctors had found. He looked strong as ever, the neck muscled and his dark eyes deep and narrow above his hawk nose. He was lighter than his mother but being out in the sun had burnished his skin to a permanent bronze.

"You know what I mean, Rick?"

"Yeah, I understand, Pop," Rick said, emptily. Wanting to change the conversation, he asked how his younger sister was doing in school.

"She's doing good, Ricky," his father said. Without turning away from the stove his mother said that Christina had gone downstairs to finish her homework with her friend Elizabeth.

"She coming up soon?" His mother stopped stirring the pot of beans, looked at the clock on the wall, nodded and resumed stirring. As if she were simply making small talk, she asked if Rick had ever met his sister's girlfriend. "They just moved into the building," she said. Ever on the alert, his father caught on immediately.

"For Chrisake, Margarita," he said. "Leave him alone. He's only twenty-six." Rick searched for sarcasm in his father's remark but found none. "Geez, I didn't have the guts to ask for your hand until I was a year older."

"She goes to Hunter College with Christina," his mother went on, paying no attention to his father's reproach of her matchmaking. "She wants to be a kindergarten teacher."

"Ma, she's a baby," Rick protested. "What is she, nineteen? She's Chris' age, right?"

There had been no malice in the words but there was little doubt in Rick's mind that his father was enjoying his discomfort. He laughed and, pointing the long knife at him, told him to watch out. "It's a conspiracy," he said. "You don't know it but they get together late at night and decide who's going to get this guy or that one. You can't get away from them. You can go anywhere you want and think they ain't gonna find you, but they do. They're worse than the CIA. How do you think they got me? If it wasn't for the conspiracy I'd be a free man today."

His father had finished paring the thick skin off the plantains, sliced them diagonally and placed the slices into two bowls of salted water. The green ones went into one and the ripe into the other. With a deft motion of the knife he swept the plantains' skins off the table and into a garbage bag and, standing up, asked Rick if he wanted a beer. Rick asked if he was going to have one.

"¡Seguro que sí!"[5] he said. "This thing with the heart is nothing," he added, pounding his chest with the palm of his hand. "Your mother probably told you I was ready for the grave. Whatta they gonna do, open me up and gimme a new engine?"

Over his father's broad shoulders, Rick looked at his mother. Her eyes wore a pleading look and Rick knew she was repeating a silent prayer. Rick answered quickly that all she had said was that he needed rest.

"That was all, Pop."

"C'mon," his father said in Spanish, handing him a can of beer. "Let's go sit in the living room. If we stay here people are gonna start saying your mother's got me sitting on the trunk." He said all of it in Spanish, adopting the fraudulent, tough guy image, the reference to the trunk being the equivalent of the henpecked husband. Rick followed his father into the living room and sat down on the couch. His father took the big chair opposite him. For a while they said nothing. Rick could hear the frying in the kitchen, the smells wafting to him in waves of memories of cold winters, before they moved into the projects, when he would race home in the twilight of evening, zooming up the four flights of the tenement and sniffing always, like an animal, not consciously but instinctively, so that even were he blind he could've reached home

---

5. Yes, of course!

on the aroma of his mother's cooking, on time each day, no matter what meat it was except on Thanksgiving, always with rice, white, red, mixed with beans or *gandules*,[6] even black rice, black from the ink of the *calamares*, the canned squid, and beans in sauce, *salsa*, like the music now, thick and spicy, making you forget disappointments.

They sat in silence still, two strangers. Outside, darkness had taken over and way out on the channel a boat was making its way out to sea, the lights of its superstructure shimmering like tear drops over the dark water. A *marintaiga*,[7] Rick thought. The "Marine Tiger" returning unhappy victims of an experiment back to their homeland. It was a make-believe ship which traveled in his consciousness bringing spics from the island to the city. He'd never seen the ship, had never met anyone who admitted having arrived on it; everyone always claimed entrance into the great land on Eastern or Pan Am; the ship thus passed from the reality of its dank, crowded quarters and rough seas, to the level of myth. And yet he recalled the word *marintaiga* being used in *bodegas*,[8] in school, outside the church on Sundays, at parties, playgrounds, and in the halls of his adolescence when he was undecided about accepting the *yerba*, the sweet smelling smoke which seemed as much a part of their existence as the language he shared with the others. The word was applied to the ship primarily, but also to any newly arrived person whose English was inadequate or whose manner was backward. They were now called hicks. The *marintaiga* had vanished and in its place and undernourished, the pencil-thin mustaches razor-sharp, the Yardley-slick, brilliantined haircuts singling them out as outcasts, their funny black and white shoes, the mud of that wretched island still encrusted on them, making them caricatures to be ridiculed. They bred each year and reproduced hip, sophisticated, English-speaking replicas of themselves, males and females, their eyes hungry and pleading.

His father finally broke the silence by asking about Kathy Bauer, how he was doing with her. He said he guessed she was all right, that he had stopped seeing her at the end of the summer and that she had gone home the previous month. His father seemed surprised and then the corners of his mouth turned down, his brows went up and he nodded, reflecting for a moment before he took another sip of beer.

"She was a little silly, wasn't she?" he said, smoothing his mustache with the back of his hand. "*Boba*,[9] you know, Ricky. *Medio apendeja.*"[10]

Rick laughed in earnest. For the time being the ice had been broken and things were forgiven between them. One thing about the old man, Rick thought, he had guts.

---

6. pigeon peas
7. Marine Tiger (name of a ship)
8. grocery store
9. dummy
10. somewhat stupid

"Yeah, Pop," he said, truly having no argument with his father's assessment of Kathy. "She was a little silly."

"I'm not kidding," his father said, confidentially, leaning forward in his seat. "I'm speaking to you man to man. You need a strong woman. You know, no crap. All business. The house and the kids." He sounded like one of his Italian buddies from the docks of South Brooklyn. "You wanna woman you can respect. Somebody you don't have to worry about watching where she goes and who she talks to. Me, I was lucky with your Ma."

"I understand, Pop," he said.

"I know you understand, Rick," his father replied, leaning back once more as if the effort had tired him. He reflected a moment, choosing his words. "I wasn't mad at you for living with the girl. Not even your mother was mad. We understand how things change and young people want freedom. In my day freedom was being able to pick your own clothes or the kind of trade you wanted to take up. Your mother and me may not have an education like you but we're not stupid people. It wasn't even that she was an American."

"I know, Pop."

"You believe me, right? I'm not prejudiced, you know that. You brought all your friends to the house. Negro, white, Jewish. I didn't care. People are people. Some are good and some are rotten. But silly women are nothing but trouble and in that the color doesn't matter."

"I guess I found out the hard way," Rick said, relenting, avoiding the argument.

"Sometimes that's the only way," his father said, nodding philosophically. "That's why I didn't say nothing to you. I wasn't happy about you and the girl but I wasn't mad at you. Why did she go home?"

"I don't know. I guess breaking up with me had something to do with it. I think the neighborhood finally got to her. She thought she was really going to solve the problems on her block. You know, the drugs and illegitimate kids and the rest of the crap. It was too much for her. Hell, it's too much for the people themselves, let alone some young kid who's been sheltered all her life and the only time she ever saw people who weren't white was in the movies."

"You miss her?"

"At first. You know, you get used to a woman."

"Yeah, I know." His father was agreeing but the subject was obviously causing him discomfort. The generalization included him and therefore his own relationship to Rick's mother. "She was a good looking girl, that was for sure," he said, perhaps regretting, or so Rick conjectured, that he had been the cause of the breakup between him and Kathy. He realized the speculation was made only to soothe

himself and the impotent anger he had experienced when he didn't tell his father to
tend to his own affairs.

He wasn't able to explore the feeling, for at that moment the door of the
apartment swung open and Christina came in, trailed by another girl. His sister was a
young replica of their mother: small, thin, pretty in a kind of acceptable way, attractive
to males but not threatening to women. In contrast to the almost bland nature of
their mother, however, Christina was full of their father's brash enthusiasm. Her eyes
opened and she let out a squeal of delight upon seeing Rick. Before he had a chance
to greet her, she was next to him on the couch, touching his face and curling up
against him. She was still like a kid, Rick thought, awed by him. Even though she had
become more direct in speaking to him, she still lapsed into childhood, reaching back
to the times when her only desire in life was to emulate him. She had followed him
everywhere and had tried outdoing his friends in sports, raging when she fell short of
her goals and they laughed benevolently at her zest for competition. But all that had
passed, and with the years she had grown gracefully into womanhood, the driving
spirit which was her trademark, transformed into her need to prove herself
academically. She traveled nearly two hours each morning to attend Bronx High School
of Science, something which she did for three years. Their parents at first had been
worried but sensed that to attempt to dissuade her would break her spirit. The drive
urged her to study and become a person to be reckoned with, a credit to their people,
as their father had put it on numerous occasions. She spoke rapidly, excited at seeing
Rick again, changing back and forth from English to Spanish, some sentences rising
and falling with the peculiarity of rhythm which Yiddish gave English in Brooklyn.
One might call it Bruklin Borincano, so that describing a history professor at school
she once said: "*Ay no,* Ricky! I can't stand him. *Y tan antipático.*[11] Such a schmuck!"
Rick wondered if his father thought Christina was a silly woman.

"Oh, my God," she said, scrambling from the couch and rushing to her friend,
whom she'd left standing by the door while she had been nuzzling him. "Elizabeth,
this is my brother Rick." And taking the girl's hand she brought her forward. "Rick,
this is Elizabeth Conde."

The girl said hello but avoided looking directly at him. She was one of those
withdrawn, slowly maturing girls who looked as if they had never seen anything more
serious than a minor traffic accident in which the drivers get calmly out of their cars,
inspected the slight damage and exchanged insurance information. Elizabeth was a
head taller than his sister, about the same Indian-tinted complexion. She was pretty
but there seemed to be a veil of rules and regulation which she had accepted and
which clouded her eyes with impossible innocence. Also notable in his assessment of

---

11. And so unfriendly

Elizabeth Conde was the inoffensive plumpness which would eventually render her passive. She reminded him of some of his clients. Like his sister, Elizabeth was dressed in bell bottom trousers and platform shoes and newly applied purple lipstick. Rick smiled at her, feeling for a moment as if he was about to do an intake on someone at the settlement house. Christina asked Elizabeth to sit down. "Don't worry," she said. "He won't bite." She winked at Rick and told him Elizabeth was studying to be a teacher. "Early childhood education major," Christina said. "She's really great with kids." Turning to her friend, she informed her that Rick was a social worker on the Lower East Side.

"Really?" she said.

"Not really," he said, "but I'm working on it."

There had been no surprise in Elizabeth's voice. Rick was certain his sister had already given her a big buildup about him. The subject of his job was a touchy one, but he had never discussed it with Chris and there was no sense going into it now. He was not a MSW[12] like Weintraub and his girlfriend Louise, or even Escobar with all his jargon and Irish wife.

"I'm taking classes at the New School at night. The settlement is paying the tuition," Rick had said. It was his defense against committing himself to the job. What the hell was he anyway? He had majored in Literature and Psychology and for a while had dabbled unsuccessfully in poetry. Goldstein, the director, had hired him to serve as a "buffer" between the staff and the neighborhood, on the promise that he'd pursue studies towards a MSW. Color him brown and *verde esperalo*,[13] the color his father gave all that one had little chance of obtaining, in his own case, because he had seen the futility of working in the field. But at least going to school at night postponed his being branded with the idiotic letters. MSW stood for Master of Stupid Work.

Elizabeth smiled weakly and sat at the other end of the couch. "Do you work with children?" she asked, looking as if at any moment he'd ask her to leave the room and fill out a form that would give her license to speak without being spoken to.

"Sure," he said smiling patiently at her. "Families come in and we work with the whole unit." He hated the words, much as he hated "client," "low income," "economically deprived," "inner city," and "educationally handicapped." They were empty words, sounds devoid of meaning and, more insultingly, euphemisms for the multitude of problems and the horror which they produced in human beings.

"I bet it's interesting work," Elizabeth said. "Have you read María Montessori?"

Rick answered that it had been required reading for one of his courses in college and suppressed his amusement at Elizabeth's earnestness.

---

12. Master's in Social Work
13. green of hope

"Liz is our resident intellectual," Christina said. The remark made the girl blush deep purple. With the years she would be grotesque, Rick thought. His father was right, silly women were nothing but trouble. "I'm only kidding," Christina said, quickly. She rushed and sat between the two of them. "No, really, Rick," she said turning to him. "Liz's going to be a terrific teacher. *Bien chevere.*[14] She's got fantastic ideas about children."

"I'm sure she does," he answered.

"I'm not kidding, Rick," said Christina. "And she writes, too. I mean not poetry but essays and stuff. I kid around but I bet one of these days people are going to be using Liz's ideas. They make perfect sense. I mean, she believes children should be treated like princes and princesses during their formative years."

"What years?" Rick said, raising his eyebrows and squinting at his sister.

"I know, I know," she replied. "You don't like to hear jargon, but I think it makes sense."

Rick nodded patiently and wondered what the hell had gotten into his sister. She was definitely pushing Elizabeth on him. Maybe his father was right and they had already conspired to marry him off to her. Princes and princesses? All of a sudden his mind snapped and he saw the joke inherent in Elizabeth. He wanted to share it with his sister but it would be petty and cruel. What was purple and ruled Early Childhood Education? Answer: Elizabeth the Grape. He smiled inwardly and decided to change the subject.

"And you, Chris," he said. "What are you going to do? You thinking of becoming a teacher too?"

"Me? Das no my yob, men," answered his sister, affecting a Spanish accent and imitating the latest TV personality, one of their own who has apparently made it. She mimicked the comedian, rolling her eyes and shuffling a quick dance step after jumping up from the couch. Everyone laughed, including their father, who prided himself on speaking "good English." After the laughter died down Christina turned deadly serious. "I really don't know," she said. Her concern was genuine and Rick was touched. "I have another year before I have to decide on a major."

"What's your favorite course?" Rick asked, lapsing into his best counseling voice without feeling self-conscious.

"All of them except history and sociology."

"Out of all of them, which one really turns you on? That's really the question," he said.

"I don't know. Lit., Psych., Anthro. I'm even getting into Philosophy. Wait a minute, for a guy who doesn't like labels, you sure are hell bent on pinning one on me."

---

14. really great

"Yeah, I guess you're right," he said, and wondered if her displeasure was part of her disappointment at his disinterest in Elizabeth. "Girls don't really have to be anything," he said, as if the question bored him. He was joking but Christina jumped back to the couch and not exactly playfully held her small fist to his face. He laughed and she slumped back on the couch, shaking her head.

"Boy, are you a class A chauvinist," she said. "Who would've thought it! My brother, the liberal, is really an MCP."[15]

Their father had been sitting back, enjoying their quick give-and-take, but Rick's words made him sit up and offer his opinion. "Rick's right," he said. "It's okay for a girl to go to school but she should also think about setting up a home."

"Oh, Pop," Christina said, rising dejectedly from the couch. "Don't start that again, okay?"

"No, it's true," he answered. "Look at your sister. She got her degree and is raising a family, too. In a few years, when the kids are a little bigger, she can get her license and teach."

"C'mon," said Christina. "Becky'll be tied to those kids until she's gray."

Their father laughed and slapped his knee.

"She's something, ain't she, Rick?" he said, looking to him for support.

"Go ahead and laugh," Chris said, defiantly. "This is one *corazoncito lindo*[16] who's not getting caught up in all that marriage-house-children baloney." Their father stopped laughing and a hurt look appeared on his face. Chris, however, had no intentions of allowing herself to be manipulated into silence. "No, really, I mean it. That's all we're programmed for. One generation after the other. From house to school to church and back to the house. Engagement, marriage and babies. We might as well be a bunch of hicks. Look at Rick. You think he'd be married by now, right? Wrong! He knows better. Why do you think he only takes out American girls?" When Chris got going, thought Rick, she was merciless. Regardless of consequences, anything which bolstered her argument was employed. One thing was certain, she wasn't pushing Elizabeth at him for the purposes of hooking him up. Realizing that perhaps his sister was honestly trying to expose her friend to the world she enjoyed through him made him feel guilty that he'd been so thoughtless. Chris had now moved to the middle of the living room and was all of a sudden the street-wise tomboy who'd known little fear growing up. She was up on her toes, her head turned arrogantly to the side and her right index finger stabbing down to make her point. And yet the pose was innocent, devoid of any malice, the words lacking in venom. Nevertheless, Rick was annoyed that she'd brought up the subject of his preference for American

---

15. male chauvinist pig
16. beautiful heart

girls. It seemed impossible she had forgotten the last scene with his father. To spite him he had begun toying with the idea of marrying Kathy Bauer. He had talked generally around the subject, testing Kathy but in effect teasing her with the possibility. She had waited patiently, accepting the change in him. After a while, feeling deceived, she moved out and in time was gone out of his life, another in a string of broken white hearts, he later thought in false self-deprecation.

"I'm telling you," Chris said, to no one. "I'm not going to stand around and let it happen to me. I'll kill myself first."

"That's enough, Chris," Rick said, suddenly. As if she had been slapped, the tone of his voice made her recoil, her theatrical arrogance shattered. She held back her tears and shook her head, not quite believing his betrayal. She quickly regained control but the hurt in her voice made the words mockingly bitter and filled with vengeance.

"Oh, Rick, not you too," she said, smiling pityingly at him. "You know what I'm saying is true. You're scared too. You know that."

"Why don't you try to relax, Chris," he said, already regretting that he had not been able to see her need for his support. They were both in the same boat and he should have known better. "I'm sorry, I really am," he said. But she was beyond the point at which she could accept his apology and went on.

"Who was the last P.R.[17] you went out with?" she said. "Margie Betancourt, right? In your last year of high school, right? You met her at that camp you worked at as a counselor. She was from the Bronx, wasn't she? And she wasn't any little hick, was she? She had her thing together. Getting ready to go to City College, hip, articulate, pretty and proud, honey. It scared you, didn't it? You knew she meant business from the giddyup. Maybe she didn't want to get married right away but she wasn't into no light romance, either. I almost didn't recognize her. That's right, she's at Hunter. Not because she had changed or nothing. She's still pretty and hip, but because she's got a Ph.D. in Math and her name is Professor Margaret Betancourt Draper. That's right, she just got married last year. Some WASP M.I.T.[18] genius. But back then she saw something in you and you couldn't be bothered. Am I right?"

Rick answered that she was right, that he had no defense against her argument. He looked to Elizabeth, seeking neutral ground. She had shrunk to child-size and, fearing involvement in the turmoil, stared blankly at the wall behind him.

"Rick has to get established first," their father said, as if it behooved him to defend the male point of view. "He has to take care of his studies. The economy isn't what it used to be. Look at Ralph. He and Becky got another kid coming and his

17. Puerto Rican
18. Massachusetts Institute of Technology [i.e., Ivy League]

salary isn't gonna be enough to support the four of them. He's gonna have to risk his life eight hours a day fighting crime in Harlem and find himself something else on the side, moonlighting."

"Good for him," Chris snapped. "Serves them both right. If you want to dance, you gotta pay the piper."

Whether their father misunderstood the phrase was not clearly apparent to Rick, but he imagined the saying being lost in translation, possibly inferring sexual connotations and making the matter of the piper, somehow, obscene to him.

"I'm gonna pretend I didn't hear that," he said. "One thing I'm not gonna stand for in my house is that kind of talk, especially about your own sister."

Vanquished, her argument useless, Chris stood up in the middle of the floor biting her lip and looking down at her feet. Their mother, who had been listening to the argument, gauging the tones of the voices as they shifted from the usual bantering to more heated words, called Chris into the kitchen. Rick imagined that once in there she would be reminded of their father's condition. Chris turned and motioned Elizabeth to follow, but the girl shook her head and said she had to return downstairs and help her mother. When the door was closed, Chris came back through the living room, her head still down, avoiding Rick's eyes and those of their father. She disappeared behind the wall which served to separate living room and kitchen in housing projects all over the city, reappearing periodically as she went about setting the table. Rick tried to reassure their father that Chris hadn't meant anything by her words.

"People say crazy things when they're worried," he said.

"I understand," said his father.

"It's just an American saying."

"Yeah, I know, Ricky," his father replied. "I know what she's talking about. I know she didn't mean no harm."

Rick was certain that his father still didn't understand and that under some highly complex pretext he would take the train to South Brooklyn to see his buddy, Angelo, at work and ask him, again in some convoluted way so that his ignorance remained hidden, about paying the piper. What pride! He was the man, the head of the family, and under no circumstance should he appear weak to any of its members. And yet he was wise in his own way. If he found nothing amiss with the saying, within a week it would be part of his repertoire of clichés and Chris would know that everything was all right between them.

The rest of the evening went as well as could be expected. Before their mother called them to eat, Chris returned to the living room and apologized to their father. She sat on the arm of his chair and smoothed his hair, not saying anything until he put an arm around her. When he did so she slid to his lap and cried and said she was going to be good and not to worry. "I know, baby," he said, holding her like he had held all his children when they were afraid or lonely, allowing his heart to expand to take them in. Rick felt a twinge of jealousy as he watched Chris bury her face in their father's shoulder, but he could not identify the source of his feelings other than to ascribe them to that all-encompassing category labeled "sibling rivalry."

As always, the food was delicious. As if their mother possessed a deeper instinct, the pork was extremely lean and very little shortening had been used on the *tostones*. Rick found himself savoring every bit of his mother's cooking, relishing the taste of the red beans as they mixed with white rice in his mouth. As they ate they talked about the food, comparing how it stacked up against other cuisine, Latin or otherwise. Their mother urged everyone to have seconds, which she always did as a matter of course, lamenting how thin everyone was and how everything would be left if they didn't eat. When everyone had again heaped their plates, the conversation turned away from food and the present, to the past, the words weaving in and out of celebrated Christmases, birthdays, baptisms, Easters, vacations, both of their parents recalling anecdotes about him and Chris. Listening to his father, Rick tried recalling his father making a kite for him when he was seven but could not.

"We used to live near Prospect Park," his father said, urging him to remember. "I made it right in the apartment. On the island we used to make them out of bamboo and I found this old bamboo chair down on the docks and brought it home and bought some colored paper. *Papel de seda*,[19] we used to call it back home. Silk paper, you know. It was green and yellow. A big box kite. You remember, Ricky!"

"I think so," he said, but couldn't remember.

His father's manner had become totally open, vulnerable, as he recalled those days. He turned to their mother. "You should've seen us, Margarita. Everybody had those store-bought kites. It was in the spring. April or May, and there was a lot of wind. A weekend. Saturday morning and here we came, me and Ricky with our monster kite with the long ten-foot tail made out of strings and *trapos*.[20] Rag strips that I tore up from one of your old slips, Margarita. People stood around watching us like we was crazy. Some kids even said the kite wouldn't fly because it was too big." He now turned to Rick. " 'You just watch,' I said to them. Rick, I gave you the kite and told you to walk away from me and I began unwinding the string and you kept going back until you was the size of my pinky you was so small. And then I started running and told you to let go. I could feel the string getting tight in my hands but I didn't look back until I could feel the kite take off. When I stopped running it was way up in the air like a big green and yellow bird, a dragon maybe, with its tail waving in the

---

19. tissue paper
20. rags

wind. You came running to me and I let you hold it and we let it fly for about three hours. Half a mile up in the air and it still looked like a building, it was so big. Three hours." He laughed now. "We got hungry but luckily there was a big crowd watching us and a hot dog man came over and we bought two of them. You didn't like sauerkraut in those days," he said, winking knowingly at him. Neither Chris nor their mother understood their private joke and he smiled sadly at his father's attempt at manly camaraderie. "Pretty soon people start asking all kinda questions about where I bought the kite and how much it cost. I laughed and told them I could make kites that looked like airplanes, cars, boats, birds, fish and anything else they could think of. The kids stood there with their mouths open, their little blue eyes asking more questions but not saying anything. You remember now, don't you, Rick?"

"Sure, Pop, now I remember," he said, but still felt the emptiness where the kite should've been. "It's just that I was small."

"Sure, I understand. It was beautiful. After a while we took down the kite. People still couldn't believe how such a big thing could stay up in the air. On the way home through the park it started to rain. We ran as fast as we could but by the time we got home all the silk paper was messed up and ripped and you cried."

His father was silent then, sensing that perhaps Rick could not recall the incident. Chris broke the silence by suggesting that their father make kites again.

"Boy, I bet they'd sell like crazy. It's not just a kid thing anymore. Everybody flies them. You know, custom-made kites. People pay good money for stuff like that. You should go to F.A.O. Schwartz and see the prices for really junky stuff Pop. Wow, you could work right here in the house. Plenty of people do that now. You could use Rick's room. Right, Ricky?"

"Sure, Pop," he said, halfheartedly.

It had been the wrong thing to say but he was caught. If he disagreed he would hurt Chris. But with his agreeing, all his father could feel was that Rick didn't understand him. He watched his father's face grow troubled as he was reminded that he could no longer work at what he loved and worse, he'd have to work alone in the house, like a woman.

"No," he said, mournfully. "I mean, I think it's a good idea but I couldn't make things like that for money. That's not work. It's like playing the guitar or something. You make a kite like that and it's like having a kid. You take it out and let it fly and hope the string doesn't break and you lose it. And then you bring it home and put it in a safe place and if there's a little rip you fix it and check the tail to make sure it isn't ripped up. And each day you look at it until you bring it out and fly it again. Selling it would be like letting your own kid go live with somebody else. You know that, Rick. You have to see it everyday."

Rick did not answer. All at once his father looked very old, defeated, done in by the pace he had kept up all those years of slaving away to have a good life. The meal had been over more than twenty minutes and all at once the apartment was very quiet. Rick could hear the whirring of the refrigerator's motor and the electric clock making the curious vibrating sound each time the second hand went past the eight. His father got up from the table, went into the living room and turned on the television set. Chris and his mother slowly began clearing the table and Rick walked over and sat on the couch. Everything had become clouded and he wasn't sure if the kite incident had taken place or if his father had invented it. He sat, letting his mind relax, not wanting to say anything, hoping it would come to him.

When Chris and their mother were finished in the kitchen they came in and sat down but still no one would say anything. After some time, Rick looked at his watch, got up and went over to his father. "I have to leave now, Pop," he said. His father got up and after Rick kissed his mother and Chris, promising to see them again soon, his father walked him out of the apartment and down the hall to the elevator. The distance, the respect, was still there between them but they both knew Rick had no recollection of the kite. They put their arms stiffly around each other and said goodbye.

"Don't stay a stranger, Ricky," his father said when the elevator came. "You know, your mother worries about you," he added, self-consciously, aware that his son had finally seen through him, but that mentioning his mother was the only way he could express his own concern.

"Okay, Pop," Rick said. "Take care of yourself." He meant it so that in saying it he felt the ache his father also felt at the uncertainty of the future. "I'll see you soon." He rode the eleven flights down, feeling as if he had been on an extended roller coaster ride. It was always like that whenever he came over to see him. Even when everything went well between them, he felt as if he had gone back in time and was being asked to scrutinize every aspect of his life in the minutest detail.

The ride from the Coney Island terminal into Manhattan on the "D" train was usually a tiresome, sleep-inducing trip. At ten o'clock at night, the express had stopped running and each station was nearly deserted. People on the train seemed, each one, to be feigning sleep. It was a New York way of being wary while at the same time relaxing so that if one were a mugger, a molester or a pickpocket, one would have to decide whether the person was in fact off guard or playing at it. He had gotten this information from one of his clients' son, who, at fourteen, was already a chronic thief. It was a silly game, playing possum. In spite of precautions, things always happened when one least expected them. When he boarded the train, Rick found himself a twin seat at the end of the car, opened a book he had begun reading the previous night and let the words carry him to the time of slavery in Cuba. *La Historia de un Cimarron,*[21] he had decided, was a propaganda tract and anybody with half a brain could see through it. He had no quarrel with its purpose and as a matter of fact found it fascinating. Beyond that, however, he enjoyed his ability to let the Spanish language flow through him without his having to translate into English and back again as had happened for a time. The problem had caused him some anguish and kept him forever asking himself why he had to exist between two languages. As the doors opened and he looked up to check on the new passengers, he saw a young woman enter the car, then seat herself directly across from him.

She was attractive, Latin, New York, hard. Something else compelled him to look at her more closely. The girl appeared to be on her way to something quite special and yet he immediately felt as if that event or place for which she was headed existed solely in her mind. As soon as the train doors closed, she began grooming herself, unconsciously, resembling but lacking the grace and fluidity of an animal. Her large brown eyes seemed empty, her awareness detached, as she brushed her long hair, dyed a deep auburn. After some five minutes she replaced the brush with a pocket mirror and began examining her face. Although made up rather heavily, she again applied lipstick to her mouth and then proceeded to remove her eyelashes. With great ceremony she replaced them with a more luxuriant pair, which, adding to the vacuousness of her eyes, gave her a perfect, babydoll-like appearance.

So precise and intense was her concern with her looks that Rick thought she might be a male. He looked closely at her face but found no traces of masculinity. She was not a male but neither was she a female. He tried returning to the book, could not concentrate and looked around the train to see if anyone else had noticed the strange young woman. The car had filled up considerably as it approached the heart of Brooklyn. The passengers, however, appeared oblivious to everything but their "Night Owl" edition of the *Daily News,* or their own thoughts, the steady clacking of wheel against rail serving as a hypnotic instrument to their lethargy. Only the warning bell which preceded the closing doors on the new train activated them and in unison they bobbed their heads to the two-tone warning.

Only one person seemed conscious of the drama being played out between himself as an observer, and the image of humanity across the aisle. For, Rick Sánchez thought, if the young woman's compulsiveness could have been called insanity, then surely it was nothing more than an exaggerated pantomime of life and the quiet pretense under which humans labored, forever toiling towards no apparent end, knowing only they were traveling with increasing rapidity in the same direction but busying themselves with whatever role each had been assigned. The other observer with whom Rick felt

---

21. The Biography of an Escaped Slave

immediate kinship was another young woman. She was wearing a long green coat, knitted green hat, matching gloves. *Verde que te quiero verde,*[22] he thought, recalling Garcia Lorca's poem. She was what Rick had learned to classify as a good, goodlooking girl. He looked at her, back to the glamour queen and back again. She understood and smiled, almost with compassion, as if in finding the scene tragic, she could nevertheless share in its absurdity.

For the moment, he was thankful that someone was not afraid to share this knowledge. He tried returning to the book but found himself looking up again. This time his gaze went directly to the girl in green. Without a trace of reserve she smiled openly at him. It was the sort of smile one gets from a person with whom something of value has been shared, a mutually discovered secret. A love smile, he thought. Not sexual love but love founded on trust. The thought disturbed him immensely. She continued to smile. It was a game and she was an expert, never letting the smile come at him from the same angle. Whereas the other girl had drawn attention to herself by heavy and repetitious movement, this one tilted her head slightly, or else raised it, one time smiling fully, the next, the smile barely on her lips but slowly filling her eyes as if the mixture of joy and mirth were a delicately blended liquid which rose from mouth to eyes by means of valvular manipulation. He imagined an exotic, green and cream-colored tropical fish, rising and falling in the deep blue water. She was a child, he thought, like his sister, full of ideals and romance. His admiration for her turned to pure lust and he imagined her naked beneath him, realizing almost immediately how resentful he had grown of the innocence of others in the past year.

As the train neared Atlantic Avenue, the girl stood up and approached the door near him. She was saying goodbye, smiling, her eyes still playful. She carried books and a light tan bag, the smooth leather matching her delicate complexion. He smiled and only when the doors opened and she was out of the train did he realize he would never see her again. As the warning bells went off, he followed her out just managing to avoid the closing doors. Not knowing what he was to say, he raced after her. Once he made sure she was not transferring to another train, he slowed down his pace. "That was something, wasn't it?" he said, as he caught up to her. It was as if she had been expecting him to follow her. She nodded, smiled, her teeth very small and even. He was now walking beside her and a faint trace of an exquisite fragrance heightened his awareness of her. He had never seen a face like hers. Never. The skin was very clear and smooth and pulled tight to her cheekbones, causing her eyes to appear deeper, greener.

"I see her almost every night on my way home," she said.

"You're kidding!"

---

22. Green, I love you green.

"It's true. I think she's a topless dancer or something. Sometimes she looks like she's rehearsing and she moves her shoulders to the beat of the train."

He loved her voice. It had a strange, reedy quality, much as if she were playing an instrument. They had walked through the tunnel, the turnstile, up the stairs and out into the night. The street was deserted, the icy wind blowing papers in crazy whorls across the cobblestone. Only the man at the newspaper stand, clapping his hands, clad in fingerless gloves, destroyed Rick's feeling that Brooklyn had been evacuated and he and the girl were the only ones left.

"Do you go to school?" he asked, buttoning his overcoat against the cold.

"Yes."

"Evening school?"

"Sort of. Nursing school."

"Aren't you afraid coming home so late at night?" She shook her head and laughed. "I take karate lessons on Tuesday and I carry a long letter opener." She stopped walking and took the weapon out of her handbag. The word "Toledo" had been inscribed on the blade of the tiny sword. "I took it from an Iberia office in Manhattan."

"The airline?"

"Yeah," she said, and laughed again. "I boost things. I'm real dangerous, so watch it," she added, taking back the letter opener. She resumed walking and about halfway down the block stopped under the streetlight, looking up at him, her face still open, smiling, her cheeks already reddened by the cold. All at once he felt foolish. Never at a loss for words with women, he'd been silenced by her. "I have to wait for my bus," she said.

"Can I walk you home?" he asked, feeling as if he were back in high school. She shrugged her shoulders and said she'd be all right.

"I have to take the bus. It leaves me a block from the house. You can wait here with me if you want. Sometimes it takes forever."

"How about a cup of coffee, then?"

She acquiesced, returning the offer with a smile in her eyes.

"What's your name?" she asked once they were seated in a booth in a diner–coffee shop. When he told her, she said, "My name's Lolín. María Dolon Pacheco to be exact."

"You're Spanish?" he said, incredulously. What an idiot he was. All the clues had been there. The way she smiled, her sureness, the way she used the word "boost." She was now shaking her head at him disapprovingly.

"Puerto Rican," she said. "What did you think I was?" And then she lapsed into street Spanish. "¡Adiós, mire éste! ¿Qué es lo tuyo, m'ijo? Dig him! ¡Parejero![23] You mean you couldn't tell?"

---

23. God, look at this one! What's your thing? Dig him! Stranger!

"No, I thought you were Italian or something."

"Italian?"

"Yeah!"

"You're kidding. *¡Qué arrebate, m'ijo!*[24] Italian?"

"Yeah, or I thought maybe you were from the Middle East when you got off at Atlantic. You know, Armenian or Lebanese. You know, your eyes, they're almond shaped."

"What does that mean!"

"It's supposed to be a sign of beauty."

"I bet," she replied, not quite believing him.

She had him coming and going, tongue-tied half the time and the other half staring dumbly at her face. She had taken off her hat, revealing loosely curled, shiny black hair which framed her face and made her twice as alluring. He couldn't recall how long they sat in the diner, smiling mostly and talking nonsense about high school stories, movies, clothes, and the topless dancer. They exchanged ages. She was twenty and when he told her his age she called him a *viejo,*[25] and then amended it to "experienced," at which point he looked her in the eye and she blushed slightly. It was the first time he'd had the upper hand. At a quarter to twelve they decided it had grown late and walked back to the bus stop. When they were on the bus she sat next to him, still mischievous, arguing with him but without any of the sarcasm she had first displayed, her face glowing with excitement.

"I'm sorry," he said at one point. "I was reading and thinking about that girl. You know, trying to figure out what was the matter with her."

"Sorry about what?" she said.

"Mistaking you for an Armenian."

"Listen, I forgive you," she said, laughing and moving closer to him, not caring that their bodies touched. "But it's the last time you look at foreign girls."

He laughed, embarrassed by her aggressiveness, still not knowing when she was serious, but convinced now that she had been. He could feel all of her. Through the heavy clothing he felt her body and all of him grew warm and pleasant. The air felt charged with her and everything had become dreamlike.

"You don't live in Brooklyn, do you?"

"No, I couldn't help it," he said. "Getting off the train, I mean. I would've never seen you again."

"I know," she said. "I felt sort of sad, but that's New York. I'm used to it."

"You're not sad anymore, are you?"

---

24. What a mistake, son!
25. old man

"No, just tired," she said, and without warning, rested her head on his shoulder. "I feel like I've just finished running. Do you like to dance?" He said he did and she asked if he'd take her.

"I hear about those places but I've never been. I can't even imagine what it's like when people tell me about it. Not for nothing but I'm a real hick. A regular *marintaiga.*" The word sent a shudder through him and memories of his childhood came flooding into his mind. He hadn't heard the word in years. And she'd used it as if she heard it every day. She had been born and raised in New York but was still a *marintaiga. La mancha de platano,*[26] his mother called it. Once you were stained by the plantain, thus you remained, indelibly branded for life, generation upon generation. "You'll take me, won't you?" she pleaded sleepily. "My mother's so strict but she'll let me go with you when she finds out you're a college graduate and everything. She's so old fashioned. It's just me and her and my grandmother and I don't feel like hurting them. They're angels really. Mami just works and saves her money to buy a little house in P.R. for her and *abuela.*[27] They both worry I'm going to end up like Mami. You know, pregnant and without a man. Are you political?" He asked her what she meant and she explained. "I started going to these discussion meetings and I'm reading about P.R. and what's happened down there. I don't read Spanish well, but I force myself if I have to. I want to know everything about the island. You know, the history and the culture. What I said about boosting is silly. It doesn't make any sense and I'm not going to do it anymore. I mean, they did steal a lot from us. First the Spanish and then the Americans."

He explained that he wasn't very political. "I believe in independence for Puerto Rico," he said, although he wasn't sure what he really meant in saying that.

"Would you live there? If it was independent?"

He couldn't answer her, unable to understand the significance of the question and finally said he didn't know. She said she didn't know either. She didn't press the issue. Automatically, her hand went up to the cord to signal the driver.

The next few minutes were like a nightmare. One second she was holding to his arm, then she was clutching it. Her books lay scattered on the sidewalk. As the bus pulled away she let go of his arm and ran down the street and around the corner. It was then that he smelled the smoke and heard the rush of water from the hoses and the pumper's engine. He picked up the books and raced around the corner after her.

Across the street, along a row of old frame houses, a wall of flames roared against the night sky, lighting up the entire block as if one were looking at it through red

---

26. Literally, the plantain stain. Figuratively, the mark of Puerto Rican identity.
27. grandmother

cellophane. The water from the fire fighting equipment hit futilely at the wind-swept flames and, like dancing demons, enormously angry at being disturbed, the columns of fire exploded upwards, sending a shower of sparks forward into the street and into the firemen aiming the hoses. People gasped at the sight and he felt a blast of heat hit his face. Not sure what to make of it, he began looking for Lolín.

He finally found her at the other end of the block. She was being held back by two policemen. In the confusion of her flight she'd lost her hat and her purse and was fighting the two cops, her voice already hoarse. He managed to disentangle her from the two officers, explaining that he was a friend. At first she didn't recognize him and fought him with the same intensity she'd directed at the police. All around them voices explained that it had been a flash fire, electrical or something. He held her, talking all the while until she went limp and all the fight left her. And then as if she once more realized the extent of the fire, she was digging her fingernails into his arm, her hand becoming rigid and her face distorted by the knowledge that it was impossible for anyone to get out of the house alive. "Oh, my God," she kept saying, even when he held her to him, soothing her. "Oh, my God. Oh, Mami. What am I going to do?"

When the fire was finally brought under control an hour later and the morgue wagon came to take away the two bodies, he remained with her, riding in the police car, holding her books and hat while she clutched her wet pocketbook to herself, staying with her throughout the long night and the identification of the charred bodies and the questions, crying with her and feeling her pain and her loss, smoothing her hair, caressing her face, ravaged now by the tragedy, the light in her eyes nearly dimmed as she fought to accept that her mother and grandmother were gone forever.

"What am I going to do, Ricky?" she asked, momentarily lucid. He had not been able to answer her and once again, as if the fire had suddenly touched her she shuddered and screamed. Wailing, keening, her pain came in long, shrill cries, and cut deep into him and left him raw; his father's own impending death was dwarfed by her sorrow. He told her over and over that he would take care of her somehow. The words were coming without any control on his part calling her *mamita*, like she was his own flesh and blood, joined, nay, fused, wedded many years before, and the knowledge, stored in his mind, coming slowly alive.

By five that morning they had left the morgue and he managed to get her back to his apartment. He made her drink warm milk and cinnamon, laced with a shot of whiskey, and made her lie down. He wasn't able to sleep and every couple of minutes he got up out of the couch to look in on her in the bedroom. When she finally fell asleep and her face began to gain some semblance of tranquility, he dozed off. Towards sunrise he was up again. He looked out the window and watched the light of the new day, the water of the East River like a silver mirror and the bridges to Brooklyn faintly drawn in the winter mist.

At eight o'clock he phoned his parents' home, knowing his mother would be up preparing breakfast for Chris. Chris answered the phone and he explained briefly what had happened.

"Is Pop awake yet?" he said.

"Yes, he's up. Do you want me to tell him?"

"That's all right, Chris. Let me talk to him." He waited, and when his father came to the phone, he said, "I need your help, Papi," dropping the English "Pop" for the more tender name he had used for addressing him in his childhood.

"Anything, Ricky," said his father.

He explained the situation and then waited in the apartment until his father and mother came to stay with Lolín. His mother touched Lolín's cheek as soon as she saw her and then held her when she began crying again, talking to her in Spanish and crying with her as if they had known each other before and the girl's loss was her own. His father wasn't able to look at him directly, his eyes averted as if to guard against breaking down and crying, maintaining even then the stoic pose, nodding philosophically and telling him he had always known Rick had a good heart and that he would have done the same thing.

Now, as he sat at his desk drinking hurriedly-bought coffee, Rick Sánchez once again pondered the events of the previous day. His head ached. The two hours of sleep he had managed would not be enough to see him through the day. More than ever he wished his job were simple. Before too long, an avalanche of distraught mothers would descend on his office to demand an explanation for not being able to obtain food stamps or why their rent had been increased. Referring them to the proper agencies had proven useless. Invariably, people came back with renewed bitterness and a longer list of complaints, their pride restraining the desperation of years of futile struggle, created, Rick had decided, by their own ignorance and inflexibility, and they sought solace in him.

But it wasn't just them. It was everything. The settlement house was a testing ground, a laboratory in which chronically neurotic "professionals" examined the exquisite form human misery took among the "new immigrants." Another of their favorite phrases. Later that morning there would be a meeting with Goldstein and the rest of the staff to plan the children's Christmas party. In well-meaning but condescending language, Goldstein would explain the importance of the season to the Puerto Rican family, while VISTA volunteers, full-fledged social workers, psychologists, family planners and the rest of the vultures who daily picked over the bones of a culture in its death throes, asked their usual silly, middle-class questions about themes and communication. It was their own personal sociology seminar, created through some obscure process to offer relief for their guilt.

Rick stood up, opened the file cabinet behind his desk and extracted several files. After a few minutes of staring at them on his desk he pushed them away. It was useless. As if the upcoming problems of the day weren't enough, he now had Lolín to worry about. Although he recoiled from the horror of the previous night, he felt drawn to it, hoping that within the series of events leading up to the tragedy, there was a way out, some minute and seemingly unimportant detail which would absolve him of culpability. Perhaps if he hadn't insisted that Lolín come with him to the diner she would've arrived in time to save her mother and grandmother. Then again, he thought, she may have perished with them. The thought produced horror in him as he recalled the limp body bags being removed from the smoldering skeleton of the house and placed in the morgue wagon. He was jarred away from the image by the ringing of the telephone. It was Mrs. Thomas, Goldstein's secretary. She wanted to know if there were any last-minute items which he wanted included in the agenda for that afternoon's meeting. He said he had nothing but that she shouldn't forget his item about the need for a drug orientation clinic. Mrs. Thomas made an oblique statement about the resistance his suggestion had met at the last meeting. On the verge of screaming, Rick insisted. He hung up the phone, tried to become interested once more in the files but again met with failure.

Suddenly, the nearly empty coffee container he brought to his lips became the object of his wrath and in controlled anger, wishing more to hurl it against the postered walls or crush it in his hand, he placed it in the trash can next to his desk. The throbbing behind his eyes had become more intense in the past half hour and he wished he had remained home. He could've called in sick but he suffered from the same guilt which assailed the others. At some point he had passed through that magic door which transformed ordinary human beings into Americans and, having done so, he now had to carry a similar burden. Excuses were not part of the intake process. And yet, if he had to make excuses he could have, having listened to them each day for the past two years. No matter how clearly neighborhood people were in the wrong, they always had an excuse.

His thoughts again turned to Lolín. Her grief, the outpouring of pain, was more than he had ever experienced, the loss so immense that he couldn't imagine how she'd bear it the rest of her life. And now he was part of it, his life and hers and his parents and the ones who each day came to him, intertwined. All of them were cast together like so many leaves blown by the wind, never knowing and yet suspecting, odious as the notion seemed to his otherwise clear and unsuperstitious mind, that destiny had played a part in bringing all of them together. The thought filled him with hatred and once again he felt trapped. The emotion choked him and he wished to run from it all. But he couldn't now. He was linked to Lolín, to her grief, to his parents and their ceaseless toiling. He must tell them.

Resolutely, going beyond his anger, he dialed his own number. The phone rang several times before his father answered it. The voice on the other end sounded strangely subdued, new, much as if in the hour which had transpired since he had left his apartment his father had undergone a transformation.

"Pop?"

"Yes, Rick."

"You all right?"

"Sure, son. What's the matter?"

"Nothing. I just wanted to know how Lolín was doing."

"She's okay, Rick. Your mother fixed her some breakfast and she ate. We're getting ready to go back to Brooklyn. Ralph and Becky just got here with the car."

"Thanks, Pop."

"She says she doesn't have any other family," his father said, sadly.

"Yeah, I know."

"She can live with us if you want. I mean, until she can get herself a place."

"I'd like that, Pop. Let her have my room."

"Sure, Rick. It's a good room. It's got plenty of light and you can see the ocean from the window."

"Yes, Pop, it's a beautiful room," he said, and all at once he felt very tired as he remembered it all and was again in Prospect Park with his father, flying the kite against the brilliant spring sky.

"She's a very serious girl, Rick," said his father.

"I know, Pop," Rick answered, smiling at his concern for him.

"You and Mami take care of her until I'm ready. I'll see you tonight."

He hung up the phone. The tiredness was being replaced by a languorous feeling and once more he recalled the kite and why it had faded from his memory. His father and mother had quarreled, and his mother had cried. It was the first time he'd seen her cry and he hated his father for it. Even after the two of them made up and things had gone back to their usual pace, he had found it difficult to talk to his father. The kite had been a peace offering from him. Now, in his mind's eye, Rick saw Lolín's face clearly once again, her beautiful smile and playful eyes filling him so that a strange new power invaded his body, making his skin tingle. He felt his own smile come from deep within him, hurting the muscles of his jaw as if they hadn't been used in years.

He opened the top drawer of his desk and from it took out a pad of yellow paper. On it he began drafting a letter to Goldstein, explaining why he had to resign. He saw his task clearly now. Although he felt sympathy for the suffering in the neighborhood, he had to go beyond the daily routine of putting people's lives in order, if not for them, at least for their children. Somehow he had to find a way of letting them know what he saw and in so doing, show with his effort that not all of life was despair. When he finished writing the letter he walked down the hall to the Social Work secretary's office and had her type it.

Returning to his own office he once again sat at his desk, picked up his pad and in block letters, in the middle of the yellow pad, he wrote:

THE MARINTAIGA KITE

by

Rick Sánchez

It was a monster kite, blue and yellow, its tail like a comet against the blazing April sky . . .

Roberta Fernández

(b. 1940)
Mexican American

Roberta Fernández is a well known writer, editor, and promoter of Hispanic literature and third world women's literature. Born in Laredo, Texas, Fernández received all of her primary schooling and her college education in Texas. In 1990 she received a doctorate in Romance languages and literatures from the University of California at Berkeley. Since the late 1960s, Fernández has served as a teacher, lecturer, and researcher at universities around the country, including Brown University, Carleton College in Minnesota, the University of California at Santa Barbara, the University of Houston, the University of Massachusetts, and Mills College, where she founded and edited Prisma, *a literary magazine.*

Through her creative writing, Fernández has embarked upon a two-decade-long search for a Hispanic third world feminist aesthetic. Her stories have come out of this diligent artistic inquiry and ideological commitment. Her beautifully crafted short stories—which have been written in both English and Spanish and published in magazines throughout the country—are comparable in detail and intricacy to the art of filigree. Such stories as **"Zulema"** *and others in her book* **Intaglio: A Novel in Six Stories** *(1990) construct a literary style and approach to writing that derive from handicrafts and trades that have been traditionally considered "women's" work in Hispanic culture: dress-making, braiding hair, orally recording the family history. For Fernández, there is art in much of women's "culture," much that can form the basis of a feminist aesthetic. For her pains, Fernández was awarded first prize for* **Intaglio** *by the Multicultural Publishers Exchange. In* **Intaglio** *Fernández uses the device of a writer and narrator who is trying to piece together her own adult identity by remembering the women who most influenced her development. The* Houston Post *concluded that* **Intaglio** *"is a beautiful story of beautiful women who are powerful in their weakness, wise in their ignorance, steady in their volatility.... These are the women who have, to a great extent, shaped Mexican-American society and therefore have helped shape South Texas."*

Zulema

I

The story Zulema heard that November morning in 1914 changed her forever, and for the rest of her life she had to deal with the consequences of what she was told on that long-ago Tuesday morning. All during the previous night she listened to sporadic gunshots across the river where the *Federales*[1] were shooting at the *Villistas*.[2] The noise and the unfamiliar bed had made her wake up long before the bells of San Augustine Church pealed their daily calling to the faithful, and at six o'clock when the

---

1. National Guard Army
2. Rebel Army of Pancho Villa

first sounds from the belfry echoed in the distance, Zulema got up, blessed herself, then knelt down to say her morning prayers. She heard her aunt Mariana moving around in the next room and wondered if the disturbances in the night had also made her get up earlier than usual.

Mariana looked different that morning, puffy around the eyes and rather tense as she prepared the coffee and tortillas. Zulema sensed she had interrupted her aunt as she came into the kitchen but Mariana instinctively left her *comal* to kiss the child. "I have a lot to tell you," Mariana whispered as she put her arms around Zulema's slender body. Then, as she moved back to the stove and stirred the chocolate she was preparing for the child, Mariana told her the story.

Her voice sounded a little forced and her face looked weary. Zulema would later try to recall the scene but all she could remember was Mariana's palor and the voice that had been pitched higher than normal. In this tone Mariana had told her that her new brother had arrived during the night, tired from his journey but happy and fat and kicking with gusto.

The night had been full of activity, she continued, for not only had the new baby arrived and the shooting continued on the other side but a messenger had also come from San Antonio. He had informed Zulema's mother that her other sister, Carmen, had come down with a serious case of pneumonia. Isabel had left right away with the messenger, leaving her new-born baby behind with the rest of the family. "Give my Zulemita and Miguelito a kiss and tell them I'll be home soon." Those had been her last words as she departed, Mariana said.

"You will stay with me for a while," she continued. Miguel would stay with his father and his grandmother, and the baby would remain with Doña Julia who lived across the street and also had a small infant she was nursing. It had all been arranged.

II

Thirty-five years later, sitting on some thick pillows Zulema had special-made for me, I heard many different versions of what I later realized was the same story. During my afternoon visits I listened to Zulema's calm, deep voice as she invented one tale after another with superbly eccentric characters who continued to dance and whirl about in my own accelerated imagination. Some of the stories were simple duplications of tales Mariana had told her but most of the narratives were Zulema's own inventions. Often Mariana would join us, sitting on the rocking chair with her eyes closed as though she were reliving the episodes which Zulema was describing.

Now and then Mariana would open her eyes, then lean forward to listen more closely. Then she would shake her head and correct Zulema. *"No, no fue así,"*[3] and

---

3.   No, it wasn't like that.

she would turn to me with her own version of the story I had just heard. It was difficult for me to decide whose narrative I liked the most, for they each had their way with description and knew just when to pause for the maximum of effect but I suppose at that time I tended to think that Mariana's *"bola de años,"* as she referred to her advancing age, gave her an edge over Zulema's rendition.

I soon learned that Zulema had a favorite story. It was the one about the camp follower Victoriana, who, at the height of the revolution, had crossed to this side to wait for her lover Joaquín. For a while people coming from her pueblo in Zacatecas confirmed her belief that Joaquín was still alive but as the years passed, everyone simply forgot about Victoriana. She continued her vigil until that unexpected afternoon when the people had found her thirty years later, sitting in the same chair where she had first sat down to wait, covered with cobwebs and red dust but with a glowing expression on her face and her rusted rifle at her feet.

I never got tired of Zulema's *cuento*,[4] for each time she'd recite it, she would pretend it was the first time she had confided to me about Victoriana and she would embellish the story with a few more details. The climax was always the same, though, as she'd describe how Victoriana was unable to recognize the man whose memory she had loved all those years, for when the newspapers had printed the story about her long wait, out of curiosity, Joaquín had come to see Victoriana and she had not singled him out from all the other visitors she had greeted that afternoon. No longer the *campesino* she had fallen in love with but a very important businessman, Joaquín was alternately amused and mortified by all of the moths and butterflies entangled among the cobwebs in her silvered hair.

Zulema would conclude the story with Victoriana boarding the Ferrocarriles Nacionales Mexicaños, while the townspeople waved a sad farewell to the splendid and flamboyant figure who had enlivened their routine lives for a brief while. She, too, waved to the people as the train pulled away, taking her back to her *pueblo*[5] where she hoped to locate some of the relatives she had last seen in Bachimba claiming their rifles and riding off into the distance to be swept into the force of the revolution.

Unknown endings, unfinished lives. That was the subject of most of Zulema's narratives but I cannot remember when I first began to notice this. On the day after my sixth birthday I sensed something different, for Zulema changed the story from fantasy to biography and for the first time mentioned Isabel to me. She took a photograph from her missal and passed the edge-worn picture to me. "Do you know who she is?"

---

4. story
5. town

Immediately I recognized the photo as a copy of one my mother had. *"Es tu mamá,"*[6] I responded right away. *"Mí abuelita Isabel."*[7]

I often opened the top drawer of my mother's dresser just to steal a peep at the young woman in the tucked lace blouse who looked back at me with soft, gentle eyes. No one had ever told me much about her except that she was my father's mother who had died when my uncle Luis was born. Each of the boys had been reared by different relatives who did not find it appropriate to talk to them about Isabel, possibly to spare the children from the memories the adults did not want them to have. Up to then I knew very little about her.

"She died when she was only twenty-four. I was six then," Zulema spoke very deliberately. "Mariana really pulled the wool over my eyes, telling me Mamá had gone away with Tía Carmen."

Zulema's shoulders began to rise up and down. Suddenly she started to sob uncontrollably, holding the photo to her breast. Through my own tears I heard her describe how she had waited for days on end for her mother's return during that first winter when Isabel had gone away without a word to her. The minute she'd hear people pass by on the street she'd run to the door on the chance her mother would be with them. The streetcar that clanged in front of the house seemed to sound especially for her and every time she'd see Julia nursing the baby she'd wonder if Luisito was hungry for his own mother. Feeling abandoned she began to talk about her feelings; yet, everyone maintained the story which Mariana had uttered. When, when, when she had asked her aunt, and Mariana had finally said, "When the war is over, she'll be back."

And so the eight-year old Zulema had become interested in the war. At night whenever she heard gunshots or sirens she'd cry herself to sleep. The bugles of the infantry across the river woke her up every morning and in the afternoons after class she'd go down to the river to look across its banks at the war-weary nation on the other side. Then she would wish the war away, praying with her eyes closed while she imagined her mother running towards her with outstretched arms. But Zulema could sense that Isabel would not be back for a long time, for every day she was aware of the dozens of people who crossed the bridge with their belongings in wheelbarrows or in suitcases of every sort. Some even had knapsacks slung across their back, looking tired and worn from the personal anxieties they too were experiencing. Sometimes her father would give work around the store or at the ranch to some of the people who had just arrived, and before they moved on farther north, Zulema would take advantage of their personal accounts to ask them questions about the war. No one

---

6.   It's your mother.
7.   my grandmother Isabel

had any idea when the fighting would end and many of them no longer cared about the revolution except for the manner in which it had altered the course of their lives. They were mostly preoccupied with the death and destruction over which they had absolutely no control.

With all the talk of death, Zulema soon became apprehensive. When the newly-arrived talked about the death of their loved ones, she began to associate their experiences with her own loss and slowly began to doubt the story about her mother's return. On her ninth birthday, in 1917, she had let everyone know she realized the war was supposed to be over and still her mother had not come back. "I know she is lost," she concluded. Then she looked directly at Mariana and stated in a tone of finality. "I no longer have a mother."

And that same day she had started to tell her own stories. She took Miguelito and Luisito to her room and sat them down on the floor, while she lay on her bed looking up at the ceiling. *"Les voy a contar un cuento de nunca acabar,"*[8] she began, then started to narrate her own version of the Sleeping Beauty, who had been put under a spell by her wicked stepmother. Sleeping Beauty was supposed to be awakened by the kiss of a gorgeous prince but that never really happened. She turned to her brothers and asked them if they knew why the prince had not found Sleeping Beauty. Then, without giving them a chance to answer, for this was supposed to be her very own story, she continued with melodramatic gestures.

The prince could not find Sleeping Beauty, she whispered, because a revolution broke out just as he was setting out on his journey. Word soon arrived that his white horse had been confiscated by Emiliano Zapata. So now the prince had to find his way around on foot, and not being accustomed to looking out for himself, he had no idea what direction he should take. Finally, he headed towards his castle but when he got there he found that it had been blown to pieces, and the revolutionaries had proclaimed that he could no longer be a prince. And so he was unable to complete his mission. Poor Sleeping Beauty was left forgotten in the woods but since she could not live without the prince, for they needed each other to exist, she simply had no future and remained out there in the dark woods forever and ever. Pretty soon no one could remember, much less care, about the troubles of that poor little Sleeping Beauty, foolish enough to think she needed to live with a prince in a castle. So, without realizing what they had done, the revolutionaries got rid of all those charming princes and the silly, pampered Sleeping Beauties as well.

That afternoon I listened for a long time as Zulema recited one such story after another. From the beginning, she said, her brothers did not like her plots because they considered her endings to be strange, even morbid at times. Once in a while she had tried to tell her stories to her father but he did not seem the least bit interested

---

8. I'm going to tell you an unending story.

in them. Mariana, who perhaps best understood what she was really trying to say, assumed she could change her endings. So, for lack of an audience Zulema felt she had been fated to keep them to herself all those years. I was the only one who had let her tell the stories the way she wanted.

"Zulema, I like your stories," I reassured her as I undid her braids, then ran my small fingers through her hair.

I then looked at her in a whole new way. Unlike Mariana and the picture we had of Isabel, Zulema seemed quite ordinary, with her long hair parted in the middle and plaited into thick braids which she wore criss-crossed on top of her head. She did not look like my mother either, whose hair was swept up, away from her face and wrapped around a hair piece that was pinned around her head in keeping with the fashion of the day. I much preferred Zulema's hair, which I loved to unbraid, then brush out in waves which reached down to her waist.

That afternoon I gave her particular attention weaving a red satin ribbon into her braids which made her look prettier than usual. Finally animated, she continued with the narrative that had gone unshared all those years. She skipped the elaboration she gave to her other tales and was direct and terse as she described the main event that had shaped her life. She really could not blame Mariana or her father, she said, for they had simply been trying to save her from the very pain they had inadvertently caused. By the time she was twelve she had given up altogether on her mother's return although occasionally when she opened a door in her father's house, for an instant she felt she had caught a glimpse of her mother sitting there in her rocking chair. That was about the time she took to leaving all the doors in the house ajar. Gradually she became fascinated with opening trunks and boxes as well.

One day while she was visiting her father and Amanda she found herself alone in the room where he kept his papers. Slowly, she began to poke into his desk and in a drawer, underneath some photos, she uncovered the announcement which she unknowingly had been searching for all those months. She picked up the card, looked at its black borders, then read: *ISABEL MENDOZA-DEL VALLE, esposa de José María Cárdenas*[9]—1890–1914. The rest of the announcement stated that Isabel was survived by three children—Zulema, Miguel, and Luis.

Zulema put the card back where she had found it. After that she lost her interest in rummaging through boxes and drawers. She began to rise at six o'clock in order to attend daily mass where she remained until it was time for school. Gradually she began to lose interest in her classes, and one day she decided to stay in church all day. For several weeks she sat in the immense church where the incense soothed her memories and the candles she lit brightened the semi-darkness. Soon el Padre Salinas began to notice the disappearance of the candles. Concerned that almost no money

---

9.   wife of José María Cárdenas

was being left in the offering box to cover their cost, he staked out the various altars and, shortly thereafter, caught her sitting in the front pew facing the virgin and child. He watched as she lighted two or three candles at once, then when those burned down, he saw her light new ones.

Just about the time el Padre Salinas approached Mariana about the expense, the teacher paid José María a visit. José María did not take the trouble to discuss the matter with his daughter; instead, he talked to Mariana who related to Zulema that her father now wished to keep her at home, for she could no longer be trusted to go out on her own. From then on she would not be allowed to go anywhere without being accompanied either by one of the cousins or the aunts.

Zulema had not minded the restrictions at all. In fact, for the first time she felt she was the object of everyone's attention. Mariana taught her the secrets that went into cooking traditional dishes. For their *mole de gallina*[10] they would spend a good part of a day grinding sesame seeds, peanuts and *pastillas de chocolate*[11] on the *metate*[12] and once the ingredients for the sauce were ready, they would simmer it for hours. It was then that they would go to the chicken coop to pick out two or three chickens. At first Zulema was squeamish but she learned to wring a chicken by the neck before chopping off its head with a *machete*. For dessert she loved to make *capirotada* and *leche quemada* and the first time she prepared the entire meal for a table of twelve, she relished all the compliments she got for her *calabaza con puerco*.

Doña Julia taught her to crochet, little squares at first, then larger items like tablecloths and bedspreads which she made as gifts for *fiestas de quinceañeras*,[13] engagement showers and weddings. When she turned fifteen she too was honored with a dance attended by all the relatives, their friends and friends of her father. Everyone danced to the music of a local band until the early hours of the morning and between dances they kept going back for more *tamales* and steaming cups of cinnamoned coffee. Before the night was over, all the spread on the table—*barbacoa, guacamole, arroz, frijoles borrachos*[14] and freshly grilled *gorditas*[15]—had been eaten up.

That was the first time she had met Carlos who danced all evening with her. A few days later, he had called on her father requesting permission to visit with her at home. Soon she began to be kidded about having a sweetheart and when the *comadres*[16] in Mariana's quilt-making group asked her about Carlos, Zulema smiled

---

10. chicken in mole sauce
11. chocolate bits
12. mortar
13. 15-year-old coming-out party
14. barbeque, guacamole sauce, rice, bean stew
15. fat tortillas
16. godmothers

and pretended to be concentrating on her stitches. After a while, she filled her trunk with the essentials for her future life and when she married Carlos, she brought to her new home all the exquisite handmade items that a seventeen-year-old bride needed. A few weeks after Zulema's and Carlos's first child was born, Mariana came to live with them, and for more than twenty years the three of them saw the family expand, then contract again, as the older sons went off to study at the university and the youngest daughter married, at seventeen, like her mother.

Zulema had tried to get each one of her children interested in listening to her stories but all four thought the stories were silly and repetitive. So, it wasn't until I started making requests for recitations about her extravagant characters that she began to ponder about this particular vacuum in her life.

Now, as the afternoon light softly faded, Zulema paused to reflect on everything she had told me. Finally, she sighed, "Telling stories. That's what I've enjoyed the most."

"Me too," I smiled, tucking at her red ribbons.

Just then the door opened and my cousin Maruca turned on the light. Surprised, she asked "How come you're sitting in the dark?"

Neither of us answered her. Then, she burst out, "Ay, *Mamá*, why are you wearing those silly ribbons? You look as if you were about to dance *el jarabe tapatío.*"[17]

"She looks great with her hair like this," I responded.

Maruca waved her hands as if to brush my comment aside. "You two live in your special little world, with all your *cuentos*. Come join us now. I've brought a big trayful of fried chicken and potato salad."

"We'll come in a minute," Zulema answered. "Just let us finish here."

As soon as we were alone again, Zulema looked at me very intently, tapping her index finger against her mouth. "Nenita, let's keep this to ourselves. Poor Mariana. It's been such a long time since mother died. There's no point in creating problems now. All this was just between you and me, okay?"

III

Earlier that day, my sister Patricia had called to inform me about the heart attack. In my rush to the bus station I had forgotten my sunglasses and the bright light of the afternoon was now blinding me. Closing my eyes, I tried to sort out my feelings but I couldn't focus on anything. Instead, I tried leafing through the magazine I had picked up at the Greyhound shop. News of Czechoslovakia, Viet Nam and Cambodia flashed by me. A picture of Joan Baez. Many anti-war demonstrators. Unable to concentrate, I set the magazine aside.

---

17. a dance from Jeilisco, Mexico ("Mexican hat dance")

Leaning against the bus window I stretched out my legs across the two seats and studied the passengers closest to me. Two rows up on my left was a woman with very teased hair. She reminded me of Florinda's Cuban mother whom I knew only through my sister's vivid description. I looked around at the other people, then fidgeted with the journal I had on my lap. Feeling its smooth leather cover, I remembered how pleased I had been the previous Christmas when Mariana and Zulema had given it to me. On its first page, they had inscribed: "Make this a memory book of your very own dreams and aspirations." It was the first thing I grabbed when I started to pack for this journey home but at the moment I did not feel like looking at it.

I concentrated instead on the woman with the teased hair. Florinda's mother must have looked like that when she left Cuba ten years ago. In anticipation of the day when the family would leave the island, she let her hair grow for more than a year. Then when the moment for their departure arrived, she had carefully teased her hair, then divided it into three layers. The first section had been twisted into a tight French roll fastened with pins encrusted with precious gems. A small fortune, I was told. The tiny twist had been covered with a larger one held up by more jeweled hairpins. Finally, the top outer layer neatly covering the cache had been sprayed several times with a heavy lacquer. As if to mock fate, she had attached thin wires with pink and white gauze butterflies all over her hair. According to my sister, Florinda had said that her mother looked so outrageous no one bothered much with her and she had smuggled a sizeable sum which the family had used to set up a fabric store. Several years later, it was a thriving business.

For reasons I didn't quite understand, Florinda's mother's story always made me anxious. So, I lit a cigarette and watched the smoke whirl upwards. From the angle the sun was hitting me, the smoke resembled the tumultuous vapors in the film version of "Pedro Páramo." In that film, as Juan Preciado searched for his father, the vapors kept getting thicker and thicker the more he travelled inside the land of the dead.

"This is my favorite novel," I had pointed out to Zulema and Mariana on the previous Thanksgiving holiday. "But I'm sure there's a lot in this novel I don't understand," I had warned as I introduced them to the spirits, the *espíritus,*[18] of Comala.

We had been reading from the paperback copies of *Pedro Páramo* that I had given to each of them. Mariana and I did most of the reading, although Zulema sometimes took her turn. Sipping Cuervo *añejo,*[19] we had commented on the novel, pointing out the scenes we had particularly enjoyed. Mariana, especially, was enthralled with the characters at the Rancho Media Luna, for they were part of a period she still remembered well. And Zulema, as I had expected, identified with Susana, the character whose fate had also been shaped by the early death of her mother.

18. spirits/souls
19. aged

"The spirits always continue to influence those who live after them," Mariana had sighed. "Just right here, we have the example of Zulema, who suffered so much after the death of Isabel."

Zulema and I had glanced at one another. Fifty-five years after the death of her sister, Mariana was finally commenting on it.

"Why do you say that?" I had softly questioned.

"It's just that the murmurs get stronger by the day," she had answered, extending her hands on the armrest. She had closed her eyes rocking herself back and forth, letting us know the conversation had ended for the moment. Finally, she had murmured, "It is time now" and to our astonishment she said she would take us to Isabel's burial place.

As I drove to the cemetery in silence, my mind was full of questions. Like the rest of the family, I had succumbed to the story of Isabel's departure and had not even asked where she had been buried. For twenty years, since Zulema had told me her version of her mother's death, I had learned to think of Isabel as a spirit living the special life of the dead. I wondered if Zulema was as shocked as I was since she too had not uttered a word.

"*Vamos por este camino.*"[20] Mariana led us through the old part of the cemetery to an enclosed plot. There, a red tin can with a cluster of marigolds lay half-buried in front of a tombstone marked with the same inscription as on the death announcement which Zulema had read so long ago: ISABEL MENDOZA-DEL VALLE, 1890–1914.

I was stunned, realizing that for all these years, Isabel had been within reach. Zulema's lower lip started to tremble and little whimpering sounds began to come out of her mouth. Mariana put her arm around Zulema's shoulder, then rested her head on it.

"I never knew how to remedy what had happened," Mariana said simply. It was obvious she finally wanted to break the silence surrounding Isabel and in order to get her off her feet, we moved to a nearby bench.

For a while we sat quietly. Then Mariana began to tell us about the difficulty she had experienced in repeating the story the family had chosen for the children on the night Isabel had died. From the very beginning she had made adjustments in her life, for she had stayed home with Zulema while the rest of the family attended the novena for her sister. Later, when the child's suspicions were aroused, she had started to doubt the decision to protect Zulema from the truth.

Yet, after a few years they themselves had almost accepted the story as fact and tacitly believed it would be much more difficult to adjust to a new reality than to live with the pattern that had been set. "I don't know what to do," Mariana repeated over and over.

---

20. Let's go down this road.

Then she told us about her weekly visits to the cemetery and how she considered those visits her personal ritual in keeping the memory of Isabel alive. For years she had snuck away on the bus with her little bouquet of marigolds. But, as she got older, her visits became more and more sporadic. Still, only a few days before, she had brought the flowers we had just seen.

I looked at Mariana's rheumatic limbs and wondered how she had managed to honor her sister for so long.

"*Uno hace lo que tiene que hacer,*"[21] she affirmed as they headed back to the car. I repeated those words to myself, "One simply does what one has to do."

For the rest of the day I tried to fit together all the pieces of the story and started to write long entries about Mariana, Isabel and Zulema in a loose-leaf journal. When I got back to my apartment I continued writing and one day in early December, I stuffed my notes into an envelope and mailed it off to them, with instructions to save the pages for me. A few weeks after that, they gave me my blue leatherbound book as a present.

I reached over to feel it, then opened my eyes. We had arrived. As soon as we pulled into the terminal I saw my sister Patricia waiting for me.

"How is she doing?" I asked.

"She's been hanging on but she won't last much longer. Late this morning she had another heart attack and the doctor does not think she'll pull through this time."

IV

As I opened the door I heard Father Murphy reciting the prayers of Extreme Unction and saw him blessing the small body on the hospital bed. My mother leaned towards me and whispered as she put her arm around me, "I'm so sorry. She died about fifteen minutes ago."

I felt everyone's eyes on me as I walked up to the bed. As tears streamed down my face I kissed the smooth sallow cheeks, then looked at the body for a long time without saying anything. It was useless for me to remain there, I thought, and slowly I began to envision what it was I had to do.

In my sister's car I drove across the border to the church by the first plaza, then walked towards the adjacent small shop which sold religious articles. As I had hoped, its window display was full of saints with tin *milagros*[22] pinned to their clothing. Inside I found hundreds of *milagros* for sale in many different shapes, sizes and materials. Immediately I by-passed the larger ones and the gold ones which I could not afford. Looking at the half-inch tin offerings, I carefully selected from those in the shape of

21. You do what you have to.
22. miracles (indulgences)

human profiles, hearts and tongues of fire. The volunteer at the shop seemed surprised when I said I wanted five dozen of each, then waited patiently while I made my selection. Eventually, she divided the offerings into small plastic bags.

With the *milagros* on my lap I drove a few blocks to the flower market. There I purchased bunches of marigolds and asked the vendor to divide them up into small bouquets which he tied together with white ribbons. They took up most of the back seat, making the custom inspector remark on my collection of *flores para los muertos.* [23] My next stop was the stationery shop where I bought a small box of red cinnamon-scented candles. Then, on my way to the funeral parlor I passed by a record shop. Slamming on the brakes, I double-parked and ran in to inquire if they sold small 45s that were blank. The clerk thought they had three such records left over from an old special order. As soon as he found them I rushed back to the car and made my way to the funeral parlor. The administrator listened rather dubiously to my plans, then reluctantly gave me permission to do as I wished.

I went home to rest for a while, then at the agreed-upon hour I returned to the funeral parlor and for the next three hours I carried out my task. My back hurt from being bent for so long as, between tears, I carefully sewed the *milagros* on the white satin which lined the inside cover of the casket. Applying three stitches through the tiny hole on each tin sculpture I made a design of three arcs—the faces were on the outer row, the tongues in the middle and the hearts on the inner row. Once I finished with the *milagros* I stepped back to get a better view. Seeing how pretty they looked, each with its accompanying tiny red ribbon, I cried once more, yet felt a little relief from my sorrow knowing that when the lid was closed the *milagros* would be a lovely sight to behold from inside. Then, with the marigolds, I created a halo effect on the space above the corpse, hoping its spirit could savor the smell of the flowers. I arranged the candles in a row in front of the casket and felt myself tremble as I placed the three records on the left side of the body. *"Llénalos con tus cuentos favoritos,"* I whispered. "Fill them with your favorite stories."

For a long time I sat in the semi-darkness, mesmerized by the smell of the flowers and perfumed glow of the candles. Recalling the many *cuentos* which had inspired my youthful imagination, I felt I could stay there forever. But I knew I did not want to see anyone tonight, and soon someone would be coming to sit out the early morning vigil.

Slowly, I got up and walked to the coffin once again. The *milagros* and the flowers looked splendid but I wondered what the rest of the family would say when they saw them. I touched the dear figure for the last time, then walked out into the night knowing I would not be going to the burial ceremony the next afternoon.

---

23 flowers for the dead

Instead I went home and immediately began to write in my journal. For two days I wrote, filling all its pages. Then I gave my thick blue book to Patricia so she could read what I had just finished.

She started reading right away and did not move from her chair for hours. At times I would see her shake her head and make almost audible sounds. Finally, when she finished, she closed the book but kept her hand on its cover.

"No," she said. "No *fue así.*"[24] A stern expression crossed her face. "It's not been at all the way you've presented it. You've mixed up some of the stories Mariana and Zulema have told you, which might not even be true in the first place. I've heard other versions from Tía Carmen and, in fact, from Zulema herself. Mariana would never even recognize herself if you ever show this to her."

"I'm not sure what you are trying to do," Patricia continued, "but what you have here is not at all what really happened."

"Lo que tienes aquí no es lo que pasó."

I smiled at Patricia, then took my journal back. As I did so, I remembered that my mother always said that her own memory book had been a collection of images of our family's past both as it was and as we all would have liked that past to have been.

"You know," I responded. *"Uno cuenta de la feria según lo que ve en ella.* Each of us tell it as we see it."

---

24. It wasn't that way.

Alejandro Morales

(b. 1944)
Mexican American

Alejandro Morales is one of the leading Chicano novelists, having published substantial novels in both Spanish and English in the United States and Mexico and having created through them a better understanding of Mexican American history, at least as seen from the vantage point of working-class culture. Born in Montebello, California, on October 14, 1944, Morales grew up in East Los Angeles and received his bachelor's from California State University at Los Angeles. He went on to complete a master's (1973) and a doctorate (1975) in Spanish at Rutgers University in New Jersey. Today Morales is a full professor in the Spanish and Portuguese Department at the University of California at Irvine.

Morales is a recorder of the Chicano experience, basing many of his narratives on historical research. He is also an imaginative interpreter of that experience with his memorable and dynamic characters and language. His first books were written in Spanish and published in Mexico due to the lack of opportunity here in the United States. These were later published in the United States as **Old Faces and New Wine** *(1981), which examines the conflict of generations in a barrio family, and* **Death of an Anglo** *(1988), which is a continuation of the earlier novel but is set against the backdrop of actual occurrences of Chicano-Anglo conflict in the town of Mathis, Texas.* **The Brick People** *(1988) traces the development of two families associated with the Simons Brick Factory, one of the largest enterprises of its type in the country. Morales' novel* **The Rag Doll Plagues** *(1991), while still incorporating a historical structure, follows the development of a plague and a Spanish-Mexican doctor who is forever caught in mortal battle with this plague in three time periods and locations: colonial Mexico, contemporary southern California, and the future in a country made up of Mexico and California united together.*

In all of his works, Morales shows himself to be a meticulous researcher and creator of novelistic circumstances that are symbolic of Mexican American history and cultural development. His novels have an epic sweep with strongly cinematic and highly literary qualities.

The Curing Woman

This is the story that Doña Marcelina Trujillo Benidorm told her friend Concepción Martinez when they met in Simons, California.

Marcelina was born into a rich family in Spain. Her highly respected parents dedicated their lives to serving the public and the Church. However, the Trujillo Benidorms never associated with the people who benefited from their generous financial gifts. They kept company with other aristocratic families; even then, only a few other families were deemed worthy of their attention. The Trujillo Benidorms had four children, three sons and Marcelina, who was conceived by her father and one of the beautiful young servants who dedicated ten years of their lives to total obedience to the family. When Marcelina's mother was forced to leave the estate at the end of her ten-year term, she begged to take her nine-year-old daughter with her. But Mrs. Trujillo Benidorm denied the request, choosing instead to keep the child herself. She had grown to love Marcelina and, besides, the child was a reminder to her husband of his sins of infidelity. Mrs. Trujillo Benidorm also believed that Marcelina's mother could never afford to educate her daughter properly.

Both women had always loved Marcelina and both had treated her well, but, when she saw her real mother leaving the estate for the last time, Marcelina was heart broken. She ran in tears to an upstairs window to catch a last glimpse of the woman who had given birth to her. Marcelina's mother smiled with joy and pride at the beautiful brown-eyed child framed by the ivy growing around the window. At that moment Marcelina realized that looking into her mother's face was like looking into a mirror, that her mother had given birth to an identical twin, had in fact given birth to herself. Marcelina ran to the mirror; she looked exactly like her mother. With a cry, she rushed back to the window. Her mother was gone.

For four years Mrs. Trujillo Benidorm gave Marcelina everything a child could want. She was well cared for and educated in an excellent school. But she never heard a word about her mother. Then one chilly, damp morning while she strolled the rocky Altean beach, a servant came to her with a crumpled piece of green paper. With the first light of the next morning, Marcelina stepped onto the road to Granada and began a journey that would eventually lead her to Simons, California.

Marcelina found her mother in the caves of the hills overlooking Alhambra. Although she had never heard her mother's name spoken aloud, on the day she approached the cave where her mother lived with her husband, Marcelina heard a voice call out "Yerma." It was the name of Marcelina's mother/twin. Yerma walked toward her daughter, and Marcelina felt a surge of energy run through her body. Neither of them spoke. As their fingers touched, their minds were joined, and they stood smiling and looking out over the world. The clasp of their hands became a harmony, a song.

Marcelina spent seven happy years with her mother. Yerma bore no other children. Her husband, a hard-working man of the earth, damned the Trujillo Benidorms for his beautiful wife's infertility, but he accepted Marcelina as his daughter and taught her all that he knew of the earth to which he was born and to which he would one day return. Yerma dedicated her life to the study of cures. She learned from Moslem, Jewish, and Christian practitioners. She mastered chants, formulas and procedures which gave her access to natural and supernatural powers. She investigated the positive and negative, good and evil, masculine and feminine forces of the cosmos. This duality she discovered and controlled in herself, and this knowledge she offered to her apprentice daughter/twin, who would one day become a *curandera*.[1]

---

1. healer

Marcelina learned her craft well, and one day Yerma realized she had taught Marcelina all she knew. With infinite sadness, Marcelina and her ageless mother were separated forever on this earth. The young woman made her way south to the Mediterranean port of Cadiz, where she boarded a ship bound for Veracruz on the Gulf Coast of Mexico. Marcelina was only twenty years old, but she was fearless and confident. She had her mother's beauty and an intelligence second to none.

The voyage to Veracruz was invigorating, as Marcelina concentrated on the forces of the sea. Nourished by the mysteries of the Mediterranean, baptized by the sea, Marcelina knew she would grow even stronger in the New World.

In Veracruz Marcelina was met by a man called "El Gran Echbo,"[2] who introduced her to the magical, marvelous realities of the Caribbean. For several years she cultivated the energies of this new vision of the world, adding them to her already considerable knowledge of enchantment. Towards the end or her apprenticeship with "El Gran Echbo," Marcelina met María Sabina, a saintly woman renowned for her curative powers. María Sabina communicated with the negative and positive forces of the cosmos through her knowledge of plants and animals. She spoke the language of the ancient doctors of the land—Nahuatl[3]—which she taught to Marcelina. María Sabina travelled with her powerful pupil to Mexico City, following an ancient secret path known only to a chosen few. As the two women journeyed through thick, hot jungles, majestic mountains, and treacherous swamps, Marcelina became aware of the universal duality of Ometecuhtli-Omecihuatl.[4] Her mind roamed through the four suns of the mandala, each passage making her stronger in the movement of the energy time-space concept of Mexican cosmology. But the journey took its toll, and Marcelina fell into a trancelike state.

When she opened her eyes, she was in María Sabina's shack in Tepito, the poorest section of Mexico City. She heard the sounds of explosions somewhere in the city. María Sabina explained that each day the city grew more dangerous and soon they would have to leave. But they would not be going together. As Marcelina stared into the other woman's cataract eyes, she saw immense sorrow. María Sabina told her to journey north, and to leave within four days. Then María Sabina was gone.

Marcelina felt a heartbreaking emptiness. For the first time in her life there was no one to guide her. She conjured up images of her lovely mother, and soon she had the strength to prepare for her journey. Marcelina left the city in the early morning of the fourth day, amidst the echoes of rifle fire.

As she proceeded north, the lands of Mexico appeared before her like a violent carnival. The Revolution[5] continued to ravish the soil and the people. While passing

---

2. The Great Echbo
3. the language of the Aztecs
4. Aztec gods
5. Mexican Revolution of 1910

through Güiseo de Abasolo, in the State of Guanajuato, she heard talk of a city in California, a fantastic city called Simons, where Mexicans lived and worked in happiness and contentment. Marcelina felt a growing conviction that she would end her journey in that city. For four months she travelled with the armies that moved ever northward, paying her way by treating the sick and wounded. The torn and bloodied bodies of the people she tended showed her the absurdity of the violent forces prevailing in the land, and she used her own powerful resources to steal many souls from Death.

In tattered and bloodstained clothes, Marcelina finally penetrated the border at Ciudad Juarez/El Paso. Never losing sight of her goal, she travelled by train for three months across the vast southwest territory. When the train stopped in Simons, California, Marcelina Trujillo Benidorm stepped off, never to leave again.

Concepción Martinez and her eldest son, Delfino, walked along Vail Street towards Doña Marcelina's home. As they walked, Concepción reflected on her friendship with Marcelina, and on how their lives had intertwined since they had met in Simons years ago. Her awe of Marcelina's knowledge of the natural and supernatural had somehow never interfered with their friendship. But today was different. Today Concepción was taking her first-born to Marcelina, to the *curandera,* for treatment.

Delfino did not know if he was angry or relieved that he was finally going to see Doña Trujillo Benidorm. She was truly his last hope. Ever since the fire that consumed his home, and the terrible shock of believing it had consumed his family as well, something was wrong. All the doctors said he was well. The psychiatrist ascribed his condition to the deep shock of thinking his family was dead, but he too said there was nothing physically wrong with him. Why then was he steadily and relentlessly losing weight? He was becoming weak and delirious, even though he ate enough to satisfy two men. He was frightened by the unknown force inside him. At the moment, though, he wasn't sure which frightened him more. Doña Trujillo Benidorm had always been a mystery to the townspeople, someone the children stayed away from. The fact that she was also his mother's friend did not lessen Delfino's anxiety about seeking her help.

Mother and son moved silently down Vail Street. They passed men on their way to work. On that street few women were out so early in the morning, so Concepción attracted immediate and polite attention. The men greeted the pair somberly, then moved along to their jobs. As Concepción and Delfino passed the church and came into sight of Marcelina's home across from the American Foundry, their steps slowed and stopped. A breeze came up and played in Concepcion's black hair. Behind her, Delfino stared at Marcelina Trujillo Benidorm's house. He felt as if he were about to step into a photograph.

Doña Marcelina greeted them briefly. They all knew why they were there. Delfino looked at her and in an unsettling moment saw both an old woman and a beautiful young girl. The moment passed, and Doña Marcelina ushered them into an immaculate white room, empty of furniture but full of brightness. The room was large, the ceiling higher than they had expected. Evenly spaced on three of the walls were images of the Passion of Christ. In the center of the fourth wall was a door to another, smaller room. Concepción bid her son farewell.

Delfino looked around. On the wall in front of him was a painting of a man sitting in a wheelbarrow with a woman sitting on a block in front of him. Both seemed to be praying. The painting was dark; storm clouds dominated the distant horizon. Sitting on the floor under the painting was a wheelbarrow, and in front of that was a black block. In the corner of the room was a standing cross.

Doña Marcelina asked Delfino to sit in the wheelbarrow. As he obeyed, he saw his mother watching them from the doorway. Her face was carefully devoid of emotion. Then his view was obscured by a quilted, multicolored jacket and black skirt as Doña Marcelina sat on the black block in front of him. With her hands lying quietly in her lap, she smiled at him reassuringly and began a litany of prayers and incantations, all the while preparing several potions. Occasionally she made the sign of the cross before preparing yet another potion.

From the doorway, Concepción watched the *curandera* work. She noted with fascination as Doña Marcelina began her struggle to gain control of and dominate the spirit which thrived on Delfino's body and soul. As the battle evolved, Delfino took on Doña Marcelina's physical characteristics. A transformation occurred. In this way was Doña Marcelina able to explore his/her body and locate her enemy. Concepción stared as her son became her friend. After some time a large grotesque form appeared on the lower back of the *curandera*. The shape grew distinctly into an octopus with powerful tentacles wrapped around Doña Marcelina's waist. The *susto*[6] was alive, pulsating, furious at being torn from its lair. Now it clung to her. But Doña Marcelina knew how to destroy evil, and before long it disappeared. Gradually Delfino reappeared in his own body. He was no longer tired, and his spirit felt light and free again. He realized with surprise that hours had passed since he entered the room, but he recalled nothing of what had happened since Doña Marcelina began her prayers. Looking down, Delfino was startled to find he was wearing Doña Marcelina's quilted jacket. Smiling at his mother, he took off the jacket and placed it in the wheelbarrow. He never asked how he had come to be wearing it. Some time later Doña Marcelina gave Concepción nine small pouches and instructed her to give Delfino potions for nine more days. Doña Marcelina was again herself as she walked Concepción into the large white room.

---

6. scare [an affliction]

Delfino waited in the center of the room while his mother and the *curandera* conversed quietly. He looked through the doorway into the room where he had been cured. As he studied the painting on the wall, he saw to his astonishment that the composition had changed. The man had disappeared. Everything else remained the same. When he turned around to tell Concepción of his discovery, he found himself in front of his home waiting for his mother to open the door.

Denise Chávez

(b. 1948)
Mexican American

Denise Chávez is a novelist, playwright, and poet who has brought to life entire populations of memorable characters in the Southwest, both Mexican American and Anglo-American. Chávez was born on August 15, 1948, in Las Cruces, New Mexico, where she attended schools. In 1974 she obtained a master's degree in theater arts from Trinity University in San Antonio, Texas, and in 1984 a master's degree in creative writing from the University of New Mexico. During her career she has taught and been a writer in residence at numerous institutions in New Mexico and elsewhere.

Denise Chávez has won numerous awards and fellowships, including Best Play Award for **The Wait** from New Mexico State University in 1970, the Steele Jones Fiction Award in 1986 for her story **"The Last of the Menu Girls,"** two fellowships from the National Endowment for the Arts in 1981 and 1982, a Rockefeller Foundation Fellowship in 1984, and the Creative Writing Arts Fellowship from the Cultural Arts Council of Houston in 1990.

Denise Chávez has been highly productive as a playwright, but it is her published works of fiction that have contributed most to her national reputation. Chávez has published short stories in magazines and has two novels in print, **The Last of the Menu Girls** (1986) and **Face of an Angel** (1994). The first of these, from which the following story was selected, is a series of interconnected stories centering on the coming of age of Rocío Esquivel. While still centering on the life of a female central character and her development, **Face of an Angel** is completely different from her first novel. It is unrestrained, bawdy, irreverent, and hilariously funny as it explores some of the major themes of the women's liberation movement as represented in the life of a waitress, who is an author in her own right. Soveida Dosamantes, it seems, is one of those people who is destined to repeat over and over the same mistakes in their choice of a partner. The novel consists of her experiences with a number of lazy, good-for-nothing men who are irresistible to her.

The Closet

I

When I close my eyes I can see Christ's eyes in the darkness. It's an early summer afternoon, and I should be sleeping. Instead, I'm standing in the silence of my mother's closet holding a luminescent sliding picture of the Shroud of Turin.[1] One image reveals Christ as he might look fleshed out; the other shows shadows of skin pressed against white cloth. A slant of light filters through the closed door.

"It's my turn! Let me in! I want to see!" Mercy whispers impatiently from behind the door. In the half-tone darkness my eyes travel from the wedding photograph at

---

1. A garment believed to have wrapped the body of the dead Christ.

the back of the closet to the reality of my mother's other life. Shoes crowd the floor, teacher's shoes, long comfortable plastic loafers, sandals and open-toed pumps in blue and black, the sides stretched to ease the bunions' pressure. They are the shoes of a woman with big feet, tired legs, furious bitter hopes. They are the shoes of someone who has stood all her life in line waiting for better things to come.

"Mother! Mother!" I yelled one day across the Downtown shoe store. "Is size ten too small?" She answered with an impatient pinching-under-the-sweater look reserved for nasty children who have the audacity to perform obscenities in public. She scowled across the crowded room, "No! And don't yell, your voice carries!"

Mother was married at age thirty-two to a man who bathed twice a day. Juan Luz Contreras was very clean. He was the town's best catch, a descendant of the Contreras family of west Texas. Head 'em up. Round 'em up. Ride 'em out. Dead. Juan Luz was poisoned by an unscrupulous druggist—oh, unwittingly. He was forced to drink acid. Someone poured it down his throat, but why? He had a wife and a child but three days old. His wife was my mother. For many years I wondered who the man in the wedding photograph was. He wasn't my father. My father still lived with us at that time, but he wasn't home much. Who was the man in the photograph if he wasn't my father? Later I found out he was Juan Luz, my mother's first husband. Ronelia's father.

When my father finally left our home, it was Juan Luz's face in the crowded closet who comforted me. From all accounts he was a perfect man.

Standing in the closet I can smell mother, all of her, forty-eight years old in her flowered bathrobes and suits of gradually increasing girth. It is the soft, pungent woman smell of a fading mother of three girls, one of them the daughter of the unfortunate Juan Luz.

In the darkness there is the smell of my mother's loneliness. Next to me the portrait of my mother and Juan Luz is hidden behind piles of clothes which are crowded into the house's largest closet. All those memories are now suffocated in cloth. So whoever comes, whatever man comes, and only *one* could, he would not feel alarm. But would my father come, being gone so long?

I remember the nights my father was home, sitting in his favorite red chair, reading the evening newspaper and later telling stories to Mercy and me.

"A is for Aardvark and In the Name of the Father and The Son and Little Lulu and Iggy went to the store ... and what did you learn today, baby?"

Sometimes, alone on the arm chair or on his lap, I recounted tales of Dick and Jane and little blond-haired Sally.

"Please, Daddy, tell me the story of the two giant brothers, Hilo and Milo."

When I open my eyes I return to the darkness of the closet. With small feet I stand on my mother's shoes. I could never fill them even if I tried.

If I didn't hold the body of Christ in my hands and if there wasn't anything to glow in the dark and then to disappear, I could still see faces in the closet and hear people talking and feel alone. I'm afraid in the middle of the day. Me, supposed to be taking a nap in August and it being the hottest month to be born in and with a crying baby sister outside the door yell-whispering, "Come on, it's *my* turn!"

And there I'd be, holding on to the brass-colored knob with one hand, and Mercy yanking with both, and the Shroud of Turin in my left hand getting crumpled and there I'd be, whispering, "Shut up, shut up! She'll hear you and so I'm looking, okay? It's *my* turn! Okay?" The boxes are open and soon scarves and hats will be all over the floor and I'll have to get a chair and put them up on the top rack and while I'm up there I'll look at the cloth flowers and feathers and I might want to play dress up with the hats.

"We'll listen to the records on the top shelf, Mercy. 'The Naughty Lady of Shady Lane' and 'Fascination.' We'll dance like we like to dance."

"We'll be floating ballerinas meeting each other halfway under the tropical bird light fixture. You can practice your diving while I count the flowers, arranging them in rows and humming. 'Let me go, let me go, let me go, lover,' while you rest from your long swim."

"It's my turn, Rocío, you get to look at the Christ eyes all the time!"

"There's no eyes. Only sockets."

"If I squint Chinesey, I can see eyes."

"Yeah?"

"So let me have the thing, it's my turn. You always look too long."

"You might get scared, baby."

"Me, no—you *promised.*"

"Baby, Baby, Baby! There's no eyes, only sockets!"

"Open that door, you promised!"

"Go ahead, baby, come inside, here's the light!"

I turn the light on Christ and Juan Luz and my mother and all my dark secret young girl thoughts and face my little Sally sister with her baby limp hair.

"Go ahead Mercy Baby! Take the stupid thing. But let me look one more time." I yank on the old pink and chartreuse belt that has become my mother's light cord, and go back inside the closet for one last look. I stumble across the gift box, full of vinyl wallets and heart-shaped handkerchiefs and a plastic container of car-and-animal-shaped soap. The gift box is regularly replenished by my mother's elementary school students' Christmas and birthday gifts: "Merry Christmas, love Sammy. To Teacher from Mary. You are nice, Mrs. Esquibel, I'll never forget you. Bennie Roybal. 1956."

I turn off all the lights and close the door as tight as I can. I look at the glow-in-the-dark Jesus card and slide it back and forth. The skeleton color of yellow-white bone is electrified, and I can feel and see the Christ eyes in the almost total darkness.

"So here it is, Baby! Leave me alone. I'm going to lie down on the bed and rest. Don't bother me and remember, this is the invisible line, your side, and mine. Don't cross over like you do, with those rubbery hairy spidery legs of yours. Here, see this pillow? Gosh, if we had a yardstick it would be good, but anyway, this pillow divides me from you, my side from yours, okay, Baby? I want the side by the wall and the pictures. So that when I'm drifting off to sleep, I can look at Ronelia in her wedding dress when she was seventeen years old and just married. She wore Mother's dress and Mother's veil, well, maybe not the veil, but the little plastic pill box crown with wax flowerbuds. Maybe you and I will someday wear that dress, Mercy, okay? Okay? What do you think?"

"Oh, leave me alone!" she says.

As I lay in bed, Mamá Consuelo and her husband stare at me from across the room. Their faces are superimposed on wood. It's more than a photograph. It's a carved picture of two people, one of them a stranger. I don't ever know what to call my grandfather. I never called him and he never called me. So he doesn't have a name. He's my grandfather. He was strong. He was good. He worked hard during the Depression. He was better off than most. He died in his sleep from a blood clot or brain hemorrhage. All I know is that he had a headache, leaped over my sleeping grandmother in the middle of the night to take an aspirin and then went back to sleep and never woke up. About Mamá Consuelo I know more.

"Oh Mercy, sleeping in the afternoons makes me tired. Without something to do or think about I'll really fall asleep. I might as well get the crown of thorns down from the crucifix and try them on."

"Are you sure, Rocío, shouldn't you leave them alone?"

Over mother's bed there's a crucifix and on the crucifix there's a crown of thorns. Real thorns, like the ones Christ was crowned with, only these are very small and they cover just the center of my head, the baby spot. It doesn't matter that they're baby-sized, because when I push them down I feel what Christ felt. Oh, they hurt, but not too much. I never pushed them down all the way. But I can imagine what they feel like. They have long waxy spikes with sharp tips. I can imagine the rest. I've been stabbed by pencils in both my palms. The one on my right looks like the Stigmata.

Naps. I hate naps because there's so much to do and think and feel, especially in August. If I have to sleep, I like it to be quick and over with before I know it, or long and happy with a visit to the Grey Room.

The Grey Room is a place I visit when I'm alone. The Grey Room was before my little-ness, before my fear of cloth shadows from clothes on chairs, and of the dark animals the shadows made.

It began when I was a little girl. I was never afraid. Every day I visited a world which the others knew nothing about. Not Ronelia, not my mother, not my father, not even Mercy.

No one knew I lived in the Grey Room or that I flew through air and time. I entered the Grey Room late at night when the house was quiet and I was alone. I'd crawl through the hall closet and into the concrete passageway that was our house's foundation. Down I would go, into the enormous basement, inching my way into the awesome darkness, alone, unhampered, guided more or less by a voice that pulled and drew me, further, further, into the concrete maze. The space became larger, a room of immense proportions, a high room, an altar room, a sanctuary where I was the only Devout. Higher, higher, I climbed, past the attic, to the labyrinth that was the Grey Room. This world was my refuge—this world unknown to all!

One day I began to live two separate lives. One magical, the other fearful. I'd wake up screaming, "The animals! The animals!" I heard the foggy mist of concerned voices. "But even you don't understand, Mercy! You always say, 'The Closet! There's nothing under our house, no rooms, no space for you to crawl through. There's no house above or underneath our house. There's no huge room without a ceiling!'

"But Mercy, I've *been* there. I've spoken to the Keeper of the Room. He's an animal and brown. He wanted to make the room smaller, but I said, no. 'There's no space for you, go away.' Now the room is white and blue and mine, alone.

"All this came to me in dreams. I felt presences and heard voices and the sound of breathing and music far away, then near. There was smoke in my room. I couldn't breathe. The animals crowded into corners. I woke up in the middle of the night trying to run away. Mother turned on the hall light to check in on me and gave me a baby aspirin. I drifted off again. 'Walking in your sleep,' mother called it.

"Mercy, would you believe me if I told you that I was born in a closet?"

"Rocío, you're crazy!"

Mother was forty years old. She'd been a widow nine years. A table was brought into the room, but the legs were removed because the doorway was too small. When I was born, Mother and I came crashing down. I shot into a closet full of shoes, old clothes. It was 4:48 A.M. on a hot August day. Ronelia hung outside the door. She was ten years old, too young to see such things.

Later, I imagined the wood, the splinters, the darkness and the shoes. And yet, on playing back the tape, Mercy, I always play back love. The things that we imagine support us never do. The world takes us quickly, handles us harshly, splinters us, casts us down and sends us forward to more pain. And yet, when I play back the tape, Mercy, I always play back love, much love.

I hear voices that say: "We are the formless who take form, briefly, in rooms, and then wander on. We are the grandmothers, aunts, sisters. We are the women who love you."

"Oh my God, Mercy, do you understand these things?"

No amount of tears will ever wash the pain or translate the joy. Over and over, it's the same, then as now. Birth and Death. There's me, in the Grey Room, or in the closet with the shoes.

"Mercy, remember the closets, remember them?"

II

The bathroom closet was full of ointments, medicines, potions to make us softer, more beautiful, less afraid. It held vials to relieve us, deceive us. It was the mysterious healing place, place of bandages, Mercurochrome and cotton balls. The center part contained the "good" towels, only used for company. They sat in their special pile, waiting for the occasional party, the welcome stranger, the annual holiday. Below this were kept the special blankets and the sheets, all folded tidily. They waited for that overnight guest or beloved family member, for nights of rearranged beds and noise and laughter. On the higher shelf were filmy containers of generic aspirin that were consumed candy-like by Mother, for headaches, backaches, heartaches. In the corner was an unused snakebite kit, with its rubber hand pump and arm tie. We fantasized this ordeal and practiced what to do if that time should ever come. The *one* time presented itself, but we were in Texas, on the way to the Big Bend National Park. The two of us had gotten off the crowded car to stretch. We heard the sound of a rattler and there we were, kitless, three hundred miles from home!

After I talked to that snake, what did you do, Mercy? I ran, wildly, madly all the way back to the car. I knew we could have died. One of us at least. It would have been me, for I was closest to the snake and saw him first. We drove on, the boy cousins up front, the girl cousins in the back. I know it would have been me.

The snakebite kit is still there, next to a greasy baby oil bottle. We never had suntan lotion until we were older, as we never had artichokes to eat, or eggplant or okra. We had summer dreams of swimming all day long, until our eyes were red, our toes and fingers pruney and our crotches white and soft and surrounded by tanned skin. Earlier we'd taken a shortcut near the Marking-Off Tree. The shortcut led to a world of water games: Splish-Splash, Tag, Dibble-Dabble. You were the swimmer, Mercy, and I the observer. In my dreams I was always just surfacing to air, having swum from an almost fatal underwater voyage. Later I stood in the darkened shade of the small blue and white bathroom, peeling off my bathing suit like a second layer of skin. My body was ice-cold and excited, slightly damp.

I stripped to summer clothes, shorts and cotton tops, and thongs. My hair was wet, in strips, my lips red, my cheeks browned, my eyes wild and smaller than normal size. My wet, slithering body found solace in cloth. I felt a great and immense hunger, as swimmers do, especially children. I took a towel from the closet, the white ones bordered in black that we were allowed to use, and saw from the corner of my eye a "miniature," placed there by my dad, who was always hiding them. I found his bottles everywhere, in his chest of drawers, under his bed. The bathroom smelled of my cool flesh, of Vicks and liquor, of old prescriptions for ever present maladies.

In the closet were remedies for women's ailments, hardened waxy suppositories, blood pressure tablets, weight pills, sulfa drugs, cough medicines, and aspirins of all sizes and shapes. There were medications for the head, the rectum, the stomach, the bladder, the eyes, the heart. The old shaving lotion was a reminder that we lived in a house of women.

An enema bag, salmon-colored and slightly cracked, the nozzle head black and foreboding, was poised and ready to be used. The last time Mother gave me an enema I was twelve, not yet a woman, but old enough to be embarrassed. I was sick, too tired to fight. Vicks and the smell of my discomfort all intermingled.

At age sixteen, I sucked in the hot, pleasant forbidden cigarette smoke and blew it out of the wire screens, hoping it would disappear. The butts were dispatched of in the usual two ways—flushed away, or wrapped in kleenex. I lit matches hoping the sulphur smell would mask my sins. But Mother knew. Mother took her aspirin not to worry about me while I smoked nude on the toilet blowing out smoke through the meshed wire.

The bathroom was a closet. It held sexual adolescent dreams. It was full of necessities and bodily functions. Everyone hid there. Some letters from lost lovers, others, old used diaphragms.

III

I smelled Johnny. Johnny again. Johnny's blue sweat shirt jacket that he accidentally left in the living room over Christmas vacation. It was mine for three long weeks. I hung it in my closet, along with my clothes. When I closed the door I smelled Johnny, the undefinable sweetness of his young masculinity.

"Oh God, Rocío, you are so gross, you are the grossest woman I know!"

"Oh settle down, just settle down, Mercy, will you?"

The smells of the closet are lusty and broad: the smells of a young woman's body odors and special juices and the memory of slithering afterbirths. This was where I slid—into the closet full of shoes. The closet smelled of summer and long nights and red lips and drying out burnt bobby socks. I washed them every night and dried them on the floor surface. They were my one and only pair. One day they were burned beyond hope. I took them up to the attic to be hidden. My passions and fantasies were lost in time that way—stuffed into dark corners. And yet, the truth I speak is not an awkward truth. I treasured the smells and touches and the darkness of those closets. All were receptacles for a me I always wanted to be, was.

IV

The t.v. room closet was Ronelia's. Her old strapless prom dresses were there, her evening gowns of tulle, with their spaghetti straps. The closet was immense and covered the entire side of the wall. It was built by Regino Suárez. The wooden doors never opened without a struggle but got stuck midway, so that you had to push one way and then the other to get inside. In this closet were stored long dresses, costumes and party shawls, with Mother's notations, "Summer Long. Ronelia's Party. Wedding Dress, Nieves'." Alongside were her initials and the date. "Ronelia FHA Queen, 1955, Yellow Tulle, N.E."

The long cardboard boxes were crammed onto the top shelf, below them in pink and blue clothing bags were the furs, the beaver Tío Frutoso trapped himself, the suede with the fur neck piece, the imitation beige coat Mercy wore, and Mamá Consuelo's muff. The closet smelled of old petticoats and musty fur. Its contents included two wedding dresses, a new one and an old one. The new one Mother picked up at a sale for five dollars. The old one she wore when she married Juan Luz. Ronelia and Mercy later wore that dress, but at that time it was carefully sealed in plastic at the very bottom of the top shelf. Anything to do with him—photographs, articles of clothing, papers—was sacred and off-limits. To me, they were the Ark of the Covenant—deep and full of mysterious untouchability. I was ignorant of the past and the relationship of my mother to this man, long since dead.

Children assign mystery to small objects and create whole worlds from lost objects, pieces of cloth. This closet, then, was a glistening world of dances and proms and handsome dates. It was Ronelia's wedding at the age when most of us are still

e. It contained my Zandunga costume,
' as my "male" partner for bazaars and

ios ... Ay Zandunga ... Zandunga ..."[2]
finest, and Mercy in imitation beige fur
les, one eternally wedded, the other,
;y and dreams—and it was Regino's: ill

umbrella in rainbow colors. For many
urdy, friendly. It came out late summer
. It welcomed and dispatched guests,
...nus who had come to visit. It protected us in early fall rain storms. It shielded us
in the early evening times when the fierce wildness of the unleashed summer tensions
rose and fell. This closet was rain, the hope of rain. To desert souls, rain is the blessed
sex of God. It cleanses and refreshes. It is still the best mother, the finest lover.

The rainbow umbrella emerged, unhooked from its long nail and was opened
outside. It dried on the porch, each time a little greyer. One day it was replaced in
black, by one of its funereal sisters.

This closet was the "guest" closet. It held all coats except Johnny's, which had
found a dearer resting place. The overflowing "good" clothes, from the fancy dress
coat closet, were placed there too. In it Christmas and birthday gifts were hidden
along with the gift box. Later, paper bags full of rummage and used clothing were
placed inside, on their way south. This closet was a clearinghouse—the "out-going"
closet, the last stop before dispersal—to needy families, young marrieds, senior citizens
who used the hand-sewn lap rugs Nieves made. It was a closet full of seasonal smells:
summer rain, dark winter clothes, the faint odor of Avon perfume like dried, autumn
flowers, the spring smell of soap and freshness. The closet smelled of luggage and
time, of faded newspapers and old passports. Behind the door were dated check
stubs and unused prayer books. The door smelled too, of wood and fingerprints.
The ceiling had a trap door that led to the Grey Room. This closet was but another
valve leading to the many chambers of the house's heart—where inside, beat my
other life.

---

2. words from a Mexican folk song, "La Zandunga": Oh, Zandunga, Zandunga, oh
    mother, by God ...

VI

Nieves' closet was her life, her artery of hope. Those corners were hers, unviolated. In the back, on the right, behind her clothes, was her wedding photograph. She and Juan Luz, both slim, with bright, serious faces, stared out to the photographer. Behind them, leading to vast spacious rooms, was a stairway, a mirror on each side. From one wall hung the lasso, symbol of marriage. Nieves clutched a white glove in her left hand, her right arm was at a ninety degree angle. Nieves stood next to Juan Luz and both of them faced right. Her hair was short, in the style of the twenties, with soft loose curls, not as she later wore it, in a bun, austere. Juan Luz was handsome, with a full head of hair that on second glance seemed subject to thinning, if not local baldness. His hand was tightly clenched, as hers was relaxed. They gazed forward, loving, bright-eyed, with hand-painted pink cheeks. They were sealed in time—a photograph on their happiest day.

One year later, Juan Luz was dead, Nieves was a widow, Ronelia was born, and Mercy and I were still in limbo.

Moving back and up, Nieves' world was full of old records, "The Singing Nun," Augustín Lara, mementos of her teaching days, her work with children. Hers was a closet packed with scarves, new shoes, old photograph albums, a chipped statue of San Martín de Porres,[3] tapes of the Living Bible and charismatic church revivals, as well as home movies of us as children standing by the Willow Tree.

The closet floor is strewn with paper, boxes. When Mercy and I stand in there, with the Christ eyes, we have to be careful.

"Leave me alone! It's my turn!"

"Give me the Christ eyes, Rocío!"

"Oh, go lay down, Baby."

"Don't pull that knob, Mother's gonna find out and get mad. You made me knock something over."

"Okay, okay, let me find the cord. There, see. That didn't take so long. Hey, Mercy, if you crouch down like this, it's better. That way, you feel darker."

I crouch in the closet wanting to know what it is like to feel crucified, to carry the sins of the world. I feel as if I'd already earned my crown of thorns. I imagine the splinters, the wood.

Each step into a closet was a step forward into that other world, the world of concrete corridors, the endless labyrinths, a soundless foray into the maze of faceless

---

3. a black Saint of the Catholic Church

forms, living spirits. Up there, down there, in there, they were all the same, they lead into the heart and spirit of the house. When the spirit was sick, the nocturnal journey was long, the gasping for air at the bottom of an endless summer pool. When the spirit was pure, the long rope flew down from the sky and I was beamed up on an umbilical cord of light. I flew beyond the Grey Room into the Blue Room and further up, into the great vast No Room of the living sky. Up beyond worlds, I flew into a universe of change, to the No Place of dreamers who do not dream.

"And *how* did it happen, Rocío?" I wanted Mercy to say when I told her about the Grey Room.

"Do you think it has something to do with seeing the house's bones, I mean, its skeleton? The wood, the house frame, the concrete slabs?"

"Maybe it had something to do with seeing the sliced away mountain," I said. "Remember that mountain? All my life I thought mountains were soft inside."

"You're kidding!"

"Seeing that mountain changed my life! It was one of the five most important things that ever happened to me; the discovery of perspective in the fourth grade was three."

"What are two, four and five, Rocío?"

"I can't tell you that, Mercy."

"Tell me, tell me," she begged.

"God bless, do I have to tell you *everything?*"

"Look, I'll tell you about the Grey Room. Will you be quiet, then? I'm in the hallway closet. I see Grandpa's death mask wrapped in white satin. I see the box of paper dolls we got on Christmas. I see your crown from elementary school, when you were Bazaar Queen. Why did you cry? I wouldn't have cried, but then I wasn't Queen. I move aside the belt cord from Mother's green bathrobe. I uncover the box of Christmas cards. I move the old rubber rain shoes and plastic rain coats. I make room for myself and step inside. I glide past everybody. I am faraway now past the color and the noise, past the cloth shadows. I am past everyone. Alone. Alone without noise. I don't need to turn on the light."

"Oh, but Rocío, aren't you afraid of the dark?" Mercy said at last, trying on the crown of thorns and then putting them on her side of the bed. "Aren't you afraid of the Christ eyes?"

"Not of the Christ eyes," I said, "but the brown animals scare me and I don't want to be afraid."

"Tell me about the Blue Room," she said, after a long pause. "It sounds *so* beautiful."

"It is," I said, lying down to rest on the bed, not bothering to tell her she was on my side again. "It's a beautiful enormous room and it's blue. But you know, the other day I went in there and it was all white and the floor was like dry ice."

"You mean it changes?" Mercy said with surprise. "Tell me about it before it changed," she said, drowsily.

"The Blue Room is my favorite room. It's the most magnificent, incredible room you'd ever hope to see, Mercy. It has a round ceiling that goes up forever. It's so big that I have to fly back and forth to get around. It's a beautiful room and it's mine. It's all mine!"

"Golly," Mercy said, yawning.

"Watch it! You almost made me turn over on the thorns. Put them up, would you?"

"Rocío, Rocío, if that's *your* room, *what's mine?*"

"I don't know, Mercy, everybody has their *own* rooms, their *own* house."

"They do?" she said with a faraway voice.

"Gaaa, Mercy, do I have to tell you *everything?*"

Roberto Fernández

(b. 1951)
Cuban American

Roberto Fernández is in the vanguard of Cuban American literature, having made the transition from the literature of exile to a literature very much of the culture and social conditions of Cubans in the United States as well as the transition from producing works in Spanish to writing in English. Born in Sagua la Grande, Cuba, on September 24, 1951, just eight years before the Cuban Revolution, he went into exile with his family at the age of eleven. His family settled in southern Florida, not in the Cuban community of Miami but in areas where Anglo-American culture was dominant. This sometimes seemed like a hostile environment to the young boy, which may account for some of the culture conflict that is narrated in his writings.

Fernández became interested in writing as an adolescent, and this interest led him to college and graduate school. In 1978 he completed a doctorate in linguistics at Florida State University; by that time he had already published two collections of stories: **Cuentos sin rumbo** *(1975,* Directionless Tales*) and* **El jardín de la luna** *(1976,* The Garden of the Moon*). At this point he also began his career as an academic, teaching linguistics and Hispanic literature at Florida State University in Tallahassee.

Roberto Fernández is the author of three open-formed novels that have given him the reputation of being a satirist and humorist in the Miami Cuban community. In all three, he is also a master at capturing the nuances of Cuban dialect in Spanish and English. **La vida es un special** *(1982,* Life Is on Special*),* **La montaña rusa** *(1985,* The Roller Coaster*) and* **Raining Backwards** *(1988) are all mosaics made up of monologues, dialogues, letters, phone conversations, speeches, and other types of oral performance that, in the composite, make up a continuing tale of the development of the exile community and its younger generations of increasingly acculturated Cuban Americans.

Miracle at Eighth and Twelfth

Me and Manolo were walking toward Eighth and Twelfth after we left Pepe's Grocery 'cause I needed a few things for Sunday when the grandchildren would be over. I know what you are thinking, but it's my very own shopping cart. I'm no thief. Well, I was guiding my Manny and thinking how hard life had got ever since he went blind after lighting that old kerosene kitchen. I warned him, but he's always been so hard headed. You want some coffee? It's not American coffee. It's not watery. So the kitchen exploded right in his face, and my poor Manny pretended for weeks that he could still see and he even tried to drive the car and ended up smashing it against Mr. Olsen's porch. Mr. Olsen never knew Manny did it 'cause he was vacationing in Georgia at the time. Let me tell you, life then was a lemon and I didn't have no sugar to make it a lemonade.

So we were walking and it was Good Friday. Wait a second, I think something is burning in the kitchen. Manny, is that you, my little heart? I wonder what he is doing in the kitchen. Last week, he turned on all the burners and nearly burned the house down. Now that he can see again he still likes to pretend to be blind. I guess he enjoyed all that extra attention. I always took care of him, like the king of this house he is. So we were walking along Eighth and Twelfth and it was Good Friday. It must have been around a quarter to three since it was really getting dark and windy. I was saying a rosary, just to do something, and I was admiring this huge mango when I noticed next to the mango tree, near the fence, Mr. Olsen's sea grape crying. It wasn't really crying, but sap was oozing from its branches. Somehow I was inspired and I helped Manny jump the fence and then I jumped. Actually, it wasn't really that easy since Manny's privates got tangled in the fence and I had to help him. I remember he screamed: "Barbarita, they are useless. Let's leave them there."

I went straight to the tree, gathered some sap in my hands and rubbed it all over my poor Manny's sightless eyes. At first, he cursed me, but then he knelt, lifted his arms and shouted: "Coño,[1] I can see. Barbarita, I can see!" I thought he was kidding, so I asked him what color my blouse was. "Red, white, and blue," he said. I wasn't convinced yet, so I asked him again what color his shoes were. "Blue sneakers," he said with a grin. I quickly knelt and was beating my chest in gratitude when Mr. Olsen came out with his shotgun and threatened to kill us for trespassing. I tried to explain, but he wasn't interested.

Finally, I had to bribe him with some bubble gum. You know how Americans go crazy for stuff like that. He let us go, screaming that only Superman could save him from this foreign plague. While he was shouting, I was trying to scoop up some more holy sap in case Manny had a relapse, but he saw me and placed his gun right in my nose and said, "Lady, put that sap where it belongs ... you ... you tropical scum, or I'll blow your head off."

We were very scared of Mr. Olsen, but very thankful for Manny's sight, and now we go everyday at a quarter to three to pray across the street from Mr. Olsen's house, facing the tree, while a watchful Mr. Olsen keeps his gun cocked. " 'Scuse me, just a minute. Manny is that you, my little heart?" It's Manny, all right. Every time he goes to the toilet he closes his eyes like he's blind and misses. I always have to go clean up after him. I want you to promise me by your mother's body lying in her funeral casket that you will tell everybody you know about this divine happening, so the faithless can become believers. But what I told about Manny's privates, keep it to yourself.

---

1. damn

ATTENTION PLEASE. MAY I HAVE YOUR ATTENTION PLEASE: WOULD YOU PLEASE DISPERSE AND GO HOME. GO CASA![2] THIS AREA IS BEING CORDONED OFF BY ORDER OF THE POLICE. POR FAVOR, GO AS QUICKLY AS POSSIBLE. PRONTO![3]

That sure is a big helicopter up there! Please, ma'am! Please, ma'am, don't push. Let me go by, please. Please don't push, don't you see I'm carrying a sick child! Who pinched my ass? Mima, where are youuuu? Hail Mary full of grace, the gentleman with the green shirt please get out of the way. Excuse me, please. Forget it, honey. I ain't moving, I saw this spot first. Out, out, out! This is private property, propiedad private! Hot dogs! Hot dogs! Get your hot dogs and cockfight tickets here. Oh, my tree! Oh Julia, if you could only see what they are doing to my tree. My beautiful sea grape! Who pinched my ass? The mother who pinched my ass! Hail Mary full of get your Bud, get your ice cold Bud here. This butt's for me. Ouch! If you touch my tree again, I'll kill you! Shut up, old man. Lois, Lois call the police! I am not. This is so much fun, ole! I swear by my little boy that I saw everything from my bathroom window. She was pushing the shopping cart with a man inside. The man had no legs. Then I saw her jump the fence and gather something from the sea grape tree and spreading it all over his stumps and the next thing I saw was the man sprouting a new pair of legs. I swear by my mother's grave that I saw everything from my bathroom window. That's why I'm here. You spic English? Yes, a little. What the police saying from the helicopter? They said that the Virgin is coming real soon. How they know she is coming? They are gringos, my friend, they know everything. If Superman could only hear me, but I can't get to my watch now. Holy cards, with the Pope blessing the holy tree, with your order of a small pizza and a Bud. Number, numbers, bolita.[4] Coke, coke. Get your coke here. Snort, excuse meee, drink your Coke here. C'mon, Manny, rub a little bit of sap on your pipi, it might make it work again. Do it for me, Manny. Okay, Barbarita, but just a little bit! Let me go by, I have arthritis. Connie, just chip off a piece. It'll keep Bill at your side. And her royal highness for the Queen Calle Ocho Festival is, may I have the envelope: Lovee Martinez, a modeling student. Hey, don't take that whole branch. Shut up, viejo. My country tis of thee sweet land of liberty. And then he sprouted two legs and an arm. Caridad, our lady, is landing. She's landing upside down on top of the tree! Who pinched my ass? Oh, Manny, that's incredible. It's so big and hard!!!!

---

2.   home
3.   please quickly
4.   a numbers gambling game

Retrieving Varadero

It had been raining non-stop for months and Eloy was doing his best to swat the palmetto bugs, mosquitoes and gnats which, drunk with rain and crashing against each other, were emerging from the puddles and trying to nest in Mirta's wavy bronze mane.

"Faster! They're driving me crazy. Faster! C'mon, you can do better than that. Fan me faster. Go to the bathroom closet and get the ostrich feather. Maybe it'll help. But be careful with it. It's the only thing my mother left me."

Eloy had been serving Mirta faithfully for the last two months in exchange for tidbits of the past. He was thirsty for information on those golden cities, those fabulous places in that enchanted island his aunt refused to mention because they were so sacred. He wanted to savor tidbits from that past he longed to relive somehow and share them in his old age with his grandchildren.

The evenings with Mirta had begun before the deluge. It all started one afternoon when Eloy, tired of folding clothes for his aunt, the laundry woman, and realizing the futility of trying to retrieve any information from her, pressed his ear against the wall and listened astonished to the discussion that Mirta was having with the radio on the other side of the wall.

"Why do you go on with your lies? Everyone knows that Varadero was the most beautiful beach, not only in the world but in the whole universe! The waters were forever changing colors, the sand had the texture of baby powder, the breezes were always warm but never hot. So how dare you say that Cancun or Sanibel are better and more beautiful. Liar! Communists! And there you go again. Isn't it enough just to say it once. You're getting me mad. I'd love to turn your program off but, you know I'm waiting for Julio's latest hit with German Garcia. But I'm losing my patience! I swear on my mother's grave that I've had it with you. I'm going to silence you forever. Liar! You're forcing me to do it."

Eloy heard a crashing noise and, overtaken by his curiosity, he sneaked out and knocked on Mirta's door. Mirta refused to open, but managed to stick her head through the kitchen window, and shout in anguish: "What do you want?" She was afraid of a rapist or, even worse, the Mastercard collector. Quickly, she muttered: "She's in Disney World in Orlando. Very, very far away from here." In her nervousness, Mirta had failed to recognize her little neighbor, the laundry woman's nephew.

---

* Varadero is the name of a beach in Havana, Cuba.

After he explained to her who he was, Mirta opened the door and, somewhat surprised by his visit, offered him a few pieces of candy which were left over from Halloween. After this first meeting, Eloy developed the need to talk to her every evening after school, and Mirta had finished her daily factory routine. Gradually, Mirta intoxicated his mind with her maze of remembrances.

"Yes. That's right, the water was always changing colors like a kaleidoscope. Each time that wind changed course the water changed color. When the wind was blowing strongly it turned into an intense violet, and when it was calm, it was as green as Ireland."

"What's Ireland?"

"It's a deodorant soap. But that's not really important. Our ocean was so delicious that even Aristotle, who is a very cultured gentleman, and who can't practice here because he never passed the board, when he tasted a sip of our waters, he left all his knowledge aside and started shacking up with El Cid, who was this enormous black woman that sold coconuts carved in the image of Mary Magdalene, but had the faces made out of bread in El Cid's own image."

"And the sand? Was it like Clearwater's?"

"You must be kidding! In all the beaches in Cuba the sand was made out of grated silver, though in Varadero it was also mixed with diamond dust. And it was definitely finer than Mennen's Baby Powder, the one with the baby inside the rose. I'm going to tell you something no one has ever told you, so you are going to become a very special person because there're only a few people that know this. Are you ready?"

"Yes, ma'am."

"The sun rose in the North and set in the South."

And thus, the days became weeks and the weeks months and Eloy came religiously every morning at dusk to hear Mirta. Very slowly, Mirta came to realize that her words had a narcotic effect upon the youth, and shrewdly opted to trade her remembrances of memories for practical favors that could ease the burden of living. She would send Eloy to Pepe's Grocery to buy a bottle of Seven-Up, or to Cabrera's Pharmacy to buy librium without prescription or benadryl to calm the constant itching that had plagued her since puberty.

One drenching afternoon, Eloy arrived and, as usual, he wiped off the mud that covered his shoes. Mirta greeted him with a list of errands; buy one jar of Bella Aurora cream; go to Clavo, the numbers man, and place $5 on 5-9-80; stop by the bank and tell them that there's a mistake in my checkbook, that my name is Miss Mirta Maria Vergara, not Mrs. Mirtha Verga; and fill out my insurance papers that I don't understand.

While Eloy read the list, Mirta promised more tales from her seemingly inexhaustible vein. Suddenly, Mirta sneezed and Eloy rushed to wipe her nose.

"Thank you, child. You are the living image of St. Gabriel the Archangel, because you're more beautiful than all the other angels. And now go and wipe the sofa cushion once more, because it still has a lot of dirt, and then go to my room and vacuum it … and the breezes were warm but never hot and there was no need for suntan lotion nor sun screens because the breezes carried the properties of aloe and they even unclogged your nose while moisturizing your skin. Now, let me tell you something very important, I watched everything from the porch. It had the best view of the beach. Besides, my mother never allowed me to go down to the beach because she said I was going to get dirty if I mixed with trash. I remember that at times, when it thundered, El Cid would take off her clothes and, with her two big breasts dancing in the air, stretch her arms, imitating a crucified martyr, and shout: "Mary Madgalene, blessed virgin. Deliver us from thunder and lightning." And then the thunder would cease and my mother would come to cover my eyes so I wouldn't see the naked Cid.

"Eloy, Eloy are you in there? Do you want to play some baseball? C'mon out."

"I can't. I'm busy."

"Could you tell me some more, Miss Mirta? I'll bet my friends don't know about El Cid."

"There were giant penguins and white seals that roamed the beach …

"Excuse me, Miss Mirta. I think it's my aunt calling me. I've got to go now. I have to help her."

"If you stay a little longer I'll tell you about Foquie, the seal with the bright green eyes. Stay, stay …

"Okay, but just a little bit more."

"But could you first squeeze the blackheads on my back, and also those little pimples that are really itching. Could you? I can't see them."

As Eloy groomed her, Mirta felt, without knowing why, a deep pleasure with each exposed blackhead, with each popped pimple.

"… and the white seals came around the Cape of Horn only because they had heard about the pleasures of Varadero, the most beautiful beach in the world. Once they got there, they would be driven mad by the one hundred waterfalls that bordered the beach and they would slide and play with the swimmers and dive for fish and pearls in exchange for bananas and papayas and could you pour some boric acid on my back and take a damp towel and put it right on my shoulder blade, and while you are at it, rub my swollen thigh with Ben-Gay."

"Really, ma'am, I've got to go. My aunt is calling me and I have to help her fold the laundry and then do my homework because last year I flunked the seventh grade."

"Why don't you bathe me before you go? I'm so tired with so much overtime at the factory that I can hardly hold the soap. Just a little shower, okay?"

"But Miss Mirtha!"

"It's not Mirtha, it's Mirta. C'mon! Be a good boy. I can even be more than your mother. Stop that nonsense and get the sponge, the avocado soap and the cologne. They're in the closet."

"Okay, Miss Mirta, but tell me more. Tell me more. Do you know about my reading aunt's farm, the one that ended where the rainbow ends?"

Mirta could only think about the pleasures that Eloy's hands would exert on her back as he bathed her, and started to tremble thinking that she would have to turn around and face Eloy in order to reach the towel that hung from the door nail. Just this thought made her salivate so profusely that the dribble threatened to inundate her neck. While Mirta was getting undressed to dive into the old tub, Eloy commenced lathering the sponge without realizing that many years later he would forbid his wife to use a sponge to do the dishes, much less to bathe the kids. That strange spongephobia would last throughout his life. Not even Dr. Kings, with her potions, balms and incantations, would be able to cure this malady. Eloy approached the tub and urged her to continue dispensing stories of the by-gone days.

"It was on Varadero Beach that I met my only fiancé. It was a week after the 1943 storm, two days before my fifteenth birthday. He was sunbathing, but he never knew that I was his sweetheart. I treasured our love with all my soul. His hair was the color of mahogany, like yours, but wavier, and when I came over here I sent him love messages in a bottle three times a week. They always read: 'I love you. Yours forever, MV' ... MV is me, Mirta Vergara ... and the breezes were warm ... a little bit more to the right, lather me right down there ... but the breezes were never hot and you didn't need suntan lotion and the white seals would play happily with the swimmers and they slid through the falls that surrounded Varadero and when it rained, it rained molasses and rice so you just needed to open your mouth and eat and if you wanted more to eat you just simply said: 'Sea creatures, I'm hungry,' and the fish and the mollusks would jump from the water to your pan and the sand had the texture of baby powder and the breezes were warm but ..."

"Miss Mirta, you already told me about the breezes and the sand," shouted Eloy, exasperated, as he retrieved the sponge and used it to wipe the sweat drops that covered his forehead.

"I'm tired, Miss Mirta. I'm tired," Eloy kept saying.

For the first time, Mirta realized that the well of remembrances that she had been exploiting was about to run dry at the precise moment when she needed to feel the skeletons of those magnificent corals, which had sacrificed their lives for her happiness, to form that joy-giving sponge.

"Yes, child, continue lathering down there," said Mirta at the same time that she turned around smiling like an old rabbit, and exposing her two udders which had sagged with the weight of virginity and were trying to rest on her reddish bush. Eloy looked at her indifferently for the first time and defiantly said, "Tell me more! If you don't continue, I won't either."

Mirta, alarmed by his attitude, tried to lure him again with her all but exhausted memories.

"The white seals then came accompanied by yodelers shouting their yodel-eeps. The women on the beach who greeted the yodelers were dressed in straw skirts and moved their hips incessantly while singing: 'waha, waha, trum, trum, waha, waha, trum trum.' And the men had wide, bronzed shoulders and were always blowing these enormous sea shells. They were sounding them to appease the volcano which stood majestically at a distance and which would let a plume of smoke escape as a sign of gratitude for the shell sounds which pleased him so much. The name of the volcano was 'Pan de Matanzas,' the Killing Bread. It got that name from the many bakers who had thrown themselves from its summit. El Cid's coconut figurines with their heads made out of bread drove the bakers mad with love, for they wanted to possess the immense maiden who denied them her body. Between the lagoon and the sea there was a mountain all covered with snow. Mama, after finishing her cleaning duties at Señora Nelia's, would swim towards the mountain to pack some snow and make herself a rum ice cream. She died evoking that mountain and whispering my father's name. He was a very rich merchant from Venice whom I never met and ah, ah, ahhhh.

"What's the matter, ma'am? What's the matter, Miss Mirta? You're sweating! Are you okay? Do you want me to call my aunt?"

"It's nothing. It's just that I get excited when I remember so many beautiful memories. But please, please don't stop lathering me, but now a little bit toward the left ... please."

"But Miss Mirta. I'm too tired and my aunt ..."

"I'll tell you more, my love. I'll tell you so much ... and when a visitor arrived they placed leis around his neck and would whisper in his ear: tiare, tiare haere mai, haere mai. And at that same time their hips would go crazy and they would take him to a heavenly hotel all made of ivory, gold and coral called El Oasis. There they would take their skirts off and, with only hibiscuses on their heads, would dive into the waves carrying with them bananas and plantains for the white seals, yodelers and penguins. Keep lathering, please keep lathering me and I will tell you how the white seals came up to the beach and how they ate from your hand and how Mama followed

Señora Nelia when she left for Miami and Mama embraced each room in the house, telling them that she had loved them more than her own family and as a souvenir she plucked an ostrich feather from a hat which the Señora had left forgotten on her bed and how the sand had the texture of baby powder and how the breeze tanned your skin and the waters were technicolor and Aristotle and El Cid were wrestling naked on the sand. Why don't you stay to sleep with me?"

Eloy didn't answer. Mirta got out of the tub, ready to force him to stay if so required. Then a cloud of palmetto bugs landed on her body, covering her nakedness like a robe. This time Eloy didn't even try to swat the gnats that were trying to invade her nostrils. Worn out, he grabbed a folding chair and sat quietly observing and listening to the emerging Mirta, who screaming madly, told him that his mother was a tramp, that his aunts slept together with his uncle in the same bed, that his father had been in jail for being a drug-pushing cuckold and that above all he was ungrateful, for if it weren't for her he would never have known about the past.

Eloy, baffled, used the sponge which he was still holding in his hands to wipe his sweaty face once more. Mirta misinterpreted his gesture and immediately started to salivate again. She knelt and told him that she would constantly talk to him about the past and the beach, and that there were still many things that he didn't know about, like his reading aunt's (as he called his other aunt) silver boat and rainbow ranch, the singing palm trees and the queen of the lizards. She implored him to stay, promising to buy his aunt a dryer and find his father a good job.

He just smiled, caressing with his right hand the peach fuzz growing on his upper lip, and hiding the sponge behind his back with his left hand, he nodded murmuring, "Tell me more, Mirta. Tell me more, baby."

Helena María Viramontes

(b. 1954)

Mexican American

Helena María Viramontes is known for her tightly crafted poetic vision of Hispanic women in American society. After serving as an editor of the pioneering cultural magazine **Chismearte,** *the coordinator of the Los Angeles Latino Writers Association, and the editor of anthologies of other writers' works, she has found the time to publish her own stories in magazines and anthologies throughout the country. But her excellent reputation rests principally on her highly praised collection of stories* **The Moths and Other Stories** *(1985).*

Viramontes was born and raised in East Los Angeles, California, which provides the setting for most of her stories. She is a graduate of the master of fine arts program in creative writing of the University of California at Irvine.

The Moths and Other Stories *portrays female characters of varying ages whose lives are limited by the patriarchy of Hispanic society and the imposition of religious values. Viramontes' stories treat such issues as abortion, aging, death, immigration, and separation. Her images range from the beautifully lyric and evocative, as in the story* **"The Moths,"** *to the violent and desperate, as in* **"The Cariboo Cafe."** *The grace and depth of these stories benefits her humanistic and caring approach to the poor and downtrodden women she depicts.*

The Cariboo Cafe

I

They arrived in the secrecy of night, as displaced people often do, stopping over for a week, a month, eventually staying a lifetime. The plan was simple. Mother would work too until they saved enough to move into a finer future where the toilet was one's own and the children needn't be frightened. In the meantime, they played in the back allies, among the broken glass, wise to the ways of the streets. Rule one: never talk to strangers, not even the neighbor who paced up and down the hallways talking to himself. Rule two: the police, or "polie" as Sonya's popi pronounced the word, was La Migra[1] in disguise and thus should always be avoided. Rule three: keep your key with you at all times—the four walls of the apartment were the only protection against the streets until Popi returned home.

Sonya considered her key a guardian saint and she wore it around her neck as such until this afternoon. Gone was the string with the big knot. Gone was the key. She hadn't noticed its disappearance until she picked up Macky from Mrs. Avila's house and walked home. She remembered playing with it as Amá walked her to

_____

1. Immigration and Naturalization Service (INS).

school. But lunch break came, and Lalo wrestled her down so that he could see her underwear, and it probably fell somewhere between the iron rings and sandbox. Sitting on the front steps of the apartment building, she considered how to explain the missing key without having to reveal what Lalo had seen, for she wasn't quite sure which offense carried the worse penalty.

She watched people piling in and spilling out of the buses, watched an old man asleep on the bus bench across the street. He resembled a crumbled ball of paper, huddled up in the security of a tattered coat. She became aware of their mutual loneliness and she rested her head against her knees blackened by the soot of the playground asphalt.

The old man eventually awoke, yawned like a lion's roar, unfolded his limbs and staggered to the alley where he urinated between two trash bins. (She wanted to peek, but it was Macky who turned to look.) He zipped up, drank from a paper bag and she watched him until he disappeared around the corner. As time passed, buses came less frequently, and every other person seemed to resemble Popi. Macky became bored. He picked through the trash barrel; later, and to Sonya's fright, he ran into the street after a pigeon. She understood his restlessness for waiting was as relentless as long lines to the bathroom. When a small boy walked by, licking away at a scoop of vanilla ice cream, Macky ran after him. In his haste to outrun Sonya's grasp, he fell and tore the knee of his denim jeans. He began to cry, wiping snot against his sweater sleeve.

"See?" she asked, dragging him back to the porch steps by his wrist. "See? God punished you!" It was a thing she always said because it seemed to work. Terrified by the scrawny tortured man on the cross, Macky wanted to avoid his wrath as much as possible. She sat him on the steps in one gruff jerk. Seeing his torn jeans, and her own scraped knees, she wanted to join in his sorrow, and cry. Instead she snuggled so close to him, she could hear his stomach growling.

"Coke," he asked. Mrs. Avila gave him an afternoon snack which usually held him over until dinner. But sometimes Macky got lost in the midst of her own six children and ...

Mrs. Avila! It took Sonya a few moments to realize the depth of her idea. They could wait there, at Mrs. Avila's. And she'd probably have a stack of flour tortillas, fresh off the comal, ready to eat with butter and salt. She grabbed his hand. "Mrs. Avila has Coke."

"Coke!" He jumped up to follow his sister. "Coke," he cooed.

At the major intersection, Sonya quietly calculated their next move while the scores of adults hurried to their own destinations. She scratched one knee as she tried retracing her journey home in the labyrinth of her memory. Things never looked the same when backwards and she searched for familiar scenes. She looked for the newspaperman who sat in a little house with a little T.V. on and selling magazines with naked girls holding beach balls. But he was gone. What remained was a little closet-like shed with chains and locks, and she wondered what happened to him, for she thought that he lived there with the naked ladies.

They finally crossed the street at a cautious pace, the colors of the street lights brighter as darkness descended, a stereo store blaring music from two huge, blasting speakers. She thought it was the disco store she passed, but she didn't remember if the sign was green or red. And she didn't remember it flashing like it was now. Studying the neon light, she bumped into a tall, lanky dark man. Maybe it was Raoul's Popi. Raoul was a dark boy in her class that she felt sorry for because everyone called him sponge head. Maybe she could ask Raoul's Popi where Mrs. Avila lived, but before she could think it all out, red sirens flashed in their faces and she shielded her eyes to see the polie.

The polie is men in black who get kids and send them to Tijuana, says Popi. Whenever you see them, run, because they hate you, says Popi. She grabs Macky by his sleeve and they crawl under a table of bargain cassettes. Macky's nose is running, and when he sniffles, she puts her finger to her lips. She peeks from behind the poster of Vincente Fernández[2] to see Raoul's father putting keys and stuff from his pockets onto the hood of the polie car. And it's true, they're putting him in the car and taking him to Tijuana. Popi, she murmured to herself. Mama.

"Coke." Macky whispered, as if she failed to remember.

"Sssssh. M'ijo,[3] when I say run, you run, okay?" She waited for the tires to turn out, as the black and white drove off, she whispered, "Now," and they scurried out from under the table and ran across the street, oblivious to the horns.

They entered a maze of allies and dead ends, the long, abandoned warehouses shadowing any light. Macky stumbled and she continued to drag him until his crying, his untied sneakers, and his raspy breathing finally forced her to stop. She scanned the boarded up boxcars, the rows of rusted rails to make sure the polie wasn't following them. Tired, her heart bursting, she leaned him against a tall, chainlink fence. Except for the rambling of some railcars, silence prevailed, and she could hear Macky sniffling in the darkness. Her mouth was parched and she swallowed to rid herself of the metallic taste of fear. The shadows stalked them, hovering like nightmares. Across the tracks, in the distance, was a room with a yellow glow, like a beacon light at the end of a dark sea. She pinched Macky's nose with the corner of her dress, took hold of his sleeve. At least the shadows will be gone, she concluded, at the zero zero place.

----

2.   Mexican popular singer
3.   my son

II

Don't look at me. I didn't give it the name. It was passed on. Didn't even know what it meant until I looked it up in some library dictionary. But I kinda liked the name. It's, well, romantic, almost like the name of a song, you know, so I kept it. That was before JoJo turned fourteen even. But now if you take a look at the sign, the paint's peeled off 'cept for the two O's. The double zero cafe. Story of my life. But who cares, right? As long as everyone 'round the factories know I run an honest business.

The place is clean. That's more than I can say for some people who walk through that door. And I offer the best prices on double burger deluxes this side of Main Street. Okay, so it's not pure beef. Big deal, most meat markets do the same. But I make no bones 'bout it. I tell them up front, "yeah, it ain't dogmeat, but it ain't sirloin either." Cause that's the sort of guy I am. Honest.

That's the trouble. It never pays to be honest. I tried scrubbing the stains off the floor, so that my customers won't be reminded of what happened. But they keep walking as if my cafe ain't fit for lepers. And that's the thanks I get for being a fair guy.

Not once did I hang up all those stupid signs. You know, like "We reserve the right to refuse service to anyone," or "No shirt, no shoes, no service." To tell you the truth—which is what I always do though it don't pay—I wouldn't have nobody walking through that door. The streets are full of scum, but scum gotta eat too is the way I see it. Now listen. I ain't talkin 'bout out-of-luckers, weirdos, whores, you know. I'm talking 'bout five-to-lifers out of some tech. I'm talking Paulie.

I swear Paulie is thirty-five, or six. JoJo's age if he were still alive, but he don't look a day over ninety. Maybe why I let him hang out 'cause he's JoJo's age. Shit, he's okay as long as he don't bring his wigged out friends whose voices sound like a record at low speed. Paulie's got too many stories and they all get jammed up in his mouth so I can't make out what he's saying. He scares the other customers too, acting like he is shadowboxing, or like a monkey hopping on a frying pan. You know, nervous, jumpy, his jaw all falling and his eyes bulgy and dirt yellow. I give him the last booth, coffee and yesterday's donut holes to keep him quiet. After a few minutes, out he goes, before lunch. I'm too old, you know, too busy making ends meet to be nursing the kid. And so is Delia.

That Delia's got these unique titties. One is bigger than another. Like an orange and grapefruit. I kid you not. They're like that on account of when she was real young she had some babies, and they all sucked only one favorite tittie. So one is bigger than the other, and when she used to walk in with Paulie, huggy huggy and wearing those tight leotard blouses that show the nipple dots, you could see the difference. You could tell right off that Paulie was proud of them, the way he'd hang his arm over her shoulder and squeeze the grapefruit. They kill me, her knockers. She'd come in real queen-like, smacking gum and chewing the fat with the illegals who work in that garment warehouse. They come in real queen-like too, sitting in the best booth near the window, and order cokes. That's all. Cokes. Hey, but I'm a nice guy, so what if they mess up my table, bring their own lunches and only order small cokes, leaving a dime as tip? So sometimes the place ain't crawling with people, you comprende buddy? A dime's a dime as long as it's in my pocket.

Like I gotta pay my bills too, I gotta eat. So like I serve anybody whose got the greens, including that crazy lady and the two kids that started all the trouble. If only I had closed early. But I had to wash the dinner dishes on account of I can't afford a dishwasher. I was scraping off some birdshit glue stuck to this plate, see, when I hear the bells jingle against the door. I hate those fucking bells. That was Nell's idea. Nell's my wife; my ex-wife. So people won't sneak up on you, says my ex. Anyway, I'm standing behind the counter staring at this short woman. Already I know that she's bad news because she looks street to me. Round face, burnt toast color, black hair that hangs like straight ropes. Weirdo, I've had enough to last me a lifetime. She's wearing a shawl and a dirty slip is hanging out. Shit if I have to dish out a free meal. Funny thing, but I didn't see the two kids 'til I got to the booth. All of a sudden I see these big eyes looking over the table's edge at me. It shook me up, the way they kinda appeared. Aw, maybe they were there all the time.

The boy's a sweetheart. Short Order don't look nothing like his mom. He's got dried snot all over his dirty cheeks and his hair ain't seen a comb for years. She can't take care of herself, much less him or the doggie of a sister. But he's a tough one, and I pinch his nose 'cause he's a real sweetheart like JoJo. You know, my boy.

It's his sister I don't like. She's got these poking eyes that follow you 'round 'cause she don't trust no one. Like when I reach for Short Order, she flinches like I'm 'bout to tear his nose off, gives me a nasty, squinty look. She's maybe five, maybe six, I don't know, and she acts like she owns him. Even when I bring the burgers, she doesn't let go of his hand. Finally, the fellow bites it and I wink at him. A real sweetheart.

In the next booth, I'm twisting the black crud off the top of the ketchup bottle when I hear the lady saying something in Spanish. Right off I know she's illegal, which explains why she looks like a weirdo. Anyway, she says something nice to them 'cause it's in the same tone that Nell used when I'd rest my head on her lap. I'm surprised the illegal's got a fiver to pay, but she and her tail leave no tip. I see Short Order's small bites on the bun.

You know, a cafe's the kinda business that moves. You get some regulars but most of them are on the move, so I don't pay much attention to them. But this lady's face sticks like egg yolk on a plate. It ain't 'til I open a beer and sit in front of the B&W[4] to check out the wrestling matches that I see this news bulletin 'bout two missing kids. I recognize the mugs right away. Short Order and his doggie sister. And all of a sudden her face is out of my mind. Aw fuck, I say, and put my beer down so hard that the foam spills onto last month's Hustler. Aw fuck.

See, if Nell was here, she'd know what to do: call the cops. But I don't know. Cops ain't exactly my friends, and all I need is for bacon to be crawling all over my place. And seeing how her face is vague now, I decide to wait 'til the late news. Short Order don't look right neither. I'll have another beer and wait for the late news.

The alarm rings at four and I have this headache, see, from the sixpak, and I gotta get up. I was supposed to do something, but I got all suck-faced and forgot. Turn off the T.V., take a shower, but that don't help my memory any.

Hear sirens near the railroad tracks. Cops. I'm supposed to call the cops. I'll do it after I make the coffee, put away the eggs, get the donuts out. But Paulie strolls in looking partied out. We actually talk 'bout last night's wrestling match between BoBo Brazil and the Crusher. I slept through it, you see. Paulie orders an O.J. on account of he's catching a cold. I open up my big mouth and ask about De. Drinks the rest of his O.J., says real calm like, that he caught her eaglespread with the Vegetable fatso down the block. Then, very polite like, Paulie excuses himself. That's one thing I gotta say about Paulie. He may be one big Fuck-up, but he's got manners. Juice gave him shit cramps, he says.

Well, leave it to Paulie. Good ole Mr. Fuck-Up himself to help me with the cops. The prick O.D.'s in my crapper; vomits and shits are all over—I mean all over the fuckin' walls. That's the thanks I get for being Mr. Nice Guy. I had the cops looking up my ass for the stash: says one, the one wearing a mortician's suit, We'll be back, we'll be back when you ain't looking. If I was pushing, would I be burning my goddamn balls off with spitting grease? So fuck 'em, I think. I ain't gonna tell you nothing 'bout the lady. Fuck you, I say to them as they drive away. Fuck your mother.

That's why Nell was good to have 'round. She could be a pain in the ass, you know, like making me hang those stupid bells, but mostly she knew what to do. See, I go bananas. Like my mind fries with the potatoes and by the end of the day, I'm deader than dogshit. Let me tell you what I mean. A few hours later, after I swore I wouldn't give the fuckin' pigs the time of day, the green vans roll up across the street. While I'm stirring the chili con carne I see all these illegals running out of the factory to hide, like roaches when the lightswitch goes on. I taste the chile, but I really can't taste nothing on account I've lost my appetite after cleaning out the

---

4.   black and white (television)

stop them, but when I go on stirring the chile, they run to the bathroom. Now look, I'm a nice guy, but I don't like to be used, you know? Just 'cause they're regulars don't mean jackshit. I run an honest business. And that's what I told them Agents. See, by that time, my stomach being all dizzy, and the cops all over the place, and the three illegals running in here, I was all confused, you know. That's how it was, and well, I haven't seen Nell for years, and I guess that's why I pointed to the bathroom.

I don't know. I didn't expect handcuffs and them agents putting their hands up and down their thighs. When they walked past me, they didn't look at me. That is the two young ones. The older one, the one that looked silly in the handcuffs on account of she's old enough to be my grandma's grandma, looks straight at my face with the same eyes Short Order's sister gave me yesterday. What a day. Then, to top off the potatoes with the gravy, the bells jingle against the door and in enters the lady again with the two kids.

III

He's got lice. Probably from living in the detainers.[5] Those are the rooms where they round up the children and make them work for their food. I saw them from the window. Their eyes are cut glass, and no one looks for sympathy. They take turns, sorting out the arms from the legs, heads from the torsos. Is that one your mother? One guard asks, holding a mummified head with eyes shut tighter than coffins. But the children no longer cry. They just continue sorting as if they were salvaging cans from a heap of trash. They do this until time is up and they drift into a tunnel, back to the womb of sleep, while a new group comes in. It is all very organized. I bite my fist to keep from retching. Please God, please don't let Geraldo be there.

For you see, they took Geraldo. By mistake, of course. It was my fault. I shouldn't have sent him out to fetch me a mango. But it was just to the corner. I didn't even bother to put his sweater on. I hear his sandals flapping against the gravel. I follow him with my eyes, see him scratching his buttocks when the wind picks up swiftly, as it often does at such unstable times, and I have to close the door.

The darkness becomes a serpent's tongue, swallowing us whole. It is the night of La Llorona.[6] The women come up from the depths of sorrow to search for their children. I join them, frantic, desperate, and our eyes become scrutinizers, our bodies opiated with the scent of their smiles. Descending from door to door, the wind whips our faces. I hear the wailing of the women and know it to be my own. Geraldo is nowhere to be found.

---

5. detention rooms for illegal immigrants
6. The Crying Lady [a folktale bogey woman]

Dawn is not welcomed. It is a drunkard wavering between consciousness and sleep. My life is fleeing, moving south towards the sea. My tears are now hushed and faint.

The boy, barely a few years older than Geraldo, lights a cigarette, rests it on the edge of his desk, next to all the other cigarette burns. The blinds are down to keep the room cool. Above him hangs a single bulb that shades and shadows his face in such a way as to mask his expressions. He is not to be trusted. He fills in the information, for I cannot write. Statements delivered, we discuss motives.

"Spies," says he, flicking a long burning ash from the cigarette onto the floor, then wolfing the smoke in as if his lungs had an unquenchable thirst for nicotine. "We arrest spies. Criminals." He says this with cigarette smoke spurting out from his nostrils like a nose bleed.

"Spies? Criminals?" My shawl falls to the ground. "He is only five and a half years old." I plead for logic with my hands. "What kind of crimes could a five-year-old commit?"

"Anyone who so willfully supports the Contras[7] in any form must be arrested and punished without delay." He knows the line by heart.

I think about moths and their stupidity. Always attracted by light, they fly into fires, or singe their wings with the heat of the single bulb and fall on his desk, writhing in pain. I don't understand why nature has been so cruel as to prevent them from feeling warmth. He dismisses them with a sweep of a hand. "This," he continues, "is what we plan to do with the Contras, and those who aid them." He inhales again.

"But, Señor, he's just a baby."

"Contras are tricksters. They exploit the ignorance of people like you. Perhaps they convinced your son to circulate pamphlets. You should be talking to them, not us." The cigarette is down to his yellow fingertips, to where he can no longer continue to hold it without burning himself. He throws the stub on the floor, crushes it under his boot. "This," he says, screwing his boot into the ground, "is what the Contras do to people like you."

"Señor, I am a washer woman. You yourself see I cannot read or write. There is my X. Do you think my son can read?" How can you explain to this man that we are poor, that we live as best we can? "If such a thing has happened, perhaps he wanted to make a few centavos for his mama. He's just a baby."

"So you are admitting his guilt?"

"So you are admitting he is here?" I promise, once I see him, hold him in my arms again, I will never, never scold him for wanting more than I can give. "You see, he needs his sweater ..." The sweater lies limp on my lap.

---

7. Nicaraguan counter-revolutionaries

"Your assumption is incorrect."

"May I check the detainers for myself?"

"In time."

"And what about my Geraldo?"

"In time." He dismisses me, placing the forms in a big envelope crinkled by the day's humidity.

"When?" I am wringing the sweater with my hands.

"Don't be foolish, woman. Now off with your nonsense. We will try to locate your Pedro."

"Geraldo."

Maria came by today with a bowl of hot soup. She reports in her usual excited way, that the soldiers are now eating the brains of their victims. It is unlike her to be so scandalous. So insane. Geraldo must be cold without his sweater.

"Why?" I ask as the soup gets cold. I will write Tavo tonight.

At the plaza a group of people are whispering. They are quiet when I pass, turn to one another and put their finger to their lips to cage their voices. They continue as I reach the church steps. To be associated with me is condemnation.

Today I felt like killing myself, Lord. But I am too much of a coward. I am a washer woman, Lord. My mother was one, and hers too. We have lived as best we can, washing other people's laundry, rinsing off other people's dirt until our hands crust and chap. When my son wanted to hold my hand, I held soap instead. When he wanted to play, my feet were in pools of water. It takes such little courage being a washer woman. Give me strength, Lord.

What have I done to deserve this, Lord? Raising a child is like building a kite. You must bend the twigs enough, but not too much, for you might break them. You must find paper that is delicate and light enough to wave on the breath of the wind, yet must withstand the ravages of a storm. You must tie the strings gently but firmly so that it may not fall apart. You must let the string go, eventually, so that the kite will stretch its ambition. It is such delicate work, Lord, being a mother. This I understand, Lord, because I am, but you have snapped the cord, Lord. It was only a matter of minutes and my life is lost somewhere in the clouds. I don't know. I don't know what games you play, Lord.

These four walls are no longer my house, the earth beneath it, no longer my home. Weeds have replaced all good crops. The irrigation ditches are clodded with bodies. No matter where we turn, there are rumors facing us and we try to live as best we can, under the rule of men who rape women, then rip their fetuses from their bellies. Is this our home? Is this our country? I ask Maria. Don't these men have mothers, lovers, babies, sisters? Don't they see what they are doing? Later, Maria says, these men are babes farted out from the Devil's ass. We check to make sure no one has heard her say this.

Without Geraldo, this is not my home, the earth beneath it, not my country. This is why I have to leave. Maria begins to cry. Not because I am going, but because she is staying.

Tavo. Sweet Tavo. He has sold his car to send me the money. He has just married and he sold his car for me. Thank you, Tavo. Not just for the money. But also for making me believe in the goodness of people again ... The money is enough to buy off the border soldiers. The rest will come from the can. I have saved for Geraldo's schooling and it is enough for a bus ticket to Juarez. I am to wait for Tavo there.

I spit. I do not turn back.

Perhaps I am wrong in coming. I worry that Geraldo will not have a home to return to, no mother to cradle his nightmares away, soothe the scars, stop the hemorrhaging of his heart. Tavo is happy I am here, but it is crowded, the three of us, and I hear them arguing behind their closed door. There is only so much a nephew can provide. I must find work. I have two hands willing to work. But the heart. The heart wills only to watch the children playing in the street.

The machines, their speed and dust, make me ill. But I can clean, clean toilets, dump trash cans, sweep. Disinfect the sinks. I would gladly do whatever is necessary to repay Tavo. The baby is due and time and money is tight. I volunteer for odd hours, weekends, since I really have very little to do. When the baby comes I know Tavo's wife will not let me hold it, for she thinks I am a bad omen. I know it.

Why would God play such a cruel joke, if he isn't my son. I jumped the curb, dashed out into the street, but the street is becoming wider and wider. I've lost him once and can't lose him again and it's hell with the screeching tires and the horns and the headlights barely touching my hips. I can't take my eyes off him because, you see, they are swift and cunning and can take your life with a snap of a finger. But God is a just man and His mistakes can be undone.

My heart pounds in my head like a sledgehammer against the asphalt. What if it isn't Geraldo? What if he is still in the detainer waiting for me? A million questions, one answer: Yes. Geraldo, yes I want to touch his hand first, have it disappear in my own because it's so small. His eyes look at me in total bewilderment. I grab him because the earth is crumbling beneath us and I must save him. We both fall to the ground.

A hot meal is in store. A festival. The cook, a man with shrunken cheeks and the hands of a car mechanic, takes a liking to Geraldo. It's like birthing you again, mi'jo. My baby.

I bathe him. He flutters in excitement, the water grey around him. I scrub his head with lye to kill off the lice, comb his hair out with a fine-tooth comb. I wash his rubbery penis, wrap him in a towel and he stands in front of the window, shriveling and sucking milk from a carton, his hair shiny from the dampness.

He finally sleeps. So easily, she thinks. On her bed next to the open window he coos in the night. Below the sounds of the city become as monotonous as the ocean waves. She rubs his back with warm oil, each stroke making up for the days of his absence. She hums to him softly so that her breath brushes against his face, tunes that are rusted and crack in her throat. The hotel neon shines on his back and she covers him.

All the while the young girl watches her brother sleeping. She removes her sneakers, climbs into the bed, snuggles up to her brother and soon her breathing is raspy, her arms under her stomach.

The couch is her bed tonight. Before switching the light off, she checks once more to make sure this is not a joke. Tomorrow she will make arrangements to go home. Maria will be the same, the mango stand on the corner next to the church plaza will be the same. It will all be the way it was before. But enough excitement. For the first time in years, her mind is quiet of all noise and she has the desire to sleep.

The bells jingle when the screen door slaps shut behind them. The cook wrings his hands in his apron, looking at them. Geraldo is in the middle, and they sit in the booth farthest away from the window, near the hall where the toilets are, and right away the small boy, his hair now neatly combed and split to the side like an adult, wrinkles his nose at the peculiar smell. The cook wipes perspiration off his forehead with the corner of his apron, finally comes over to the table.

She looks so different, so young. Her hair is combed slick back into one thick braid and her earrings hang like baskets of golden pears on her finely sculptured ears. He can't believe how different she looks. Almost beautiful. She points to what she wants on the menu with a white, clean fingernail. Although confused, the cook is sure of one thing—it's Short Order all right, pointing to him with a commanding finger, saying his only English word: Coke.

His hands tremble as he slaps the meat on the grill; the patties hiss instantly. He feels like vomiting. The chile overboils and singes the fires, deep red trail of chile crawling to the floor and puddling there. He grabs the handles, burns himself, drops the pot on the wooden racks of the floor. He sucks his fingers, the patties blackening and sputtering grease. He flips them, and the burgers hiss anew. In some strange way he hopes they have disappeared, and he takes a quick look only to see Short Order's sister, still in the same dress, still holding her brother's hand. She is craning her neck to peek at what is going on in the kitchen.

Aw, fuck, he says, in a fog of smoke his eyes burning tears. He can't believe it, but he's crying. For the first time since JoJo's death, he's crying. He becomes angry at the lady for returning. At JoJo. At Nell for leaving him. He wishes Nell here, but doesn't know where she's at or what part of Vietnam JoJo is all crumbled up in. Children gotta be with their parents, family gotta be together, he thinks. It's only right. The emergency line is ringing.

Two black and whites roll up and skid the front tires against the curb. The flashing lights carousel inside the cafe. She sees them opening the screen door, their guns taut and cold like steel erections. Something is wrong, and she looks to the cowering cook. She has been betrayed, and her heart is pounding like footsteps running, faster, louder, faster and she can't hear what they are saying to her. She jumps up from the table, grabs Geraldo by the wrist, his sister dragged along because, like her, she refuses to release his hand. Their lips are mouthing words she can't hear, can't comprehend. Run, Run, is all she can think of to do, Run through the hallway, out to the alley. Run because they will never take him away again.

But her legs are heavy and she crushes Geraldo against her, so tight as if she wants to conceal him in her body again, return him to her belly so that they will not castrate him and hang his small, blue penis on her door, not crush his face so that he is unrecognizable, not bury him among the heaps of bones, and ears, and teeth, and jaws, because no one, but she, cared to know that he cried. For years he cried and she could hear him day and night. Screaming, howling, sobbing, shriveling and crying because he is only five years old, and all she wanted was a mango.

But the crying begins all over again. In the distance, she hears crying.

She refuses to let go. For they will have to cut her arms off to take him, rip her mouth off to keep her from screaming for help. Without thinking, she reaches over to where two pots of coffee are brewing and throws the streaming coffee into their faces. Outside, people begin to gather, pressing their faces against the window glass to get a good view. The cook huddles behind the counter, frightened, trembling. Their faces become distorted and she doesn't see the huge hand that takes hold of Geraldo and she begins screaming all over again, screaming so that the walls shake, screaming enough for all the women of murdered children, screaming, pleading for help from the people outside, and she pushes an open hand against an officer's nose, because no one will stop them and he pushes the gun barrel to her face.

And I laugh at his ignorance. How stupid of him to think that I will let them take my Geraldo away, just because he waves that gun like a flag. Well, to hell with you, you pieces of shit, do you hear me? Stupid, cruel pigs. To hell with you all, because you can no longer frighten me. I will fight you for my son until I have no hands left to hold a knife. I will fight you all because you're all farted out of the Devil's ass, and you'll not take us with you. I am laughing, howling at their stupidity. Because they should know by now that I will never let my son go and then I hear something crunching like broken glass against my forehead and I am blinded by the liquid darkness. But I hold onto his hand. That I can feel, you see, I'll never let go. Because we are going home. My son and I.

Virgil Suárez

(b. 1962)
Cuban American

Born in Cuba in 1962 and living in the United States since 1970, Suárez is the holder of a master of fine arts in creative writing (1987) from Louisiana State University, where he studied with Vance Bourjaily. He is currently a professor of creative writing at Florida State University in Tallahassee. Although educated in the United States since the age of eight, Suárez has been preoccupied with the themes of immigration and acclimatization to life and culture in the United States.

Suárez is the author of three successful books and numerous stories published in literary magazines. He is also an active book reviewer for newspapers around the country. His first novel, **Latin Jazz** *(1989), chronicles the experiences of a Cuban immigrant family in Los Angeles by adopting the narrative perspectives of each of the family members. New York's* Newsday *hailed the novel as "a striking debut. A well-crafted and sensitive novel. An engrossing, honest book by a writer who cares deeply about preserving ties within the family unit and, by extension, within the Hispanic community and America. Suárez is marvelous."*

His second novel, **The Cutter** *(1991), deals with the desperate attempts of a young sugarcane cutter to leave Cuba and join his family in the United States.* Publishers Weekly *stated that "Suárez's powerful novel about one individual's response to the abuses and arbitrariness of totalitarianism shows us how ordinary people can be driven to take extraordinary risks."*

Suárez's most recent book is a collection of his short fiction, **Welcome to the Oasis** *(1992)—from which the selection for this present anthology is drawn—which portrays a new generation of young Hispanics who struggle to integrate themselves into an Americanized culture while maintaining pieces of their heritage.* Kirkus Reviews *has baptized Suárez as a leading spokesperson for his Cuban American generation, saying that* **Welcome to the Oasis** *is "a tightly controlled but affecting exploration of fundamental tensions in a community for whom Suárez is becoming an eloquent and promising voice."*

Dearly Beloved

1

Pilar sat in her corner of the worn divan sipping her coffee so as not to burn her tongue. She watched *El Maldito*,[1] the eight o'clock soap opera on channel 34.

Armando sat quietly at the other end, waiting for Julia, his wife, who had left moments before to buy a pizza, another item on her endless list of cravings. He understood that now that she was pregnant she was eating for two. The I-will-be-back-soon prolonged into what seemed hours as he sat alone with his mother-in-law

---

1. The Damned

in the stuffy living room of the old house. Julia had left, he concluded, so that her mother and he could reconcile and speak to one another. This was his first visit to the house since he and Julia had got back together.

After Gustavo, Pilar's husband, had left, the house looked messy, unkempt, like a house in the process of being remodeled or moved into. The dim lamp shed light upon the film of dust on the television console, lamp table, picture frames and coffee table under which the last issue of the telephone directory lay yellowed, untouched. The room smelled of soiled rags and fried fish, when it had at one time smelled of lilac or rose water air freshener.

2

Steam whirled from the porcelain mug to Pilar's eyes and forehead. She sat with her shoulders bent forward, her large breasts under her blue robe spilled over her stomach. She blinked to the changing pictures on the screen. The sound of rusty, static voices coming from the console's side speaker muffled the silence.

The face of an old woman appeared on the screen. Her voice, when she spoke, carried the metallic sound of make-believe despair. A soft crackle. She seemed like an old woman who at the end of her life struggles, with afflictions of sickness and solitude, to endure her suffering a little longer.

3

"I'm worried," Armando said. "She shouldn't have gone out in this weather."

"Julia can take care of herself," Pilar said, not turning from the screen.

Julia, he knew better than anyone else, was a poor driver. She drove like a crazy person: made left turns without signalling, changed from lane to lane, and tried to beat the traffic lights before they turned red.

4

Pilar had put on extra pounds since the last time he saw her, two or three months after his separation from her daughter. As she had walked through the sliding door of El Pueblo Market, she had spotted him getting out of his car. Maricela, one of the women he had dated, was with him. Pilar gave her a harsh, cold stare. Embarrassed, he turned and headed straight for the IN door. Minutes later he walked out puzzled—Maricela had followed him in and out—having completely forgotten what he had gone to buy.

Pilar looked at him through the steam as though she knew what he was thinking. He knew that she hadn't forgotten the incident. Maricela had dismissed his distraction as just another one of his absent-minded acts.

5

A couple kissed in a Colgate toothpaste commercial.

"How much longer?" Armando asked, staring at Pilar's shiny mug. All this time had passed and she hadn't offered him any coffee.

She said she didn't know, then peeled her fingers one at a time from around the mug as she regripped the handle.

"Cornelli's isn't that far."

"She must have gone somewhere else."

A moment of silence followed in which he could hear the soft rattle of the heater's fan.

6

"How can you watch that, Pilar?"

She turned from the screen. "It's the only thing I watch."

"Watch the American channels. They have variety."

"I see nothing wrong with this."

What he wanted to say, to confess, was that Maricela had meant nothing to him, that she had been a companion to make him forget what had gone wrong with his marriage. Julia wanted to manipulate him, and he needed no one to do that for him. Now he could only discard their breakup as a mishap, a misunderstanding, or, as Pilar had said, "A lesson for him to learn from."

But he hadn't learned a thing—or, well, if anything that being close to someone was better than being alone. Loneliness killed. Hurt. And it seemed, as he watched Pilar, that her loneliness stretched beyond the hurting stage.

7

"You haven't forgotten, have you?" Armando said.

"What?" Pilar said, still watching the action on the screen.

On impulse, Armando stood and turned off the annoying noise.

"What did you do that for?"

"It's time we talk. Isn't that the reason why Julia left us alone?"

Pilar tried to stand, but Armando blocked her way. "Turn it back on!"

"Talk. Get everything that's bothering you out."

"You're crazy. I have nothing to say to you," she said. The mug trembled in her hand.

"What do you want from me?"

"Nothing. I need nothing."

"Then why do you ignore me?"

"I'm not ignoring you."

"You've never forgotten that day you saw me with Maricela at El Pueblo?"

"Ask Julia if she's forgotten. I don't care."

"You didn't care that I was with another woman?"

"What I care about's that you left Julia. You got bored with her, didn't you? Then you returned, and look what has happened. I hope I don't have to raise your child. If you don't love my daughter, why did you marry her?" She stood up, pushed Armando out of her way, and turned the T.V. back on.

"It's not that I don't love her . . ."

"If you don't, why did you come back? To torment her? To make her suffer more?"

"Your daughter was an impossible person to live with," he said, trying to keep his voice down. "She wanted to run my life."

"Have you ever asked how she felt about you? I think you left her, and you're back to ruin her."

"Christ, that's not true!"

"Don't curse in this house!" Pilar shouted.

"You're not being fair."

"Armando, please, let me watch. I told you, I don't have anything against you, except when it concerns my daughter."

"Maricela meant nothing to me."

"But does Julia know that? Have you told her?"

"I thought you did?"

"Never a word. All along I've tried to stay out of my daughter's marriage."

8

Armando left the living room and went to the kitchen to cool off. His throat felt scratchy. He drank a cold glass of water, then returned. Pilar's words still echoed in his mind.

"How's Gustavo? Have you heard from him?" he asked.

"I don't want to talk about that bastard," she said, her lips unsticking from the mug slowly.

9

At their wedding, Armando had been close enough to smell the Cuba Libres in Gustavo's breath. It was during the reception (Julia and Armando had already sliced the cake and were getting ready to depart for their honeymoon) that Gustavo approached Armando. At first Gustavo fumbled with his words as though he was deeply moved by the sight of Julia dressed in white. He began by saying that Julita was his treasure, to take care of her and to love her ... Then he said, "I'm not one for sayings but ..." He paused to suck the last drops of rum from the ice cubes in the plastic cup. "A woman ... you want to know the truth, Armandito? I can't stand the sight of my wife in the morning. And she probably can't stand me, but she pretends better than I do. Her body's a constant reminder that I'm getting old, that I'm going to die ... But a woman, a woman's that darkness that prevents a man from finding the light switch. What a mystery they are." The other time he had met Gustavo, it was at the bank, during a long wait at the teller window. He revealed his plans to leave for Miami, then mentioned something about buying an apartment complex in Puerto Rico.

10

Pilar glanced at Armando. "Did Julia tell you we're looking for a house?" he said.
"No, she hasn't. She's been so busy with her first graders."
"Now with the baby we're going to need more room," he said.
"Do you have the money?"
"Little, with what I've managed to save from the construction work. But Julia was thinking of asking—"
"Tell her to get the idea out of her mind. Her father'd never lend her the money."

11

The pictures on the wall hung loosely on their wires—all pictures of Julia's evolution from diapers to ruffles to graduation cap and gown to the silk dress and veil.
"The two of you need a new beginning," Pilar said. "If only I'd have known, I would have never come here. Look what has happened to my family. What am I going to do here all by myself? You know I have nothing against this country, but ... Nonsense. Has Julia come up with a name yet?"

"No, we haven't."

"One'll come."

She ran the tip of her finger around the brim of the cup.

"Pilar, why do people change?"

She took a moment as though the question puzzled her, then answered, "If I knew, all my problems would be solved."

"I was in a bind," Armando said. "Our romance vanished in the blink of our eyes. We lost our desire for each other."

"So you thought by leaving her all your problems would be solved? You should never take shortcuts, Armando. They don't lead anywhere."

"I knew that if I didn't get away things would get worse."

"And you decided to run to another woman?"

"That just happened!"

"Just happened," Pilar repeated, then swallowed the last of her coffee.

12

She stood up and went to the kitchen. Armando heard her open the faucet and wash her mug. "He ran away," she said. "He ran away to another woman."

Watching Pilar slouch back onto the divan made Armando feel sorry for her. "He'll be back and like a fool I'll take him back."

Armando was tired of quarrels. His eyes burned as if the heater had been shoved close to his face.

"You're all the same ... And you watch, he'll be back to have me—"

"Don't. Don't do it. You don't have to take him back."

Gustavo, Armando thought, might never return; he had no reason to.

"She did," Pilar said, looking up at the pictures.

"I'm not Gustavo," he said.

"I'll take him back. I always do." She wiped the saggy skin under her eyes with the tips of her fingers. "But I'll never forgive him."

"Just like you won't forgive me," he said.

"You're her problem." She stared at him the way she had looked at Maricela that hot August afternoon, the way a snake sizes up its rat, and he knew that at that moment she was blaming him for her life.

13

A car drove up the driveway. The motor choked to a stop. The door slammed shut. Quick footsteps approached the front door, while fingers tried to get ahold of the right key. The door opened and then, Julia.

Pilar pushed herself up from the divan and walked toward her daughter as if to hug her.

Julia walked in from the cold, holding a large, grease-stained box with her mittens still on. Mother and daughter exchanged glances. Julia dropped her keys on the coffee table—a careless act Armando always hated—and walked into the kitchen.

"What took you so long?" he said, following her.

"I went shopping first," Julia said, putting the box down on the table and removing her mittens. "Mother," she shouted, her voice echoing among the dirty dishes, dripping faucet, grease-spattered stove and strewn newspapers, "would you like a slice?"

"Not hungry," Pilar shouted back.

She didn't want to sit with him, he thought, and be reminded of her misery.

"What did you say to her?" Julia said.

"Tried to settle our differences, that's all."

"Why's my mother upset?"

"Because of your father. Julia, please, let's eat."

Julia cut the largest slice. The cheese stretched in long strings until they snapped and recoiled. He moved his hand over to touch Julia's as she served him a slice. It felt clammy, cheese-greasy smooth. "I don't want to argue any more."

"What's that all about?" she asked.

He shrugged his shoulders. Here from the kitchen, he thought he heard soft weeping noises rising over the T.V.

"Mother?" Julia said, standing up and walking out of the kitchen.

Alone now, he reached for the knife and separated another slice, putting it onto his plate. He had promised so many things. So many things. To love and to honor ... He chewed his piece of crust as though it were his penance, as he told himself over and over like a litany, that a good father never abandoned his child.

POETRY

Gloria Vando

(b. 1934)
Puerto Rican

With a circus acrobat and poet for a mother and a political activist, playwright, actor, and poet for a father, Puerto Rican poet and editor Gloria Vando grew up in New York surrounded by artists, writers, and intellectuals. Her education in Texas, New York, and at the University of Amsterdam and the Academie Julian in Paris only added to the rich diversity in her background. Vando's poetry has been published in magazines throughout the country, but the publication of a book took second priority to the service that she has rendered literature and women writers and artists in particular through her editing and publishing the respected feminist magazine Helicon Nine from 1979 to 1989 and, later, Helicon Nine Editions. In 1993 Vando finally issued a complete book, **Promesas: Geography of the Impossible**, which is a personal, autobiographical encounter with the history of colonialism and her family roots and those of Puerto Rico. Vando's awards include the 1991 Billee Murray Denny Poetry Prize and a 1991 Kansas Governor's Art Award. Promesas was a finalist in the National Poetry Prize and the Poetry Society of America's Alice Ray de Castagnola contest. Vando continues her service to the field by administering, with her husband Bill Hickock, the Writer's Place in Kansas City, Missouri.

Legend of the Flamboyán

1

It was a good old-fashioned
victory—no massacres, no fires,
no children gunned down
in the streets of day,
no cameras to point a finger
and say *he* did it, or *they;*
it was calm, it was civilized—
they emerged from the ocean,
and claimed their paradise.
From the rain forest, naked and
trembling beneath scheffleras
and figs, perched like purple
gallinules among the low branches
of the jacarandas, the Taínos[1]

---

*.   The Flamboyán is a large Caribbean tree bearing flame-red flowers
1.   Pre-Colombian Indians of the Caribbean

watched the iron-clad strangers
wade awkwardly ashore, their
banners staking out their land.

Chief Agüeybana also watched,
the gold *guanín*[2] glinting
on his chest like a target.
Who were these intruders and what
were they doing on this island?
Could they be cannibals like
the Caribes?[3] Could they be gods?
Their bodies glistened like stars;
their eyes like the sea.

The Taínos met and argued
well into the night, weighing
the pros and cons of strategies—
if these were gods, to ignore them
might incite their wrath,
to fight them might invite death.
Best to rejoice then and welcome
the silver giants to Boriquén.[4]

The Spaniards responded by
taking first their freedom,
then their land, then
using them as human picks to dig
for gold—gold for the crown,
gold for the holy faith,
gold for the glory of Spain.

2

The darkness of the mines
consumed them, sapped

---

2.   ornaments
3.   Pre-Colombian, nomadic, bellicose Indians of the Caribbean
4.   The Taíno name of the Island of Puerto Rico

their laughter, their song,
locking them into perpetual night.
The women withdrew, drew in,
their hearts hard
against the longing they saw
in the strangers' eyes—
not to look, not to be seen—
they bowed their heads, folded
into themselves like secrets
whispered only in the safety
of brown arms.

3

A wrecked vessel washed ashore
at Guajataca. The children raced
down to the beach looking
for treasures, looking under
torn sails, beneath coiled ropes,
turning over loosened boards,
and suddenly—a hand, then a face,
the skin pale and mottled, the eyes
staring up at them, opaque
like a fish, the color of the sea.

Something dead. Something *ungodly*.

The island echoed their cries.

That night the Taínos planned
carefully, knowing—
like those at Masada[5] before them—
that there was no other way.
They drew straws.

The first Spaniard to awaken
was startled by the hush, as though
the earth itself had given up.

---

5.   a Biblical fortress city in Israel

He stepped out into the chill,
into the stained silence,
but saw only flowers, thousands
of flamboyáns—

splashes of blood—

blooming all over the island.

Nuyorican Lament

San Juan you're not for me.
My cadence quails and stumbles
on your ancient stones:

there is an inner beat here
to be reckoned with—
a *seis chorreao,*[1] a *plena,*[2]
an inbred *¡Oyeeee!*[3]
and *¡mira tú!*[4] against which
my Manhattan (sorry
wrong island) responses fell flat.

¡Vaya![5] How can I deal with that?

And yet ... once, long ago,
your beach was mine; Luquillo
was my bridle path to ride—
back then, before the turning of the tide
when Teddy's blue-eyed shills
secured the hill

---

1. a creole folk dance
2. an Afro–Puerto Rican folk dance
3. Listen
4. look
5. Wow

and tried in vain to blot
the language out. But *patria*[6]

is a sneaky word—it lies,
seeming to turn its back
upon itself—it lies,
through paling generations—lies
     and lies in wait:
the sleeping dog of nations
no translation can obliterate

(and when it's roused—
beware the bully
beware the apple pie).

I rode with purpose then,
back then, when
you were mine, harnessing
the strength of iron
     in my thighs—
my eyes blazing with self, my self
     with pride—

and once, at La Parguera,
I was baptized
on a moonless night in spring,
emerging purged and
reinvented, the phosphorescent
spangles clinging
to my skin, signaling
the night to bless my innocence—

then, only yesterday—or so it seems—
I spent my youth
in La Princesa's dungeon
for unproved crimes
against an unloved nation—yes

---

6.   homeland

only yesterday, I knew where I belonged,
I knew my part.

And now, you see me here,
a trespasser in my own past,
tracing a faint ancestral theme
far back, beyond the hard rock
rhythm of the strand.
I walk down El Condado, past
Pizza Huts, Big Macs and
Coca-Cola stands
listening for a song—

a wisp of song—

that begs deep in my heart.

Luis Omar Salinas

(b. 1937)
Mexican American

Luis Omar Salinas was born in Robstown, Texas, but moved with his family at an early age to Monterrey, Mexico. After the death of his mother in 1941, he moved to California to be raised by an uncle. He received his early education there and went on to obtain a junior college degree and to study at various universities, but his formal education was interrupted by nervous breakdowns. Salinas is one of the most prolific and respected Hispanic poets in the United States, beginning his writing career as a somewhat romantic, surrealistic poet during the Chicano Movement of the late 1960s and continuing to produce volumes of well-crafted work for more than two decades. Although he has been the recipient of some of the most prestigious literary awards, Salinas has not become well known in mainstream poetry circles in the United States, perhaps because he is not affiliated with a university or creative writing program, does not travel much, and does not associate to any degree with other writers around the country. His verse brings together the traditions of Federico Garca Lorca and Paío Neruda with that of Whitman and has earned him the Earl Lyon Award (1981), the Stanley Kunitz Award (1980), and the General Electric Foundation Award (1984). Included among his works are his first widely praised book **Crazy Gypsy** (1970), which was followed by **Afternoon of the Unreal** (1980) and **Prelude to Darkness** (1981). In 1987 his collected and new poems were issued in **The Sadness of Days.** Salinas is a poet of compassion and humanity whose verses will stand the test of time.

Ode to the Mexican Experience

The nervous poet sings again
in his childhood voice, happy,
a lifetime of Mexican girls
in his belly, voice
of the midnoon bells
and excited mariachis[1]
in those avenues persuaded out
of despair

He talks of his Aztec mind,
the little triumphs and schizoid trips,
the many failures
and his defeated chums
dogs and shadows,

---

1.   a Mexican musical ensemble

the popularity of swans in his neighborhood
and the toothaches of rabbits
in the maize fields.

I know you in bars
in merchant shops,
in the roving gladiators,
in the boats of Mazatlan that never anchor,
in the smile of her eyes,
in the tattered clothes of school children,
in the never-ending human burials;
those lives lost in the stars
and those lost in the stars
and those lost in the wreckage
of fingernails,
the absurd sophistry of loneliness
in markets, in hardware stores,
in brothels.

The happy poet talks in his sleep,
the eyes of his loved one
pressing against him—

When This Life
No Longer Smells of Roses

It will be raining,
the air will be blue,
my compadres[1] will be
singing rancheras[2]
and seagulls will be
dancing the "Jarabe."[3]
My loved one will come
all the way from Paris;
my creditors will

---

1. co-parents (one is the godfather of the other's child)
2. rural songs ("ranch")
3. a foot-tapping dance

denounce me.
Children will be
thrashing piñatas[4]
and in the barrio
they will be singing
"Por Una Mujer Casada."[5]
A would-be nun
will slash her wrists.
A gypsy will have
his guitar stolen.
My poems will turn up
in Mazatlan, starched
as napkins in good cafes,
and I'll be rehearsing
a ballad by Negrete,
dreaming of villages,
the white breasts
of the sea, and there will
be plenty of laughter.
When this life no longer
smells of roses,
I'll have left
on a tour with Don Quixote[6]—
I'll leave no forwarding
address.

My Father Is a Simple Man

I walk to town with my father
to buy a newspaper. He walks slower
than I do so I must slow up.
The street is filled with children.
We argue about the price
of pomegranates, I convince
him it is the fruit of scholars.

4. a decorated gourd filled with party favors and candy
5. title of a popular song, "For a Married Woman"
6. the famed chivalrous knight created by writer Miguel de Cervantes

He has taken me on this journey
and it's been lifelong.
He's sure I'll be healthy
so long as I eat more oranges,
and tells me the orange
has seeds and so is perpetual;
and we too will come back
like the orange trees.
I ask him what he thinks
about death and he says
he will gladly face it when
it comes but won't jump
out in front of a car.
I'd gladly give my life
for this man with a sixth
grade education, whose kindness
and patience are true ...
The truth of it is, he's the scholar,
and when the bitter-hard reality
comes at me like a punishing
evil stranger, I can always
remember that here was a man
who was a worker and provider,
who learned the simple facts
in life and lived by them,
who held no pretense.
And when he leaves without
benefit of fanfare or applause
I shall have learned what little
there is about greatness.

I Am America

It's a hell of a world.
I go like a schoolboy stepping
through the murderous countryside,
a bit of rhyme, a little drunk
with the wonderful juices of breasts,

and the magnificent
with their magician-like words
slipping into the voice of America.
I carry my father's coat,
some coins,
my childhood eyes in wonder—
the olive trucks plucky
in their brash ride
through the avenue,
the wino in a halo of freedom,
the shopkeepers of Democracy.

I am brave, I am sad
and I am happy with the workers in the field,
the pregnant women
in ten dollar dresses,
the night air supping
and stopping to chat
like a wild romantic lady.
Children's voices and dogs,
the bar, the songs and fights.
I go ruminating in the brothels,
the ghettos, the jails.
Braggart, walking into early
cafes confessing naiveté
and love for the unemployed.
I'm a dream in the land
like the Black, Mexican, Indian,
Anglo and Oriental faces
with their pictures of justice.
I go gaudy into movie houses,
flamboyant spectator.

Angela de Hoyos

(b. 1940)
Mexican American

Angela de Hoyos is one of the outstanding pioneers of the Chicano literary movement, a woman breaking barriers inside and outside of that movement. *Born in Mexico and raised in San Antonio, Texas, de Hoyos became a professional painter and poet at an early age. She began publishing her poetry in the early 1960s in international venues. By 1965, she began to accumulate international awards, and in 1970 and 1971 she was awarded two citations—magna cum laude—from the World Poetry Society International, for which she also served as a poetry translator. In addition to publishing poems in various languages in periodicals at home and abroad, de Hoyos has collected her works in various books, all of which correspond to her complete embrace of the Chicano literary movement:* **Arise Chicano and Other Poems** *(1975),* **Chicano Poems: For the Barrio** *(1976),* **Selecciones** *(translated to Spanish by Mireya Robles, 1976), and* **Woman, Woman** *(1986). In her poetic works, de Hoyos is known for sweet satire with a feminist and political edge. In service of the literary movement, de Hoyos administers a small publishing house, M & A Editions, and an occasional literary and cultural periodical* Huehetitlan.

You Will Grow Old

forever comparing me
with your dream woman
—that goddess
of fantasy
of matchless perfection
defying correction
yet always
so conspicuously absent—
while I go about
grinding my teeth
on the thankless endless
daily task:
dusting your wings.

I too
will age . . .
for obvious reasons.

Lesson in Semantics

Men, she said,
sometimes
in order to
say it

it is
necessary
to spit
the word.

How to Eat Crow
on a Cold Sunday Morning

just start on the wings
nibbling
apologetic-like
because after all
it was you
who held the gun
and fired point-blank
the minute you saw the
whites of their eyes
just like the army sergeant
always instructed you.

—Damn it, this thing's
gonna make me sick!

—No it won't. Go on. Eat the
blasted thing
(for practice)

because you'll be sicker
later on
when your friends

start giving you
an iceberg for a shoulder.

... So the giblets are dry
and tough.
But you can
digest them.

It's the gall bladder
—that green bag of biliousness—
wants to gag your throat
in righteous retribution

refuses to budge
won't go up or down, just
sticks there

makes you wish that long ago
you'd learned how to eat
a pound of prudence
instead.

Miguel Algarín

(b. 1941)
Puerto Rican

A native of Santurce, Puerto Rico, Miguel Algarín moved with his family to New York City in the early 1950s. Algarín studied in city schools and later obtained a bachelor's degree from the University of Wisconsin in 1963; in 1965 he graduated with a master's degree in English from the Pennsylvania State University. He began his doctoral work at Princeton University but never finished. Algarín has had a successful career as an English professor at Rutgers University, but it is through his work as a poet and the founding director of the Nuyorican Poets Cafe that he has won much recognition. The cafe is dedicated to writers performing their art orally. It was particularly important during the 1970s as a gathering place for young Nuyorican writers defining their art. Algarín played in an important role in that definition as their mentor, critic, and sounding board, as well as compiling with Miguel Piñero the first anthology of their work in **Nuyorican Poets: An Anthology of Puerto Rican Words and Feelings** *(1975)*. Algarín is the author of four books of poetry: **Mongo Affair** *(1978)*, **On Call** *(1980)*, **Body Bee Calling from the 21st Century** *(1982)*, and **Time's Now/Ya es tiempo** *(1985)*. In addition, he has written plays, screenplays, and short stories. Algarín's poetry runs the gamut from jazz-salsa to the mystical. He is one of the foremost experimenters with English-Spanish bilingualism and has even penned trilingual works that incorporate French. In 1976 Algarín published **Canción de gesta/A Song of Protest,** a book of translations of the poetry of one of his great models, Pablo Neruda.

Taos Pueblo Indians: 700 Strong According to Bobby's Last Census

It costs $1.50 for my van to enter
Taos Pueblo Indian land,
adobe huts, brown tanned Indian red skin
reminding me of brown Nuyorican people,
young Taos Pueblo Indians
ride the back of a pickup truck
with no memories of mustangs
controlled by their naked calves and thighs,
rocky, unpaved roads, red brown dirt,
a stream bridged by wide trunk planks,
young warriors unloading thick trunks
for the village drum makers to work,
tourists bringing the greens,

Indian women fry flour and bake bread,
older men attend curio shops.
the center of the village is a parking lot
into which America's mobile homes
pour in with their air conditioned cabins, color
T.V., fully equipped kitchens, bathrooms
with flushing toilets and showers,
A.M. & F.M. quadraphonic stereo sound,
cameras, geiger counters, tents,
hiking boots, fishing gear and mobile telephones,
restricted signs are posted round the parking lot
making the final stage for the zoo
where the natives approach selling
American Jewelry made in Phoenix
by a foster American Indian from Brooklyn
who runs a missionary profit making turquoise jewelry shop
"Ma, is this clean water?
do the Indians drink out of this water?
is it all right for me to drink it?"
the young white substitute teacher's daughter
wants to drink some Indian water,
young village school children recognize her,
and in her presence the children snap
quick attentive looks that melt into
"boy am I glad I'm not in school"
gestures as pass,
but past, past this living room zoo,
out there on that ridge,
over there, over that ridge,
on the other side of that mountain,
is that Indian land too?
are there leaders and governments over that ridge?
does Indian law exist there?
who would the Pueblo Indian send
to a formal state meeting
with the heads of street government,
Who could we plan war with?
can we transport arms earmarked for ghetto

warriors, can we construct our street
government constitutions on your land?
when orthodox Jews from Crown Heights
receive arms from Israel in their territorial struggle
with local Brooklyn Blacks,
can we raise your flag
in the Lower East Side
as a sign of our mutual treaty of protection?
"hey you you're not supposed to walk in our water,"
"stay back we're busy making bread,"
these were besides your "restricted zones"
the most authoritative words
spoken by your native tongue,
the girl's worry about her drinking water
made Raúl remove his Brazilian made shoes
from the Pueblo Indian drinking cup.
the old woman's bread warning
froze me dead on the spot
"go buy something in the shop,
you understand me, go buy something,"
I didn't buy I just strolled on by the curio shops
till I came across Bobby the police officer.
taught at Santa Fe, though he could've gone on to Albuquerque,
Taos Pueblo Indians
sending their officers of the law to be trained
in neighboring but foreign cities like in New Mexico
proves that Taos Pueblo Indians
ignore that a soldier belongs to his trainer
that his discipline, his habitual muscle response
belongs to his drill sergeant master:
"our laws are the same as up in town"
too bad Bobby! hey could be your laws,
it's your land!
then flashing past as I leave Taos Bobby speeds
towards the reservation in a 1978 GMC van with two red flashers
on top bringing Red Cross survival rations to the Taos Pueblo Indians
respectfully frying bread for tourists
behind their sovereign borders.

Ricardo Sánchez

(b. 1941)
Mexican American

Ricardo Sánchez is one of the most prolific Chicano poets, one of the first creators of a bilingual literary style, and one of the first poets to be identified with the Chicano Movement. Born the youngest of thirteen children on March 21, 1941, he was raised in the notorious Barrio del Diablo (Devil's Neighborhood) in El Paso, Texas. He became a high school dropout, an Army enlistee, and later a repeat offender sentenced to prison terms in Soledad Prison in California and Ramsey Prison Farm Number One in Texas; he began his literary career at these prisons before his last parole in 1969. His early life experiences of oppressive poverty and overwhelming racism, his suffering in prisons, and his self-education and rise to political and social consciousness are chronicled in his poetry. Although Sánchez's poetry is very lyrical, it is also the most autobiographical of all the Hispanic poets. Once his writing career was established and Sánchez began to publish his works with both mainstream and alternative literary presses, he assumed various visiting appointments as a professor or writer-in-residence at various universities.

Sánchez's poetry is characterized by an unbridled linguistic inventiveness that not only calls upon both English and Spanish lexicon but also is a source of neologisms and surprising combinations of the sounds and symbols of both languages in single works. His work can be virile and violent at one moment and delicate and sentimental at the next as he follows the formulas and dictates of a poetry written for oral performance. Most of all, Sánchez is a poet who casts himself as a Chicano Everyman participating in the epic history of his people through his poetry.

Besides publishing hundreds of poems in magazines and anthologies, Sánchez has authored the following collections: **Canto y grito mi liberación (y lloro mis desmadrazgos)** *(1971, I Sing and Shout for My Liberation [and Cry for My Insults]),* republished in expanded form in 1973; **Hechizospells: Poetry/Stories/Vignettes/Articles/ Notes on the Human Condition of Chicanos & Pícaros, Words & Hopes within Soulmind** *(1976);* **Milhuas Blues and Gritos Norteños** *(1980);* **Amsterdam Cantos y Poemas Pistos** *(1983);* **Selected Poems** *(1985); and* **Eagle Visioned/Feathered Adobes: Manito sojourns and pachuco ramblings** *(1989).*

Soledad Was a Girl's Name

Soledad was a girl's name,
years ago
at jefferson high,
and she was soft and brown
and beautiful.
i used to watch her,
and think her name
was ironic
and poetic,
for she was Soledad Guerra,
solitude and war,
and she used to always smile
con ternura morena
como su piel,[1]
and now in this soledad
that i am leaving soon,
this callous nation
of bars and cement and barbarity,
it seems strange
that a name can call out to me
and mesmerize me,
yet repel me,
one a girl, now a woman,
and the other
a jagged prison world
where hate
is a common expletive,
seems everyone hates,
seems everyone is a convict,
even the guards and counselors
do time here
everyday trudging into
this abysmal human warehouse.
am leaving

---

1. with brown tenderness like her skin

and it hurts.
funny that it hurts;
i see the faces of my friends,
we joke about my getting out,
and they ask pleading things,
"DO IT ONE TIME FOR ME, ESE!"
just one time, carnal,
nomás una vez.[2]
hell, bato,[3] i'll go all over
and do it a million times
recalling all the sadness
that hides
within this place;
i'll do it a jillion times
for me, for you, for all of us,
and maybe the next soledad i see
is a morenita from el chuco[4]
i had been too timid
to ask out ... it's strange
that i recall her.
but then la pinta[5]
makes you think/regret.
but huachenle, batos,[6]
when i'm doing it for us
i'll probably burst out laughing,
not at you or me or even at some ruca,
but at all the pendejadas,
at all the crazy lies
that say that we are savage;
i'll laugh at mean-ass convicts
who terrify the world
yet love to eat ice cream,
i'll laugh at convicts scurrying

---

2.   only one time
3.   guy
4.   is a brown girl from El Paso
5.   the penitentiary
6.   but look, guys,

from cell block to the canteen
with books of scripted money
to purchase cokes and cookies
and candy bars as well;
i'll laugh at contradictions
and yet within i'll hurt
remembering xmas packages
and letters full of pain,
recalling those sad moments
when night became the coverlet
and darkness filtered songs,
when all alone i'd die
realizing just how sordid
a prison life can be ...

yes, i'll laugh, carnales,
just like we all want to laugh,
not to mock us nor to spite you,
just to say i understand,

pero eso sí, compiras,
no quiero regresar.[7]

---

7.   but that's true, buddies, I don't want to return

> *new panaceas abound,*
> *new promises of paradise,*
> *new to me and oddly old*
> *to others, Utah*
> *sours dreams and it should*
> *begin with a P for its*
> *perversity and putismo ...* [1]
> *been here over a week, damn ...*
> *but it seems forever ...*
> *Saltyville of a Lakeburg*
> *September 30, 1977*

Letters to My Ex-Texas Sanity

left you, Tejas,
over a week ago,
had to,
for work
is here and not there,
home
resides wherein one lives,
and i live (almost do)
in salt lake city.
it hurls its salty dust
at your soul's eyes,
burns its vapid senselessness
into the furrows
of your thoughts,
it urges you to give up
life, liberty and the
real pursuit of selfdom,
clothes, everything,
with missionary zeal,
demands
your capitulation,
bicycles you to death,
and then intones

---

1. whorishness

that heaven
merely is for those
who have renounced
all semblance of having been
salient/lively creatures
who lived to love
while loving to live.
ay, utah brutalizes
hope
with its spineless
and amorphous
gelatinous mentality.

perverse and anti-human,
your temple
manufactures
complacent/placid smiles
to keep all niggers out,
your westside of salt lake.
awash with fetid meskin smells,
it creaks and groans
with fear
that we might multiply,
your fear of loathsome Laman[2]
defines the way you see us.
a mass of swarthy people
who revel in their evil.
ay, brutah, putah, utah,[3]
whose land is so majestic.
with deserts y montañas[4]
and nature's pungency.
you fear
those who are darker,
and claim to be so saintly,

---

2. the devil for the Mormons
3. dumb, whorish
4. mountains

enslaver of the frail
and dementer of the fragile,
your sacrosantimonious
attempts at being holy
are ludicrous at best,
at worst imperialistic
and ever missionizing.

you flail, hither-thither,
the differences you fear,
and though you feel superior
and smug in your behest,
you strive like hungered zealots
to make us look your best.

oh, poor and foolish bigots,
you have no need to fear us,
for you have nothing worthy
to send us on in quest.
you see,
this land belongs
to all who wish to love it
and within it reside.
we'll be ourselves, ay, utah,
and celebrate our difference,
we'll look at you and smile
and continue on our way
to live within your valleys
while we project our name ...

Pat Mora

(b. 1942)
Mexican American

Pat Mora was born and raised in El Paso, Texas, and she also received her bachelor's and master's degrees in English at the University of Texas at El Paso. She very much sees herself as a creature of the desert and the border, and has developed much of her work around those themes. Pat Mora is the Mexican American poet who probably has had the most success in having her works included in textbooks for senior and junior high schools, most likely because of the clarity of her voice and thought as well as her ability to evoke a specific place and its culture within the perspective of a Mexican American woman. Two of her three books of poetry have won Southwest Book Awards: **Chants** *(1984) and* **Borders** *(1986). Her latest poetry collection,* **Communion,** *was published in 1991. Mora is a fellow of the National Endowment for the Arts and the Kellogg Foundation and was inducted into the Texas Institute of Letters in 1987. She is also a successful children's book author with three such books in print:* **A Birthday Basket for Tía** *(1992),* **Pablo's Tree** *(1993), and* **Tomás and the Library Lady** *(1993). She is also the author of a volume of personal essays,* **Nepantla** *(1993). Pat Mora currently resides in Cincinnati, Ohio.*

Immigrants

wrap their babies in the American flag,
feed them mashed hot dogs and apple pie,
name them Bill and Daisy,
buy them blonde dolls that blink blue
eyes or a football and tiny cleats
before the baby can even walk,
speak to them in thick English,
hallo, babee, hallo,
whisper in Spanish or Polish
when the babies sleep, whisper
in a dark parent bed, that dark
parent fear, "Will they like
our boy, our girl, our fine american
boy, our fine american girl?"

Gentle Communion

Even the long-dead are willing to move.
Without a word, she came with me from the desert.
Morning she wanders through my rooms
making beds, folding socks.

Since she can't hear me anymore,
Mamande ignores the questions I never knew
to ask, about her younger days, her red
hair, the time she fell and broke her nose
in the snow. I will never know.

When I try to make her laugh,
to disprove her sad album face, she leaves
the room, resists me as she resisted
grinning for cameras, makeup, English.

While I write, she sits and prays,
feet apart, legs never crossed,
the blue housecoat buttoned high
as her hair dries white, girlish
around her head and shoulders.

She closes her eyes, bows her head,
and like a child presses her hands together,
her patient flesh steepled, the skin
worn, like the pages of her prayer book.

Sometimes I sit in her wide-armed
chair as I once sat in her lap.
Alone, we played a quiet I Spy.
She peeled grapes I still taste.
She removes the thin skin, places
the luminous coolness on my tongue.
I know not to bite or chew. I wait
for the thick melt,
our private green honey.

Arte Popular

A hot breath among the pale crystal,
and polite watercolors of this tidy museum,
a breathing
in these new rooms,
and faint drums, whistles, chants.

Judas figures puffed with sins rise
to the ceiling ready to explode into
pure white smoke,
dragons' eyes bulge, and green claws reach
to pull your hair
as masks sneer down
at skeletons dressed as bride and groom.

In Mexican villages
wrinkled hands lure and trap
dark spirits,
snakes
slide into woven reeds
dogs
growl softly in wood
frogs
blow their wet song into clay flutes
jaguars
pant in papier-mâché

a breathing those spirits poised
to inhale deeply, fly out museum windows,
leap down steps three at a time, slither
on cool white marble into the night, into the full moon.

Old Anger

I didn't believe he loved that woman,
didn't believe he stroked her

cheek softly when she dreamed, wrapped himself
around her in the cold.

Ella. She lured him away from me
and the children years ago, into her
perfume, powder, soft, inviting skin
that held him even at the end
when she coughed herself away night after night.

But when she died, he shuffled head down
through the *rancho* with the coffin,
weaving like a dry leaf in the wind,
stood alone by her grave, wiped a tear away.
They saw. All eyes saw my *hombre macho*
wipe a tear away.

My daughters lured him back into our house.
They plead, "Speak to him. It's Christmas. For us."
Ten years he has shuffled through these rooms,
but I live alone, inside myself.

My old anger warms my bones.
ella: she
rancho: small village
hombre: man

Curandera*

They think she lives alone
on the edge of town in a two-room house
where she moved when her husband died
at thirty-five of a gunshot wound
in the bed of another woman. The *curandera*
and house have aged together to the rhythm
of the desert.

---

*   a curandera is a healer

She wakes early, lights candles before
her sacred statues, brews tea of *yerbabuena*.[1]
She moves down her porch steps, rubs
cool morning sand into her hands, into her arms.
Like a large black bird, she feeds on
the desert, gathering herbs for her basket.

Her days are slow, days of grinding
dried snake into powder, of crushing
wild bees to mix with white wine.
And the townspeople come, hoping
to be touched by her ointments
her hands, her prayers, her eyes.
She listens to their stories, and she listens
to the desert, always, to the desert.

By sunset she is tired. The wind
strokes the strands of long gray hair,
the smell of drying plants drifts
into her blood, the sun seeps
into her bones. She dozes
on her back porch. Rocking, rocking.

At night she cooks chopped cactus
and brews more tea. She brushes a layer
of sand from her bed, sand which covers
the table, stove, floor. She blows
the statues clean, the candles out.
Before sleeping, she listens to the message
of the owl and the coyote. She closes her eyes
and breathes with the mice and snakes
and wind.

---

1. peppermint

Miguel Piñero

(1946–1988)
Puerto Rican

Miguel Piñero is the most famous dramatist to come out of the Nuyorican school. Born in Gurabo, Puerto Rico, on December 19, 1946, he was raised on the Lower East Side of New York, the site of many of his plays and poems. Shortly after moving to New York, his father abandoned the family, which had to live on the streets until his mother could find a source of income. Piñero was a gang leader and involved in petty crime and drugs while an adolescent; he was a junior-high-school dropout and by the time he was twenty-four he had been sent to Sing Sing Prison for armed robbery. While at Sing Sing, he began writing poetry and dramatic works and acting in a theater workshop there.

By the time of his release, his most famous play, **Short Eyes** *(published in 1975), had already been prepared in draft form. The play was produced and soon moved to Broadway after getting favorable reviews. During and after the successful run of his play, Piñero became involved with a group of Nuyorican writers on the Lower East Side and became one of the principal spokespersons and models for the new school of Nuyorican literature, especially poetry, which was furthered by the publication of* **Nuyorican Poets: An Anthology of Puerto Rican Words and Feelings** *which was compiled and edited by Piñero and Miguel Algarín in 1985. During this time, Piñero developed his career as a performance poet who brought together the popular Hispanic and African American traditions of oral presentation. His blending of these traditions resulted in his production of what might be characterized as bilingual-jazz street poetry that has been emulated by numerous grassroots poets in the barrios and ghettos of New York, Detroit, Chicago, and other urban centers.*

Piñero died of sclerosis of the liver in 1988 after many years of hard living and recurrent illnesses. Before his untimely death, Piñero wrote some eleven plays that were produced, most of which are included in his two collections, **The Sun Always Shines for the Cool, A Midnight Moon at the Greasy Spoon, Eulogy for a Small-Time Thief** *(1983), and* **Outrageous One-Act Plays** *(1986). Piñero is also author of the book of poems* **La Bodega Sold Dreams** *(1986), which was a compilation of the poems that best lend themselves to silent reading as opposed to oral performance. Included among his awards were a Guggenheim Fellowship (1982) and the New York Drama Critics Circle Award for Best American Play, an Obie, and the Drama Desk Award, all of which were presented in 1974 for* **Short Eyes.**

A Lower East Side Poem

Just once before I die
I want to climb up on a
tenement sky
to dream my lungs out till

I cry
then scatter my ashes thru
the Lower East Side.

So let me sing my song tonight
let me feel out of sight
and let all eyes be dry
when they scatter my ashes thru
the Lower East Side.

From Houston to 14th Street
from Second Avenue to the mighty D
here the hustler & suckers meet
the faggots & freaks will all get
high
on the ashes that have been scattered
thru the Lower East Side.

There's no other place for me to be
there's no other place that I can see
there's no other town around that
brings you up or keeps you down
no food little heat sweeps by
fancy cars & pimps' bars & juke saloons
& greasy spoons make my spirits fly
with my ashes scattered thru the
Lower East Side . . .

A thief, a junkie I've been
committed every known sin
Jews and Gentiles . . . Bums and Men
of style . . . run away child
police shooting wild . . .
mother's futile wails . . . pushers
making sales . . . dope wheelers
& cocaine dealers . . . smoking pot
streets are hot & feed off those who bleed to death . . .

all that's true
all that's true
all that is true
but this ain't no lie
when I ask that my ashes be scattered thru
the Lower East Side.

So here I am, look at me
I stand proud as you can see
pleased to be from the Lower East
a street fighting man
a problem of this land
I am the Philosopher of the Criminal Mind
a dweller of prison time
a cancer of Rockefeller's ghettocide
this concrete tomb is my home
to belong to survive you gotta be strong
you can't be shy less without request
someone will scatter your ashes thru
the Lower East Side.

I don't wanna be buried in Puerto Rico
I don't wanna rest in long island cemetery
I wanna be near the stabbing shooting
gambling fighting & unnatural dying
& new birth crying
so please when I die . . .
don't take me far away
keep me near by
take my ashes and scatter them thru out
the Lower East Side . . .

New York City Hard Times Blues

NYC Blues
Big time time hard on on me blues
New York City hard sunday morning blues
yeah

Junkie waking up
bones ache trying to shake
New York City sunday morning blues
the sun was vomiting itself up over
the carbon monoxide detroit perfume
strolling down the black asphalt dance floor
where all the disco sweat drenched Mr. Mario's
summer suit still mambo-tango hustled
to the tunes of fiberglass songs
New York City sunday morning means
liquor store closed
bars don't open 'til noon
and my connection wasn't upping
a 25 cent balloon
yeah
yeah reality wasn't giving me no play
telling me it was going to be sunday
24 hours the whole day
it was like the reincarnation of the night
before when my ashtray became
the cemetery of all my lost memories
when a stumble bum blues band
kept me up all night playing me cheap
F.M.
dreams
of hard time
sad time
bad time
hell we all know times are
hard
sad
bad
all over
well I thought of the pope
welfare hopes
then I thought of the pope again
whose sexual collar musta been tighter
than a pimp's hat band
yeah

that brought a warm beer smile to this
wasteland the mirror called my face
ya see
I left my faith in a mausoleum
when my inspiration ran off with
a trumpet player
who wore double knit suits and stacy adam shoes
this girl left me so broke
my horoscope said
my sign was a dead dog in the middle
of the road
yeah
the morning will be giving up to the noon
and soon I'll hear winos and junkyard dogs
howling at the moon
made the shadows
dance
at jake's juke saloon
as a battalion of violet virgins
sang tunes
of deflowered songs
men poured their
fantasies of lust into young boy's
ears
car stolen
whizzed by
crying hard luck tears in beers
the love conflict of air conditioned
dim lit motel rooms
rumpled sheets with blood stains
explain
my yesterday night of mind
the winter fell as hard
as the smell of a brick shithouse
in the hot south
Om ...
but the hawk seeped into my home
chillin' my bones

Om ...
it didn't hear my incantation
there has to be an explanation
wasn't it true
when you
Om ...
you are one
Om ...
make me warm
Om ...
is part of god
Om ...
make the cold wind stop
Om ...
perhaps if I
Om ...
stronger
Om ...
louder
Om ...
LONGER
OMMMMMMMMMMMMMMMMMMMMMMMM
it don't work
Om ...
I feel like a jerk
I'll try once more just to make sure
OMMMMM
maybe if I pleaded on my knees
to J.C.
he'd take heed of my needs
and melt the icicles
from the tears in my eyes
but it was still cold
I'm told if you sing
"I'm gonna lay down my sword and shield
down by the river side ... down by the river side"
I get no signal
maybe if I do it bilingual

"en la cruz, en la cruz yo primero vi la luz"[1]
oh come on chuito
have a heart
take apart the winter winds from me
please … J.C ….
OM …
en la cruz
down by the river side
10 hail marys I offer
and 5 our fathers
but the cold was no further
than before
I should know it's very rare when
a prayer
gets the boiler fixed
OMMMMM
yeah
New York City december sunday morning
was whippin' my ass in a cold blooded fashion
treatin' me like a stepchild
putting a serious hurting on me
watching me bleed
thru my sleeves
as I tried to get high
shooting up caffeine without sacharine
that some beat artist sold me down
on eldredge st.
yeah
but that's the ghetto creed
that the strong must feed
yeah
brotherman
everything was happening faster than the
speed of sound
my whole seemed like it was going down
I wonder who ever wrote that tune
about being back on top in june

---

1. religious song: "On the cross, on the cross, where I first saw the light"

nigger forgot about september and december
now that's a month to remember
when each cold day becomes like a brick wall
and you're the bouncing ball
yeah I kept seeing my fate being sealed
by the silk smooth hands of the eternal bill
collector
who keeps rattling my door knob
pressing my avon ding dong bell ...
my pockets were crying the blues
telling me that I ain't fed them a dollar in years
and was it clear that they couldn't hold
anymore unpaid debts ... traffic tickets ... or promissory notes
and hey that was when I wished I was back in
L.A.
laid back
L.A.
kick back
L.A.
smog town
hollywood ... driving down to malibu
hollywood U.S.A. ... hey hey USA hollywood
seedy looking film producers smile at you
over a burrito with taco bell breath
explain the plots to fellini[2] movies
they aint ever seen
hollywood ... down to malibu
at two a.m. if you get tired
of cal worthington shit-eating grin
you walk out on him hit santa monica blvd
and watch the manicured thumbs caress the
homosexual airs of rolled up jeans and silver buckles
as westwood camaro rides very slow very low
down western ave
where neon lights scream
the latest kick in adult entertainment
masturbation

---

2.   Federico Fellini, famed Italian director

enters your thoughts
when pornographic stars with colgate smiles
whisper
inane
mundane
snides of flicking your bic
or I'm nancy fly with me national
well I'm going nowhere got nowhere to go
going nowhere fast
got me a couple of dollars a few dimes
and plenty of time
go into some bar on alvarado
and temple listen to some mariachi music
or stroll into some dive joint off sunset
sit in some naugahyde booth
with some dishwater blond
with sagging breasts
wearing a see thru blouse
and listen to all her 1930 starlet dreams
as she smokes all my cigarettes
sure what have I got back at that
refugee from a leprosy colony hotel

but a one station a.m. radio
feeding my neurological cells
with those south street philadelphia blues
she want to cruise thru griffin park
no thank you
I'd rather listen to linda ronstadt instead
and the bartender tell dirty jokes
and his customers recite 12% alcoholic aluminum
recycled viet nam horror stories
reading the signs of our times
the obituary of a dying society
the folktales of yesteryear's gonorrhea
history
hollywood going down to malibu
malibu ... pretty people and fonzi T shirts

flex their muscles spreading spiritual bad breath
and joe namath perfume
yeah
but i'm in new york city
crying the junkie blues
welfare afro hairdos sprout out
of frye boots
yeah punk rockers hitting on you
for subway fare three times
soon the mohair slick lines
at penn station are getting impatient
wanna get home
to alone
make the scene with a magazine
or with a plastic doll
cause the missus got another headache
gaze at the farrah foster poster
that adorns his horny teenage son's walls
yeah these days always
have a way of showing up
like rubber checks
I wish I could cop a bottle of muscatel
stroll thru the bowery with a pocket
full of wino dreams
but sunday morning in New York City
for the junkie there ain't no pity
we just walk the streets with loaded dice
and hear people say there goes miky
miky piñero
they call him the junkie christ . . .

Sandra María Esteves

(b. 1948)
Puerto Rican/Dominican

Sandra María Esteves was born in the Bronx, New York, and educated in New York City, where she studied art at the Pratt Institute. Esteves was one of the very few women's voices to be heard in the first generation of Nuyorican poets. From her teenage years, Esteves was very active in women's struggles, African American liberation, and the movement for Puerto Rican independence. Esteves used her poetry in performance to support her activism and to inspire other activists at rallies and conferences. In 1973 she joined El Grupo, a New York–based touring collective of musicians, performing artists, and poets and the cultural wing of the Puerto Rican Socialist Party. By 1980 she had published her first collection of her poetry, **Yerba Buena,** *which is a search for identity by a colonized Hispanic woman of color who is the daughter of immigrants from the Caribbean. All three of her books—***Yerba Buena, Tropical Rains: A Bilingual Downpour** *(1984), and* **Mockingbird Bluestown Mambo** *(1990)—affirm that womanhood is what gives unity to all of the diverse characterizations of life. Today, she continues to organize workshops and performances for poetry, and she is the resident theater director for The Family Repertory Company.*

Resurrections

We come to the dance,
our legs in pain,
muscles protruding, swollen
red from battle,
bodies limping distortion scars,
eyes veiled with inner rage,
words hot as sun.

We come to the dance
parched for miracle drops of holy water,
cures for self and the world's diseases
embedded in the unseen.

We, the lonely victims, come
deaf from the madness,
desperate for the naked sounds
of rainbow waterfalls,
wanting to drink,
partake in the treasured secrets of our ancestors.

Padrino*

for John Mason

Round sleeping-moon face
from where watchful seers interpret visions
sent by caring saints,
viewing into realms where we are blind.
Choosing to guide our steep awkward climbing
with their buoyant hands holding us secure
over the bottomless pit
where we are conquered by a skilled magician's faith,
head crowned by magic herbal wreath,
crimson berries bedded in fresh mint,
infusing sacred words through holy breath
that clears soul-clouding cataracts of illusion,
setting our spirits free
with barely a touch and gentle incantation,
causing our rebirth,
to become blessed fruit, made sweet
and ripe for offering in the final ritual
where we return to the house of our ancestors,
a grand mansion full of infinite rooms
under a chandelier of stars
pulsating precise cosmic music,
vibrations consuming darkness,
revealing what is greater within ourselves
where we live as native children
riding on tall vine swings,
suspended from the high branches of an old wisdom tree
in the mystical playground of our Great Grandfather's garden.

---

* Padrino is a Godfather

Bautizo*

for Brunie

Early Brooklyn morning
Padrino counsels initiates,
new children into his house,
spiritual survivors reclaimed from a pilfered legacy.

Silent and anxious
the *iabos* shed old clothes
that hang on and grip like tight skins
of solid lead shackles. A burden
heavier than their ability to resist.
Acknowledging need to align
cumbersome physical being with Divine power,
diminishing the weight,
implementing knowledge of metaphysical chemistry,
the natural combustion of kinetic earth, composed
and refined in the transcendental laboratory of mind.

Full of aché,
Babalorisha invokes the ancestors,
family of one-hundred-thousand names,
to join this rebirth,
sing and feast in prodigal victory,
reaffirming linkage
to bloodlines woven like luminous veils
over walls and windows of their souls,
opening to reveal the precious landscapes
and inherited panoramas of our connected intelligence.

Ocha*

Crawling through the ground,
hidden and covered in slime,
begins the metamorphosis of the butterfly.

---

* Bautizo is baptism.
* Ocha is an African deity.

Almost at the point of death,
dormant, frozen in its prison,
asleep and unaware of its future,
until its casing presses tight,
breathless against its skin
as it stirs in its initiation,
pushing at the walls that hold
like a sealed coffin,
finding need for its own rebellion,
heaving its liberation song with calculated force,
a ritual guided,
pulled forward through a slight crack
like beacon barely sighted over a stormy sea,
like the tender promise of a lover's kiss
after annihilation in the war of loneliness,
stretching out slowly,
limb after untrained limb,
emerging through its birth canal,
disoriented and dizzy,
unfolding one fan wing, then another,
to dry, visible and free over the fields,
revealing qualities of the prismatic universe
that powers it to flight,
to feast in the eternal garden,
empowered by itself
with beauty blazing mantle adorning its back,
head crowned luminous,
blessed by the eccentric wind,
blowing magnetically towards the midday sky,

receiving its final gift:
a left-sided wing,
invisible, perfumed,
trailing a direct spiral into heaven.

Pablo Medina

(b. 1948)
Cuban American

Pablo Medina was born in Havana and emigrated to the United States in 1960. After graduating from high school in Washington, D.C., he received undergraduate and graduate degrees from Georgetown University. Medina then embarked on a successful career as a writer, performance poet, translator, and creative writing teacher. He currently teaches in the master of fine arts writing program at Warren Wilson College in North Carolina. His books include **Pork Rind and Cuban Songs** *(1975) and* **Arching into the Afterlife** *(1991). His collection of personal essays,* **Exiled Memories: A Cuban Childhood,** *was published by the University of Texas Press in 1991. With Carolina Hospital, Medina published translations of the dissident poetry of Tania Díaz Castro in* **Everyone Will Have to Listen** *(1990). In 1976 Medina won the William Carlos Williams Poetry Award.*

Madame America

1. *Privy*

Midnight he entered
the dream shore where oceans pounded
and fish puckered for the kiss of maidens.

Midnight and his bladder sang.
Finished, too
tired to revel in relief,
he pushed the lever, saw Hades' mouth
fill quicker than it could swallow,
dribble over icy lips
down stony chin to toes:
islands, minnows in tidal waste,
stunned amphibians.

2. *Poker*

She lay on a crimson recliner
languorous, fully dressed. Her caftan
swelled with every breath. The candle
flickered and he thought of Jewish Alps,

Shoshone burial mounds ...
Outside hyacinths were blooming,
peonies were up.

His last card was the ace of clubs.
Her white feet arched, the night
was hers. She wagered all: her clothes,
the fillets on her hair, her crescent
custom pin. He stiffened. She yawned.
The room was still. A scent of lilac
and musk tarnished the air.
"Do you call me or raise?"
She mocked his scant mannering.

When the moon broke
and the eel's fast ended she showed her hand.

Landscape, bare yourself!

3. *Spanish Lesson*

"Ven"[1] he said, accented
but impervious, "Dame lo que das."[2]

Water she,
sluicing water,
sent him headlong to despair
where he wallowed till he woke.
She went home
with wallet and watch.
Day's work for day's wages.

Joseph the last of his names
he made his choice:
clean teeth and the radiance of failure.
"Death will wear me smiling."

---

1.   Come
2.   Give me what you give.

4. *Next-to-Last Supper*

He cooked horizons.
Star tongues slapped
the roof of night.

He lived insouciant to the end
and listened to the neighbor's dogs
yelping at the heels of time.

The pan of his thought lay idle,
lard of memory popping,
insomnia the flame.

The breeze was tar, the evening
on its steel bed sighed
for the mothers of dawn.

He closed his eyes and his hunger died
and he sank to where the fish sleep
and the earth cries.

5. *Deluge*

Under the pillow was sand,
splinters from an ancient tree.
centuries of syntax,
syllables of land, pruned mind,
heart in brine.

Words fell apart
turned Babel babe hell
tongue slither grunt
Calliope.

The angels of Freedom
gathered pieces with the up
side down
and let the punctuation loose

touch me
rub my knee
one
last
blessed
time

Après moi[3]

The Apostate

To breathe fire
in this land is a conspiracy
of wrong.

The moon outside
wanes over yellowing fields.

Only the teeth of barking dogs
give light.
There is coffee
and phones ringing
and funereal smoke.

Na na, na na sings a girl
on the road into autumn.
She stops, she turns, she goes.

Far away behind the hills—
birth, red earth.

Behind that
God's face receding.

The land is full of innocence
and comfortable slumber.

---

3.   French: After me

Na na, na na.
Few birds remain. The grass
is dying. The earth turns hard.

The Beginning

I don't know the name
where all this started:
a gathering of stone and jagged peaks,
silence like mist disguising distance.
I came to it thinking I could make my fire
glow off the moon.
There were myths, dragons' teeth,
the shadows of mute crows.
Then I tasted rose in my throat,
murmur of a growing rust.
I saw a child walking away
through mountains. I thought
he turned but it could have been
my need contriving or someone
who told me years later he must have.
I remember the planks of the world
dropping and the rain seeping
down roots to the dark bone.

Victor Hernández Cruz

(b. 1949)
Puerto Rican

Victor Hernández Cruz is the Nuyorican poet most recognized and acclaimed by mainstream literary critics. Born on February 6, 1949, in Aguas Buenas, Puerto Rico, he moved with his family to New York's Spanish Harlem at the age of five. Cruz attended Benjamin Franklin High School, where he began writing poetry. In the years following graduation, his poetry began to appear in Evergreen Review, New York Review of Books, Ramparts, Down Here, and in small magazines. In 1973 Cruz left New York and took up residence in San Francisco, where he worked for the U.S. Postal Service. Since 1989 he has lived in Puerto Rico.

Victor Hernández Cruz's poetry books include **Papo Got His Gun** *(1966)*, **Snaps** *(1969)*, **Mainland** *(1973)*, **Tropicalization** *(1976)*, **By Lingual Wholes** *(1982)*, **Rhythm, Content and Flavor** *(1989)*, and **Red Beans** *(1991)*. Classifying his poetry as Afro-Latin, Cruz has developed as a consummate bilingual poet and experimenter who consistently explores the relationship of music to poetry in a multiracial, multicultural context. Cruz has often been considered to be a jazz poet, an African American poet, and, according to the April 1981 issue of Life magazine, among a handful of outstanding American poets.

today is a day of great joy

when they stop poems
in the mail & clap
their hands & dance to
them

when women become pregnant
by the side of poems
the strongest sounds making
the river go along

it is a great day

as poems fall down to
movie crowds in restaurants
in bars

when poems start to
knock down walls to

choke politicians
when poems scream &
begin to break the air

that is the time of
true poets that is
the time of greatness

a true poet aiming
poems & watching things
fall to the ground

it is a great day

energy

is
red beans
ray barretto[1]
banging away
steam out the
radio
the five-stair
steps
is mofongo[2]
cuchifrito[3] stand
outside down
the avenue
that long hill
of a block
before the train
is pacheco[4]
playing with
bleeding
blue lips

---

1. salsa music band leader
2. mashed, fried plantains with pork rinds and garlic
3. stewed chitterlings, Puerto Rican style
4. Johnny Pacheco, a salsa music band leader

The Latest Latin Dance Craze

First
Your throw your head back twice
Jump out onto the floor like a
Kangaroo
Circle the floor once
Doing fast scissor works with your
Legs
Next
Dash towards the door
Walking in a double cha cha cha
Open the door and glide down
The stairs like a swan
Hit the street
Run at least ten blocks
Come back in through the same
Door
Doing a mambo-minuet
Being careful that you don't fall
And break your head on that one
You have just completed your first
Step.

Loisaida

To the memory of the original Nuyorican Poets Cafe on Sixth Street—To Miguel Piñero who lived it—To Tato Laviera who sings it—To Miguel Algarín who knows it—To Chela, Flicha, Papote Maggy and Cari my cousin named after Caridad del Cobre and all the Saints that got me through in safety.

By the East River
of Manhattan island
Where once the Iroquois
Canoed in style
Now the jumping
Stretch of Avenue D
housing projects

Where
Rican / Blacks
Johnny Pacheco / Wilson Pickett
Transistor
the radio night
Across the Domino sugar
sign
Red Neon on stage
It's the edge of Brooklyn

From heaven windows
megalopolis light
That's the picture
Into a lizard mind
Below the working
class jumps like frogs
Parrots with new raincoats
Swinging canes of bamboo
Like third legs
Strollers of cool flow
A didy-bop keeping step
time with the finest
Marching through
Red Bricks aglow
Hebrew prayers
inside metals
Rolled into walls
Tenement relic
living in Museum
Home driven carts
arrive with the morning
slicing through the
curtains
Along with a Polish
English
Barking peaches and melons
The ice man sells
his hard water

Cut into blocks
Buildings swallowing
coals through their
Basement mouth

Where did the mountains
go
The immigrants ask
The place where houses
and objects went back
in history and entered
The roots of plants
And became eternal again
Now the plaster of Paris
The ears of the walls
The first utterances
in Spanish
Recalled what was left
behind

People kept arriving
as the cane fields dried
They came like flying bushes
from another planet
which had pineapples for moons
Fruits popping out of luggage
The singers of lament
into the soul of Jacob Riis
The Bible tongues
Santa Maria
Into the Torah
La liturgical lai le lo le
A Spanish never seen
before
Inside the gypsies
Parading through
Warsaw ghetto
Lower East Side

Rabbinicals
Begin to vanish
into the economy
Left Loisaida
a skeleton
The works quarter

Orchard Street
garments
Falling off the torso
in motion down the avenue
It seems it could not hold
the cold back

The red Avenue B bus
disappearing down
The drain of Man
Hat on
Dissolving into the
pipes of lower Broadway
The Canals of streets
direct to the factories

After Foresite Park
Is the begining of Italy
Florence inside Mott
Street windows
Palmero eyes of Angie
Criss crossing these
mazes I would arrive
At Lourde's home
With knishes she threw
next to red beans

Broome Street Hasidics[1]
with Martian fur hats
Gone with their brims

---

1.   Orthodox Jewish sect

Puerto Ricans with Pra[2]
Pras
Atop faces with features
thrown out of some bag
Of universal racial
stew
Mississippi sharecroppers
through Avenue D black
Stories
All in exile from broken
Souths
The amapolas[3] the daffodils
were cement tar and steel
Within architectural
gardens remembering
the agriculture of mountain
and field

From the guayava[4] bushels
outside a town with a
Taíno[5] name
I hear a whistle
In the aboriginal ear
With the ancient I
that was Andalucía[6]
Arrive on a boat
To distribute Moorish[7]
eyes on the coast
Loisaida[8] was faster
than the speed of light
A whirlpool within which
you had to grab on to some-
thing

2.   a type of hat
3.   poppies
4.   guava
5.   Caribbean Indian
6.   Andalusia, Southern Spain
7.   Arabs of North Africa
8.   Lower east side of New York City

It took off like a Spauldine
hit by a blue broomstick
on 12th street
Winter time summer time
seasons of hallways
And roofs
Between pachanga and duwap
Thousands of Eddies and Carmens
Stars and tyrants
Now gone
From the temporary station of
desire and disaster
The windows sucked them up
The pavement turned out to
be a mouth
Urban vanishment
Illusion
Henry Roth
Call it Sleep.

Evangelina Vigil-Piñón

(b. 1949)
Mexican American

Evangelina Vigil-Piñón was born in San Antonio, Texas, and raised by a poor family; she spent part of her youth with her maternal grandmother living in public housing. She inherited her love of music and oral tradition from her shoe repairman father, who played the guitar and sang, and her love of reading from her mother. Vigil-Piñón is possibly the greatest Mexican American poet of barrio life. Her numerous poems published in magazines during the 1970s and her first book, **Thirty 'an Seen a Lot** *(1982), winner of the American Book Award of the Before Columbus Foundation, freely interweave English and Spanish, capturing the sounds, music, and scenes from San Antonio's West Side in celebration of and respect for the common folk and their culture. Her second book,* **The Computer Is Down** *(1987), reveals her current life in Houston with high technology and steel and glass skyscrapers masking an underworld of folk culture and poverty. Vigil-Piñón is the Associate Editor of the* Americas Review, *the oldest and most respected Hispanic literary magazine. She is also the compiler of the first successful anthology of Hispanic women writers in the United States:* **Woman of Her Word: Hispanic Women Write** *(1983).*

¡es todo!

¡ay qué mujeres mexicanas![1]
with your skinny ankles and muscular chamarros[2]
in your flowered dresses o vestidos cuadrados[3]—
half-sizes
(pa' que queden bien de la cintura)[4]
and beige-tone panty hose
(oyes, huercas,[5]
¿se acuerdan de la ligas?)[6]

¡ay qué mujeres mexicanas![7]
con sus zapatos blancos de charol[8]
(para el tiempo de calor)[9]

---

1. Oh what Mexican women!
2. calves
3. checkered dresses
4. so they fit right at the waist
5. listen girls
6. Do you remember the elastic bands?
7. Oh what Mexican women!
8. with their white patent leather shoes
9. (for the hot season)

esperando el bos[10]
de Guadalupe [11] Prospect Hill
untándose un poquito
de perfume por aquí
o de makeup por acá[12]
followed by a quick last look
through the Suntone compact mirror
followed by a skillful flip
of an Avon golden bullet
three quick scarlet dashes
coloring the waiting lips:
half-heart right
half-heart left
lower lip half-kiss
followed by el beso al revés[13]
glance at the watch
one quick final look around—
ahí viene el bos[14]
ies todo![15]

iay qué mujeres mexicanas![16]

---

10. waiting for the bus
11. for Guadalupe
12. putting some perfume on here or some makeup there
13. the reverse kiss
14. here comes the bus
15. that's all
16. Oh what Mexican women!

Tato Laviera

(b. 1950)
Puerto Rican

Jesús Abraham "Tato" Laviera is the best-selling Hispanic poet in the United States and he bears the distinction of still having all of his books in print. Born in Santurce, Puerto Rico, on September 5, 1950, he migrated to New York at the age of ten with his family, which settled in a poor area of the Lower East Side. After finding himself in an alien society and with practically no English skills, Laviera was able to adjust and eventually graduated from high school as an honors student. Despite having no other degrees, his intelligence, aggressiveness, and thorough knowledge of his community led to a career in the administration of social service agencies. After the publication of his first book, **La Carreta Made a U-Turn** *(1979), Laviera gave up administrative work to dedicate his time to writing. Since 1980 Laviera's career has included not only writing but touring nationally as a performer of his poetry, directing plays, and producing cultural events. In 1980 he was received by President Jimmy Carter at the White House gathering of American poets. In 1981 his second book,* **Enclave,** *was the recipient of the American Book Award of the Before Columbus Foundation.*

All of Tato Laviera's books have been well received by critics, most of whom place him within the context of Afro-Caribbean poetry and U.S. Hispanic bilingualism. **La Carreta Made a U-Turn** *is bilingual jazz and salsa poetry that presents the reader with a slice of life from the Puerto Rican community of the Lower East Side. In* **Enclave,** *Laviera celebrates cultural heroes, both real and imagined.* **AmeRícan** *(1986), published on the occasion of the centennial celebration of the Statue of Liberty, is a poetic reconsideration of immigrant life in New York City and the United States.* **Mainstream Ethics** *(1988) proposes transforming the United States from a Eurocentric culture to one that is ethnically and racially pluralistic in its official identity. Laviera's written and published poems have been created out of a process that attempts to re-create as much as possible the oral performance in a living epic of Hispanic people. For Laviera, part of that oral tradition and performance are the structures, spirit, and rhythms of popular and folk music, especially those drawn from Afro–Puerto Rican music.*

latero story (can pickers)

i am a twentieth century welfare recipient
moonlighting in the sun as a latero
a job invented by national and state laws
designed to re-cycle aluminum cans
to return to consumer acid laden
gastric inflammation pituitary glands
coca diet rite low cal godsons

---

* a latero is a collection of aluminum cans

of artificially flavored malignant
indigestions somewhere down the line
of a cancerous cell

i collect from garbage cans in outdoor facilities
congested with putrid residues
my hands shelving themselves
opening plastic bags never knowing
what to encounter

several times a day i touch evil rituals
slit throats of chickens
tongues of poisoned rats
salivating on my index finger
smells of month old rotten food
next to pamper's diarrhea
dry blood infectious diseases
hypodermic needles tissued with
heroine water drops pilfered in
slimy grease blood hazardous waste materials
but I cannot use rubber gloves
they undermine my daily profit

i am a twentieth century welfare recipient
moonlighting during the day as a latero
making it big in america
some day i might become experienced enough
to offer technical assistance
to other lateros
i am thinking of publishing
my own guide to latero collecting
and founding a latero's union to offer
medical dental benefits

i am a twentieth century welfare recipient
moonlighting at night as a latero
i am considered some kind of expert
at collecting cans during fifth avenue parades

i can now hire workers at twenty
five cents an hour guaranteed salary
and fifty per cent of two and one half cents
profit on each can collected
i am a twentieth century welfare recipient
moonlighting at midnight as a latero
i am becoming an entrepreneur
an american success story
i have hired bag ladies to keep peddlers
from my territories
i have read in some guide to success
that in order to get rich
to make it big
i have to sacrifice myself
moonlighting until dawn by digging
deeper into the extra can margin of profit
i am on my way up the opportunistic
ladder of success
in ten years i will quit welfare
to become a legitimate businessman
i'll soon become a latero executive
with corporate conglomorate intents
god bless america.

AmeRícan

we gave birth to a new generation,
AmeRícan, broader than lost gold
never touched, hidden inside the
puerto rican mountains.

we gave birth to a new generation,
AmeRícan, it includes everything
imaginable you-name-it-we-got-it
society.

we gave birth to a new generation,
AmeRícan salutes all folklores,

european, indian, black, spanish,
and anything else compatible:

AmeRícan, singing to composer pedro flores' palm
        trees high up in the universal sky!

AmeRícan, sweet soft spanish danzas gypsies
        moving lyrics la espanola cascabelling
        presence always singing at our side!

AmeRícan, beating jibaro modern troubadours[1]
        crying guitars romantic continental
        bolero[2] love songs!

AmeRícan, across forth and across back
        back across and forth back
        forth across and back and forth
        our trips are walking bridges!

        it all dissolved into itself, the attempt
        was truly made, the attempt was truly
        absorbed, digested, we spit out
        the poison, we spit out the malice,
        we stand, affirmative in action,
        to reproduce a broader answer to the
        marginality that gobbled us up abruptly!

AmeRícan, walking plena[3]-rhythms in new york,
        strutting beautifully alert, alive,
        many turning eyes wondering,
        admiring!

AmeRícan, defining myself my own way any way many
        ways Am e Rican, with the big R and the
        accent on the i!

---

1.   Puerto Rican mountain folk
2.   slow tropical dance
3.   an Afro—Puerto Rican dance

AmeRícan, like the soul gliding talk of gospel
          boogie music!

AmeRícan, speaking new words in spanglish tenements.
          fast tongue moving street corner "que
          corta"[4] talk being invented at the insistence
          of a smile!

AmeRícan, abounding inside so many ethnic english
          people, and out of humanity, we blend
          and mix all that is good!

AmeRícan, integrating in new york and defining our
          own destino,[5] our own way of life,

AmeRícan, defining the new america, humane america,
          admired america, loved america, harmonious
          america, the world in peace, our energies
          collectively invested to find other civili-
          zations, to touch God, further and further,
          to dwell in the spirit of divinity!

AmeRícan, yes, for now, for i love this, my second
          land, and i dream to take the accent from
          the altercation, and be proud to call
          myself AmeRícan, in the U.S. sense of the
          word, AmeRícan, America!

intellectual

so historically total
so minutely precise
so accurately detailed
so politically active
so grammatically arrogant
so academically prepared

---

4.   that cuts
5.   destiny

so literally perfect
so ethnically snobbish
so aristocratically professional
so if you want to challenge me,
be prepared to lose the argument,
for i am too humanly infallible
about my researched assertions,
so take it or leave it,
the latter is your wisest choice,
do not arouse my anger,
i will reduce you to a
bibliographical ibidem,
demoting you to childhood,
in other words,
come out to kill,
and be dead
from the start.

boricua*

we are a people
who love to love
we are loving
lovers who love
to love respect,
the best intentions
of friendship,
and we judge from
the moment on, no
matter who you are,
and, if we find
sincere smiles,
we can be friends,
and, if we have a
drink together,
we can be brothers,

---

* boricua is a Puerto Rican word referring to the Indian name of the Island

on the spot, no
matter who you are,
and we have a lot
of black & white
& yellow & red
people whom we
befriend, we're
ready to love
with you, that's
why we
say, let there
be no prejudice,
on race, color is
generally color-blind
with us, that's our
contribution, all
the colors are tied
to our one,
but we must fight
the bad intentions,
we must respect
each other's values,
but guess what,
we're not the only ones,
and we offer what your
love has taught us,
and what you're worth
in our self-respect,
we are a people
who love to love
who are loving
lovers who love
to love respect.

Gustavo Pérez-Firmat

(b. 1950)
Cuban American

Born on March 7, 1949, in Havana, Cuba, Pérez-Firmat received his bachelor's in English and master's in Spanish from the University of Miami in 1972 and 1973, respectively. He received his doctorate in comparative literature from the University of Michigan in 1979. Since 1979 he has been a professor in the Spanish Department at Duke University. Pérez-Firmat has created a dual career as a literary historian and critic and as a creative writer. His academic books include **Idle Fictions: The Hispanic Vanguard Novel, 1926–1934** *(1982)*, **Literature and Liminality: Festive Readings in the Hispanic Tradition** *(1986)*, **The Cuban Condition: Translation and Identity in Modern Cuban Literature** *(1989)*, and **The Cuban-American Way** *(1993)*. His creative books include two collections of his poems: **Triple Crown: Chicano, Puerto Rican and Cuban American Poetry** *(1987)* and **Equivocaciones** *(Mistakes, 1989)*. He is also the author of numerous articles and poems for journals and magazines.

Lime Cure

I'm filling my house with limes
to keep away the evil spirits.
I'm filling my house with limes
to help me cope.
I have limes on the counters, under the sink,
inside the wash basin.
My refrigerator is stuffed with limes
(there's no longer any space for meat and potatoes).
Faking onionship, they hang from the walls.
Like golf balls, they have the run of the carpet
(but I would not drive them away).

I stash them in flowerpots.
I put them on bookshelves.
I keep them on my desk, cuddling with my computer.
I have two limes in every drawer of every chest
of every room.
I don't bathe, I marinade.

At night, I think of their cores, plump and wet.
I imagine myself taking off the peel and squeezing

until they burst in my hands.
I taste the tart juice dripping on my tongue.
I shudder.
Then I sleep peacefully inside green dreams of lime
and when I wake, I bask in the morning's lime light.

Were it not for limes, I would not know
what to do with myself.
I could not bear this loneliness.
I would burst. But there is a wisdom in limes, an uneventfulness
that soothes my seething, and whispers to me:
think, be still, and think some more,
and when the night arrives, dream of juice.

On Whether My Father Deserves a Poem

I will never say
my father used to say.
My father never said
anything
(except dirty jokes
with each phone call).
Scratch idea for poem
with father's words.

My father did not teach
by example.
My father never acted
decisively
(he waffled and gambled
and lost).
So scratch idea for poem
with father's deeds.

Absent words and deeds
what's left me of my father
to write this orphan poem?

The Poet's Mother Gives Him a Birthday Present

Thirty masses is what I got
for my birthday. Thirty masses
and a bottle of Paco Rabanne.

Gustavo Pérez-Firmat
will share in the following
spiritual benefits for one year:
Thirty Masses
Two Novenas of Masses
Requested by Mrs. Gustavo Pérez
Signed: Father Edward,
Salesian Missions.

It must be I'm tottering on the brink.
It must be I'm in perilous condition.
It must be I'm losing my soul.
Surely these are critical masses.
Jump start my soul, ma.
Pile mass on mass till I stop fibrillating.
Drip cool hosannas into the IV.
Pump me with 42 cc's of saintliness,
one for each of my errant years.
Slip that catholic catheter into my prick
and bring my peccant prostate to its knees.
Have me break out in ejaculations, ma.

Do it.
Make me holy.
Put an end to this wanton life.
I shall sin no more.
And all for you, ma.
All for you.

May the joy of this your birthday
Continue all year through
And make each day that comes your way
A happy day for you!

Judith Ortiz Cofer

(b. 1952)
(See Judith Ortiz Cofer headnote in the Autobiography section.)

Quinceañera*

My dolls have been put away like dead
children in a chest I will carry
with me when I marry.
I reach under my skirt to feel
a satin slip bought for this day. It is soft
as the inside of my thighs. My hair
has been nailed back with my mother's
black hairpins to my skull. Her hands
stretched my eyes open as she twisted
braids into a tight circle at the nape
of my neck. I am to wash my own clothes
and sheets from this day on, as if
the fluids of my body were poison, as if
the little trickle of blood I believe
travels from my heart to the world were
shameful. Is not the blood of saints and
men in battle beautiful? Do Christ's hands
not bleed into your eyes from His cross?
At night I hear myself growing and wake
to find my hands drifting of their own will
to soothe skin stretched tight
over my bones.
I am wound like the guts of a clock,
waiting for each hour to release me.

Mamacita*

Mamacita hummed all day long
over the caboose kitchen

---

* Quinceañera is a fifteen-year-old's coming-out party.
* "Mamacita" means little mother

of our railroad flat.
From my room I'd hear her *humm,*
crossing her path, I'd catch her *umm.*
No words slowed the flow
of Mamacita's soulful sounds;
it was *humm* over the yellow rice,
and *umm* over the black beans.
Up and down two syllables she'd climb
and slide—each note a task accomplished.
From chore to chore, she was the prima donna
in her daily operetta.
Mamacita's wordless song was her connection
to the oversoul,
her link with life,
her mantra,
a lifeline to her own Laughing Buddha,
as she dragged her broom
across a lifetime of linoleum floors.

Exile

I left my home behind me
but my past clings to my fingers
so that every word I write hears
the mark like a cancelled postage stamp
of my birthplace.
There was no angel to warn me
of the dangers of looking back.
Like Lot's wife, I would trade
my living blood for one last look
at the house where each window held
a face framed as in a family album.
And the plaza lined with palms
where my friends and I strolled in our pink
and yellow and white Sunday dresses, dreaming
of husbands, houses, and orchards where
our children would play in the leisurely summer
of our future. Gladly would I spill

my remaining years like salt upon the ground,
to gaze again on the fishermen of the bay
dragging their catch in nets glittering
like pirate gold, to the shore.
Nothing remains of that world, I hear,
but the skeletons of houses, all colors
bled from the fabric of those
who stayed behind
inhabiting the dead cities
like the shadows of Hiroshima.

Under the Knife

My aunt wipes blood from her knife
across a kitchen towel, spilling
the thick contents of a just decapitated
hen into the sink.
I feel slightly nauseated but must
forbear for her sake. Childless
family martyr, renowned for her patience
with human frailty, and her cooking.
Her man drinks, she has failed three times
at childbearing. She squeezes the last
of the blood from the neck and a blue button
falls into her hand. Rinsing it, she drops it
into her apron pocket. And as she places the
pale carcass and the knife before me, she explains
how to cut the pieces with even, forceful
strokes: no hacking. She is under
no obligation to be kind.
The mothers and the daughters
have given her a lifetime license to mourn,
and like a queen in exile she acknowledges
nothing as a privilege. The pale fingers
of my aunt work with precision over
the pink flesh, showing me just how
to separate the tough from the tender.

Alberto Ríos

(b. 1952)
Mexican American

Alberto Alvaro Ríos was born in Nogales, Arizona, in 1952, to a Mexican American father and an English mother. Ríos earned a bachelor's degree and a master's degree in creative writing from the University of Arizona in 1975 and 1979, respectively. He has been a tenured associate professor of creative writing and director of the creative writing program at Arizona State University in Tempe since 1985. In 1989, he was promoted to full professor. Ríos is one of the major exponents of craft and style in Chicano poetry and short fiction. He is today one of the most respected poets in academic and creative writing circles, having won such prestigious awards as the Walt Whitman Award of the Academy of American Poets (1981), the Western States Book Award (1984), the Pushcart Prize IX (1989), the Mountain Plains Library Author of the Year Award (1991), and the Governor of Arizona Arts Award (1991). His books of poetry include **Whispering to Fool the Wind** *(1982) and* **The Lima Orchard Woman** *(1988). His prose fiction is represented by* **The Iguana Killer** *(1984) and* **Teodore Luna's Two Kisses** *(1990). In addition, Ríos' poetry has appeared in all of the major poetry reviews in the United States.*

Five Indiscretions

The Unfortunate Story of the Unmarried Flora Carrillo
And the Man Who Loved Her Before He Died his Famous Death,
From Whose Single Liaison a Daughter Was Born
And the Advice, Rather the Explanation,
Both of Them Left for Her, And the Story Also
Of What She Became, and That She Was Happy

1
Three did not count.
A fourth was forgiven by the Father Torres
In exchange for reasonable payment,
Two full days of Hail Mary.
Bigger than priests, the fifth
Indiscretion was born on a Thursday, early
Evening in a November not too cold.
No rain had fallen
And the birds had not yet gone.
She chose a black dress, this Flora, Florita

+ here evoke the names of saints +

Underneath which she carried tonight
An old blade, but of fine Toledo forging
Long as the member of this man
In love with this woman standing at his door.
Her head was filled with the vines of the jungle
The noises of a lion, the feel of ten birds
Trying with their beaks to get out.
All anger: that she had hoped he would
Come to her bedroom.
And that he had.
Faster than that she took from him his rolled tongue
Hanging there between his thin legs, his two-fingers,
This girl's wrist and fist of his
Its central tendon and skin that moved on itself,
This small and second body of his
Which had found its way to her second mouth,
This part of himself which he had given her
Then taken back on this same day, earlier
His ugly afternoon of loving her too much.
He would scream as she had
When she had taken him in first as a leg-bone
And held him there too long, too much
Until he had become a pinky-finger

+ here evoke the holy names +

Which she took now and put in the dowry
She would make for her new daughter.
With it she would write a note,

Nothing else was left to do:
   Daughter, you will be an only child.
   The story of your birth will smell on you.
   Do this: take baths filled with rosemary
   With leaves, with pinched orange peels.

Keep secret the fact of yourself
Be happy enough, happy with this much life.
Ask for nothing. Do not live for a long time.

2
He sang to her the oldest song
That he was a piccolo flute in the small of her heart
Or, if that were not convincing, too much filled with flowers,
A small noise, then, a smart, a cut which is healing
Its face feeling good to be scratched
The way even wild cats like;
A piccolo flute in the small of her heart
Nothing more, and nothing more necessary
A noise different from all the rest
Louder and more shrill, a good sound of haunting
The voice of a Muslim caller at dawn
A bird, a Saturday, four directions and a need.
He sang this and did not sing
In that manner of speech afforded the heart:
That he was a man
Came to her not from any words, not like that
    But from the measure of his breathing
    From the five-ladder depth of his left eye
    The one that did not move, his one eye which
    While his right eye could move through the every day
    Could only stay looking at her.
When she looked at this eye at first
The sight of it made a noise in her, a start,
A note somewhere at the top of the piano scales
Fear, almost; a grasped breath; a glass dropped.
In the moment was the music of being wanted.
    Or of wanting, but she could not think it.
Certainly she could only say no
The way anyone would after a glass falls
No and Jesus. And as an afterthought, that he should go away.
    Many years later she read a book and it took
    Her breath: how neatly the glasses for champagne
    Thrown by the fine heroes

Broke against the walls holding fire.
That this was a celebration.
That this was the continental, the European.
No, she said, to this thick railroad tie of a man
Who sang to her the oldest song, the one
Of being young, that he was a piccolo flute
In the small of her heart. No
She said, but said it with her mouth, not with her heart
Making no a spoken word, like all other words
So that he did not hear, so that he kept singing
Until one day it was enough, but not for her, not now:
Now, instead, the afternoon, which was kind
Which is what she was earlier, had only pretended for him
I am her, whispered it to him, let him be strong
In its arms one more time before it took him,
Holding tighter than a grandmother.
     This was not at all what he wanted
     But what he wanted he could not have,
     No, she said, and he could not get close enough
     Could not put the ear of his song heart
     Against her chest
     To know what the word meant, no.

3
He had written no note for his daughter.
It had not been necessary.
She knew now what it would have been,
What the word no means
When it is pronounced, when the last half of it lingers, o
Imagined that the o was like this
     Together as if it were now nude in the afternoon
     They must have danced the wild Apache
     Without lunch, into the hours
     Imagining themselves French, striped shirt and berets
     Two carp on a rug in the ocean of the room
     Two june beetles, two bees
     Beings with impossible wings, pulleys from the roof

Pulling the two of them up like birthday piñatas[1]
Two of them, then four: hands and legs
Tied more expertly than the best dreams of an old salt sailor
Bread dough wound round and again into afternoon cakes,
Two, four, then six of them: all the parts of the face
Then twelve of them: their two faces together
Twenty-four then and thirty-six and words and breaths
Inside each other their tongues
Like the wings of hummingbirds in flight
Like bees, his fingers, faster than possible
That it was like this exactly.

4

Her fame was as a maker of oval mats many years later
Mats for placement behind photographs,
How the old ones were, sometimes in colors
Sometimes to highlight, sometimes for support simply,
Always making the best faces.
But what she loved most, what was true for her
Was her firm putting of the tongues and most heavy parts
Of several men of the town, each on a different night
Sundays being specially reserved for the troubled boy
On a rancho several kilometers out of town,
Putting them slowly into her mouth, this best of all
And sucking there at them better
Than if she were drawing out the juice of an orange
Small hole made in it, the way children do
Squeezing out the everything.
It was, better described, this *deliverance* of her men
This taking out from their baby-arms
What it was that troubled them
So much all at once, so much like the stories
She had heard of the ghost being delivered,
Being let go, from the mouth
Exactly at the point of death.
She would trade nothing for this
For being able to say yes where others had said no.

---

1.   a decorated gourd filled with party favors and candy

To say yes, and watch her men die.
Die and then be brought back, to be strong at this
This was her power, this is what made her laugh
Being happy for them all
Never once making love to a man.

On January 5, 1984,
El Santo the Wrestler Died, Possibly

The thing was, he could never be trusted.
He wore the silver mask even when he slept.
At his funeral as reported by all the Mexican news services
The pall bearers also put on their faces
Sequined masks to honor him, or so it was said.
The men in truth wore masks as much to hide from him
That he would not see who was putting him into the ground
And so get angry, get up, and come back after them
That way for which he was famous.
His partner el atomico pretended to think
There was no funeral at all.
He would have had to help el santo be angry
Come like the Samson running against the pillars
These men were, holding up the box
In which el santo was trapped;
Would have had to angle his head down, come at them
Mount them three men to a shoulder
As he ran through the middle, ducking under the casket
Bowling them down like all the other times
Giving el santo just a moment to breathe, get strong.

He will be missed
But one must say this in a whisper, and quickly.
One knows of the dead, of their polite habit of listening
Too much, believing what they hear, and then of their caring.
One knows of the dead, how it all builds up
So that finally something must be said.
One knows of the year in which the town of Guaymas
Had its first demonstration of a tape recorder.

It confirmed only what was already known:
That people speak. And that the voice of the wind
Captured finally, played back slowly
Given its moment to say something of lasting importance
Made only a complaint.
If el santo were to hear of his being missed
He might get hold of the wind, this voice of the dead,
And say too much, the way the best wrestlers do
With all the yelling.
So one will always be responsible enough only to whisper
The best things about el santo
Out of concern for the crops and the sapling trees.
This much was decided at the funeral.

The decision to whisper was not too much.
One had to be suspicious of this man with a mask
Even as he reached out to shake your hand,
That you might be flung and bent around
Knocked on the head and forced to say
How glad you are to meet him, and his uncle:
How suspicious that hand, which he always raised
More slowly than a weightlifter's last possible push
As if he too were suspicious of you
That you might at the last second
Be the Blue Demon after all—*el demonio azul: iaha!*[1]
He recognizes you, *but too late!* that you might
In this last moment avoid his hand raised to shake
Hook the crook of your arm into his
And flip him with a slam to a cement canvas.
No, he could not be trusted
And he could not trust you.

In his last years very far from 1942
The year he gave his first bruise to another man
One received as a greeting no hand from him any longer.
A raised eyebrow, perhaps, *good morning to you,* Just visible
    through the mask on his morning walk.

---

1.   the blue devil, Aha!

This was his greeting, one man to another, now.
But even then he could not be trusted
Had not slipped with age even an inch:
As he moved the hairy arm of his brow up and down
Like a villain taking possession of the widow's house,
If one quickly did not get out of his way—
Well, then, he kept it moving up and down, had gotten you
Had made you imagine his eyebrow like that
Making the sound of a referee's hand
Slam beating the canvas ten times
Telling you that you have lost.

Jimmy Santiago Baca

(b. 1952)
Mexican American

Of Chicano and Apache descent, Jimmy Santiago Baca was born in New Mexico and raised by a grandfather after his parents had abandoned him; by age five both his parents were dead and Baca was taken in by an orphanage. At age eleven, he escaped the institution and began living on the streets, which eventually led him to a life of crime, for which he paid dearly with incarceration. In a maximum security prison Jimmy Santiago Baca taught himself to read and write, earned his GED and became interested in creating literature. Baca is known for the autobiographical content in his narrative poetry and for his sweeping Whitmanesque breadth and deep human values. With the assistance of the well-established poet, Denise Levertov, Baca was able to make the bridge from the Chicano literary movement to more mainstream venues and to see his latest two books published by the venerable New Directions publishing house. Baca's books include **Immigrants in Our Own Land: Poems** *(1979),* **Swords of Darkness** *(1981),* **What's Happening** *(1982),* **Martín and Meditations on the South Valley** *(1987), and* **Black Mesa Poems** *(1989). In 1988 Baca was awarded the American Book Award of the Before Columbus Foundation for* **Martín and Meditations on the South Valley.**

Martín III

Driving across the country
I thought back to my boyhood.
Those I'd known in New Mexico
came back to me again.

In Arkansas, on a fallen oak trunk,
half its limbs in the pond,
sat old one-armed Pepin.
"Martín, your father and I
were in the El Fidel cantina
with unas viejas[1] one afternoon.
Tú sabes, nos pusimos bien chatos.[2]
And then Sheri, your mama, walks in.
I don't remember what she asked Danny,
but la vieja that was with your father said,
I thought your wife was a cripple.

---

1. some girls
2. you know, we got smashed

Sheri started crying and sin una palabra,[3]
she turned and went out."

In September Estella Gómez appeared.
She stood mid-air in a gust of wind,
blind, dressed in black and with a religious voice, said,
"92 years, m'ijito. ¿Que pasó?[4] There was no more
beans to pick, no beans to load
on trains. Pinos Wells dried up, como mis manos.[5]
Everyone moved away to work.
I went to Estancia, con mi hijo,[6] Refugio.
Gavachos de Tejas,[7] we worked for them. Loading
alfalfa, picking cotton for fifty cents a row.
¿Y Danny? La borrachera. ¿Y Sheri? La envidia.[8]
That's what happened, Martín, to your familia."

In Ohio, December 14th, great pines
crackled icicles to the forest floor,
jarring the air with explosions of sparkling flakes.
Wrapped in my serape, snow up to my knees,
at a bend in a dirt road.
When I reached the bend, Antonia Sánchez,
La Bruja de Torreón,[9] said to me,
"¿Dónde está tu mama?[10] Safe from that madman.
Se casó otra vez y tiene dos niños.[11]
No, no te puedo decir dónde viven."[12]

Four or five months later I moved
to North Carolina
in a red brick house at the edge of Piedmont Woods.

---

3. without a word
4. my son, what happened?
5. like my hands
6. with my son
7. Anglos from Texas
8. And Danny? The drunkeness? And Sheri? The envy.
9. The witch from Torreón
10. Where is your mother?
11. She got married again and has two children
12. I can't say where they live.

Narrow red mud roads marked with tractor treads,
sultry air droning with insects and steamy
with harvest crops—
day after day in green dark shade I walked,
bending under briar riggings, my pole
with a blue rubber worm bait
dangling from 30 pound line, down deer trails,
skipping creek rocks, climbing over sagging
barbwire fences, until I found a secluded pond,
shores choked with bullrush I thrashed down,
as I tossed my line out into the sunset burning water,
big-mouth bass puckered, sending water rings
rippling through towering pines leaning over the water.
I fished until I could no longer see my bait
plop, until the far shore disappeared and the moon
bobbed in the black water
like a candle flame in a window against the night darkness.

One evening as I walked back
up a hill to the house,
I could hear all their voices
drifting through the trees—
I said aloud to myself
and the memories they lived in,
I am leaving in the morning.

Passing back through Tennessee
on the way to Albuquerque,
deep down a mountain dirt road bend,
walking barefoot on pebbles,
I see a woman talking with two men,
in the dark silence of the forest,
Señora Martinez walked toward me,
wavering like smoke in the cold air,
"Sheri was scared to go home for her purse.
So she sent me. Dios mio,[13]
I'll never forget that day, mijo.[14]

---

13. my God,
14. my son

When I opened the closet door, there was Danny,
standing with a butcher knife raised high,
ready to kill."

April in Tennessee
Merlinda Griego appeared to me—she sat
on a rock, skirt raised to her knees, her bare toes
playing with petals floating in the creek.
"You cried a lot, Martín. Dios mío cómo llorabas.[15]
A veces your jefito[16] brought you to Las Flores Cantina
where I worked. He came to see me. You played on the floor
with empty whiskey bottles.
One day I was at El Parke, sitting like now, on a rock, my
feet in the water.
Your mother came up to me and started yelling
that I gave you mal de ojo,[17] and she dipped you
in the freezing water. I thought she was going to drown you
because of Danny seeing me. Quién sabe, m'ijo,[18]
all I remember is that she was jealous."

A week after I saw Merlinda, I was looking
through an old tobacco barn in a field.
In a corner with moldy gunney sacks
and rusting field tools, peeling an apple with his knife,
Pancho Garza sat, the retired manager of Piggly Wiggly
in Santa Fe.
"I gave her bruised fruit, old bread
and pastries. Once a week I gave her a sack of flour.
Danny drank up her pay check,
so I let her have a few things.
Besides she was a good checker."

It was June in Virginia.
One evening walking through the woods

15. God how you cried.
16. sometimes your father
17. the evil eye
18. Who knows, my son.

I could see someone waiting for me
her infant straddling her hip.
I thought of my boyhood in the South Valley
where women took summer evening walks,
their children fluttering like rose leaves
at their skirts.

Through the Texas panhandle
I remembered Estancia
where harvest dust smolders and insects whiff
empty crates and vegetable boxes
stacked against the produce stands.
Transparent wings of bees
wedge board bins, cracks sticky with chili mash.
Gorged flies buzz in tin pails and paper sacks
dropped on the sawdusted earthen floor,
their feet glazed with potato guck. And parked alongside
the stands at evening, rugged eight wheelers
simmer hot rubber and grease odors, their side board racks
oozing with crushed fruits.

Finally driving over the Sandía Mountains,
on the outskirts of Albuquerque,
I thought of you, mother—long ago
your departure uprooted me,
checked the green growing day,
hollowed out the core of my childhood—
whittled down
to keep me
in your rib crib
clothed in webs—
a doll in a cradle
in a barn loft in Willard.

Your absence
is a small burned area in my memory,
where I was cleared away
like prairie grass,

my identity smoldering under the blue sand of my soul—
my appearance dimmed to smoke,
in the glowing light somewhere
beyond your house each dusk.

Night now as I come into Albuquerque,
moon's rusty rings pass through one another
around me—
broken chain of events
decaying in black sand and ash
of the empty dark past
I dig through.

An embering stick
I call the past,
my dream of a mother existed in,
I breathed on to keep light
from extinguishing
like a star at dawn.
I come to inspect the old world,
those green years burned silvery with time,
by silence in the mind.

Lorna Dee Cervantes

(b. 1954)
Mexican American

Of Mexican and Native American ancestry, Lorna Dee Cervantes was born into a very poor family but she discovered the world of books at an early age. Born on August 6, 1954, Lorna began writing poetry when she was six years old; poems written when she was fourteen were eventually published in a magazine after Cervantes had established her career as a writer. In 1990 she obtained a doctorate from the University of California at Santa Cruz, where she studied philosophy and aesthetics. She then went on to teach creative writing at the University of Colorado in Denver.

Emplumada *(1981,* Plumed), *Cervantes's first collection of poems, is made up of works published in literary magazines throughout the Southwest. The book's popularity has made it a best-selling title in the University of Pittsburgh's prestigious poetry series.* **Emplumada** *as a whole presents a young woman coming of age, discovering the gap that exists in life between one's hopes and desires and what life eventually offers in reality. The predominant themes include culture conflict, the oppression of women and minorities, and alienation from one's roots. Cervantes's poetry is very well crafted and has the distinction of using highly lyrical language while at the same time being direct and powerful. Her second book,* **From the Cables of Genocide,** *is very much the work of a mature poet dealing with the great themes of life, death, social conflict, and poverty; it has won two awards: the Latin American Writers' Institute Award and the Paterson Poetry Prize.*

Refugee Ship

like wet cornstarch
I slide past *mi abuelita's*[1] eyes
bible placed by her side
she removes her glasses
the pudding thickens

mamá raised me with no language
I am an orphan to my spanish name
the words are foreign, stumbling on my tongue
I stare at my reflection in the mirror
brown skin, black hair

I feel I am a captive
aboard the refugee ship

---

1.   my grandmother

a ship that will never dock
a ship that will never dock

Heritage

Heritage
I look for you all day in the streets of Oaxaca.
The children run to me, laughing,
spinning me blind and silly.
They call to me in words of another language.
My brown body searches the streets
for the dye that will color my thoughts.

But Mexico gags
"ESPUTA"[1]
on this bland pochaseed.

I didn't ask to be brought up tonta!
My name hangs about me like a loose tooth.
Old women know my secret,
"Es la culpa de los antepasados"
Blame it on the old ones.
They give me a name
that fights me.

The Poet Is Served Her Papers

So tell me about fever dreams,
about the bad checks we scrawl
with our mouths, about destiny
missing last bus to oblivion.

I want to tell lies
to the world and believe it.
Speaks easy, speaks spoken to,
speak lips opening on a bed of nails.

---

1.   She's a whore

Hear the creaking of cardboard
in these telling shoes?
The mint of my mind
gaping far out of style?

Hear the milling of angels
on the head of a flea?
My broke blood is sorrel, is a lone
mare, is cashing in her buffalo chips.

As we come to the cul-de-sac
of our heart's slow division
tell me again about true
love's bouquet, paint hummingbird

hearts taped to my page.
Sign me over with XXXs
and *passion*. Seal on the lick
of a phone, my life. And pay.

And pay. And pay.

Pleiades from the Cables of Genocide

for my grandmother and against the budgets of '89

Tonight I view seven sisters
As I've never seen them before, brilliant
In their dumb beauty, pockmarked
In the vacant lot of no end winter
Blight. Seven sisters, as they were before,
Naked in a shroud of white linen, scented angels
Of the barrio, hanging around for another smoke,
A breath of what comes next, the aborted nest.
I'll drink to that, says my mother within. Her mother
Scattered tales of legendary ways when earth
Was a child and satellites were a thing of the
Heart. Maybe I could tell her this. I saw them

Tonight, seven Hail Marys, unstringing:
viewed Saturn
Through a singular telescope. Oh wonder
Of pillaged swans! oh breathless geometry
Of setting! You are radiant in your black light
Height, humming as you are in my memory.
Nights as inked as these, breathless
From something that comes from nothing.
Cold hearts, warm hands in your scuffed
Up pockets. I know the shoes those ladies wear,
Only one pair, and pointedly out of fashion
And flared-ass breaking at the toes, at the point
Of despair. Those dog gone shoes. No repair
For those hearts and angles, minus of meals, that
Flap through the seasons, best in summer, smelling
Of sneakers and coconuts, armpits steaming
With the load of the lording boys who garnish
Their quarters: the gun on every corner,
A chamber of laughter as the skag
Appears—glossed, sky white and sunset
Blush, an incandescence giving out, giving up
On their tests, on their grades, on their sky
Blue books, on the good of what's right. A star,
A lucky number that fails all, fails math, fails
Street smarts, dumb gym class, fails to jump
Through the broken hoop, and the ring
Of their lives wounds the neck not their
Arterial finger. Seven sisters, I knew them
Well. I remember the only constellation
My grandmother could point out with the punch
Of a heart. My grandma's amber stone
Of a face uplifts to the clarity of an eaglet's
Eye—or the vision of an aguila[1]
Whose mate has succumbed, and she uplifts
Into heaven, into their stolen hemispheres.
It is true.
When she surrenders he will linger by her leaving,

---

1. eagle

Bringing bits of food in switchblade talons, mice
For the Constitution, fresh squirrel for her wings
The length of a mortal. He will die there, beside
Her, belonging, nudging the body into the snowed
Eternal tide of his hunger. Hunters will find them
Thus, huddled under their blankets of aspen
Leaves. Extinct. And if she lives who knows what
Eye can see her paused between the ages and forgotten
Stories of old ways and the new way
Of ripping apart. They are huddled, ever squaring
With the division of destiny. You can find them
In the stars, with a match, a flaring of failure,
That spark in the heart that goes out with impression,
That thumb at the swallow's restless beating.
And you will look up, really to give up, ready
To sail through your own departure. I know.
My grandmother told me, countless times, it was all
She knew to recite to her daughter of daughters,
Her Persephone of the pen.
The Seven Sisters
Would smoke in the sky in their silly shoes
And endless waiting around doing nothing,
Nothing to do but scuff up the Big Bang with salt
And recite strange stories of epiphanies of light,
Claim canons, cannons and horses, and the strange
Men in their boots in patterns of Nazis and Negroes.
I count them now in the sky on my abacus of spun duck
Lineage, a poison gas. There, I remind me, is the nation
Of peace: seven exiles with their deed of trust
Signed over through gunfire of attorney.
She rides
Now through the Reagan Ranch her mothers owned.
I know this—we go back to what we have loved
And lost. She lingers, riding in her pied pinto gauchos,
In her hat of many colors and her spurs, her silver
Spurs. She does not kick the horse. She goes
Wherever it wants. It guides her to places where
The angry never eat, where birds are spirits

Of dead returned for another plot or the crumb
Of knowledge, that haven of the never to get.
And she is forever looking to the bare innocence
Of sky, remembering, dead now, hammered as she is
Into her grave of stolen home. She is singing
The stories of Calafia[2] ways and means, of the nacre
Of extinct oysters and the abalone I engrave
With her leftover files. She knows the words
To the song now, what her grandmother sang
Of how they lit to this earth from the fire
Of fusion, on the touchstones of love tribes. *Mira,*[3]
She said, *This is where you come from.* The power peace
Of worthless sky that unfolds me—now—in its greedy
Reading: Weeder of Wreckage, Historian of the Native
Who says: *It happened. That's all. It just happened.*
And runs on.

---

2.   an Amazon queen in a chivalrous romance—from when California got its name
3.   Look

The Chumash who inhabited the Santa Barbara coast may have believed that they
descended to earth from the Pleiades, also known as The Seven Sisters.
The Seven Sisters also refers to the seven big oil companies.

Martín Espada

(b. 1957)
Puerto Rican

Martín Espada was born and raised in Brooklyn, New York. He received a bachelor's in history from the University of Wisconsin and a law degree from Northeastern University in Boston, where he has resided since becoming a lawyer. Espada began writing poetry at an early age and has published his works in numerous magazines and anthologies. He is the author of two books: **The Immigrant Iceboy's Bolero** *(1982) and* **Trumpets from the Islands of their Eviction** *(1987). Espada's poetry has often been recited or displayed and published with his father's (Frank Espada's) photography. They have both been concerned with documenting and commenting on the political and social conditions of Puerto Ricans in industrial and urban settings in the United States. Robert Creeley has written that "Martín Espada is a poet of great communal power and he is also, with equal resource, the voice of intensive isolation." Espada has won recognition from the National Endowment for the Arts and from the governor of Massachusetts. Like so many of the Hispanic poets, Espada is an excellent performer and activist for poetry (and a political activist, one might add), organizing workshops, groups, and performances in the Boston area. As a lawyer, Espada is an active defender of the civil rights of immigrants.*

Portrait of a Real Hijo de Puta*

*for Michael

Not the obscenity,
but a real ten year old
son of a whore,
locked out of the apartment
so mamá could return
to the slavery
of her ancestors
who knew the master's burglary
of their bodies at night,
mamá who sleeps
in a pool of clear rum;

and the real hijo de puta poses
with the swim team photograph
at the community center,

---

* A hijo de puta is a bastard.

bragging fists in the air,
grinning like a cheerleader
with hidden cigarette burns,
a circus strongman
who steals cheese and crackers
from the office
where the door
is deliberately
left open.

Revolutionary Spanish Lesson

Whenever my name
is mispronounced,
I want to buy a toy pistol,
put on dark sunglasses,
push my beret to an angle,
comb my beard to a point,
hijack a busload
of Republican tourists
from Wisconsin,
force them to chant
anti-American slogans
in Spanish,
and wait
for the bilingual SWAT team
to helicopter overhead,
begging me
to be reasonable

Colibrí*

for Katherine, one year later

In Jayuya,
the lizards scatter
like a fleet of green canoes

---

* A Colibrí is a hummingbird.

before the invader.
The Spanish conquered
with iron and words:
"Taíno" for the people who took life
from the plátanos in the trees,
those multiple green fingers
curling around unseen spears,
who left the rock carvings
of eyes and mouths
in perfect circles of amazement.

So the hummingbird
was christened "colibrí."
Now the colibrí
darts and bangs
between the white walls
of the hacienda,
a racing Taíno heart
frantic as if hearing
the bellowing god of gunpowder
for the first time.

The colibrí
becomes pure stillness,
seized in the paralysis
of the prey,
when your hands
cup the bird
and lift him
through the red shutters
of the window,
where he disappears
into a paradise of sky,
a nightfall of singing frogs.

If only history
were like your hands.

Carolina Hospital

(b. 1957)
Cuban American

Born in Havana, Cuba, Carolina Hospital emigrated to Miami, Florida, with her family in 1961 as refugees from the Cuban Revolution. Hospital was educated in South Florida and earned a master's degree in English from the University of Florida, completing a thesis on the first Cuban American generation of writers. Hospital continued her research and involvement with the writers of her generation as a professor at Miami Dade Community College. With that base she launched the first anthology to bring together the writers of her Cuban American generation from throughout the United States: **Cuban American Writers: Los Atrevidos** (1989). Like many of her fellow writers, Hospital began writing at an early age to express the contradictions of living both in the idyllic past of parental memories and the bilingual/bicultural kaleidoscope of the South Florida present. Hospital's is a powerful bilingual voice, full of lyricism and critical acuity. Hospital has published her poetry broadly in magazines in both languages: the Americas Review, Bilingual Review, Cuban Heritage, *and* Linden Lane, *with which she is affiliated as an editor.*

Miami Mimesis

Miniature porcelain clowns
crowd the heart shaped bowl,
hands and legs confused.
Their white faces painted
with russet cheeks and violet lips
and the teal eyes,
defined by penciled-in brows,
stare.
Golden ruffles crown their necks
and red, green, black lace
forms their tiny bodies.
But the radiance of these colors,
the carefully drawn smiles
do not fool me.
This small multitude overflows
with eyes that shout.

A Visit to West New York

The Virgin of Charity, in blue,
and her three fishermen rest
on the wooden dresser.
I can hear salsa on
the neighbor's radio.
I try to decipher the faces
covering the night table.
The single bed hardly fits
in this room, cluttered,
clothes hanging off the closet doors,
on the red felt arm chair. I turn
to face the flowered wall
and sleep.

The ring of the phone, her voice,
loud and energetic, waken me.
I quickly dress, follow the scent
of espresso and buttered toast.
It's Jose's mother I meet in the kitchen,
her eyes glistening with mischief.
We have just met, but she talks of life
back home, her arms waving as she
urges me to eat more toast.
Jose seems embarrassed.

Then, it is time to leave.
He opens the door.
I confront the landscape:
a lean street with urined curbs,
a jagged fence and skies of
worn and pitted bricks.

Alma Mater

Half past three at school,
in an oversized blue t-shirt,
navy polyester shorts,
she sees a crowd of mothers.

I see me,
six again with tears,
searching, my mother with a
flowering wide skirt and flats,
waiting in a 67 Ford,
under the same black olive trees.

I return to her
now
running, smiling, waving.
For hers are not hollow hallways.

They hold the echoes.

Finding Home

I have travelled north again,
to these gray skies
and empty doorways.
Fall, and I recognize
the rusted leaves descending
near the silence of your home.
You, a part of this strange
American landscape with its
cold dry winds,
the honks of geese and
the hardwood floors. It's more
familiar now than
the fluorescent rainbow on the overpass,
or the clatter of politicos in the corners,
or the palm fronds falling by the highway.
I must travel again, soon.

The Old Order

A man enters through the kitchen
and closes the door behind him,
afraid of letting the outside in.

Onions and peppers simmer,
fries and plantains sizzle,
pork grease drips off the window panes.

He places the yellow cap on the formica
and waits his turn.
Finally, he hollers above the clatter;
a young plump waitress serves him a mountain of rice.

After his meal, he wipes the grease off his lips,
gulps down his espresso and
shouts his good-byes.
Outside, now he tilts his cap and walks away with ease.

DRAMA

Dolores Prida

(b. 1943)
Cuban American

Dolores Prida is a playwright and screenwriter whose works have been produced in the United States as well as in Puerto Rico, Venezuela, and the Dominican Republic. Born in 1943 in Caibairén, Cuba, Prida emigrated with her family to New York City in 1963. She graduated from Hunter College in 1969 with a major in Spanish American literature and soon began a career as a journalist and editor for various New York publishers. In 1977 her first play, **Beautiful Señoritas,** *was produced at the Duo Theater. Since then, she has had some ten plays produced. They vary in style and format from adaptations of international classics such as* **The Three Penny Opera** *to experiments with the Broadway musical formula as in her* **Savings** *(1985). In 1981 she created a totally bilingual play,* **Coser y cantar (To Sew and to Sing),** *which has been repeatedly produced because of its success at depicting with humor and pathos the cultural and linguistic conflicts of Hispanics in the United States. In 1990 Prida debuted* **Botánica (The Herb Store)** *and as of this writing it is still enjoying a run in New York at the Spanish Repertory Theater. The play is a deft and stylistic examination of the generation gap and culture conflict in a Puerto Rican family of women. In 1991 Prida published her collected plays in* **Beautiful Señoritas and Other Plays.** *Prida is also a talented poet who in the late 1960s was a leader of New York's Nueva Sangre (New Blood) movement of young poets. Her books of poetry include* **Treinta y un poemas** *(1967, Thirty-one Poems),* **Women of the Hour** *(1971) and, with Roger Cabán,* **The IRT Prayer Book.**

Beautiful Señoritas

CHARACTERS

Four BEAUTIFUL SEÑORITAS who also play assorted characters: Catch Women, Martyrs, Saints and just women.

The MIDWIFE, who also plays the Mother
The MAN, who plays all the male roles
The GIRL, who grows up before our eyes

SET

The set is an open space or a series of platforms and a ramp, which become the various playing areas as each scene flows into the next.

Beautiful Señoritas was first performed at Duo Theater in New York City on November 25, 1977, with the following cast:

THE BEAUTIFUL SEÑORITAS _____ Vira Colorado,
    María Norman, Lourdes Ramirez and Lucy Vega
THE MIDWIFE _____ Sol Echeverria
THE GIRL _____ Viridiana Villaverde
THE MAN _____ Manuel Yesckas
It was directed by Gloria Zelaya. Music by Tania Leon and Victoria Huiz. Musical direction by Lydia Rivera. Choreography by Lourdes Ramirez.

Beautiful Señoritas opened on the West Coast April 6, 1979, at the Inner City Cultural Center's Stormy Weather Cafe in Los Angeles with the following cast:

THE BEAUTIFUL SEÑORITAS _____ Roseanna Campos,
    Jeannie Linero, Rosa María Márquez and lka Tanya Payán
THE MIDWIFE _____ Peggy Hutcherson
THE GIRL _____ Gabrielle Gazón
THE MAN _____ Ron Godines

It was codirected by Eduardo Machado and IIXa Tanya Payán. Musical direction by Bob Zeigler. Choreography by Joanne Figueras.

ACT I

As lights go up DON JOSÉ *paces nervously back and forth. He smokes a big cigar, talking to himself.*

DON JOSÉ: Come on, woman. Hurry up. I have waited long enough for this child. Come on, a son. Give me a son ... I will start training him right away. To ride horses. To shoot. To drink. As soon as he is old enough I'll take him to La Casa de Luisa. There they'll teach him what to do to women. Ha, ha, ha! If he's anything like his father, in twenty years everyone in this town will be related to each other! Ha, ha, ha! My name will never die. My son will see to that ...
MIDWIFE: (MIDWIFE *enters running, excited.*) Don José! Don José!
DON JOSÉ: ¡Al fin! ¿Qué? Dígame, ¿todo está bien?[1]
MIDWIFE: Yes, everything is fine, Don José. Your wife just gave birth to a healthy ...

---

1. Finally! What? Tell me, is everything okay?

DON JOSÉ: *(Interrupting excitedly.)* Ha, ha, I knew it! A healthy son!

MIDWIFE: It is a girl Don José ...

DON JOSÉ: *(Disappointment and disbelief creep onto his face. Then anger. He throws the cigar on the floor with force, then steps on it.)* A girl! ¡No puede ser! ¡Imposible! What do you mean a girl! ¡Cómo puede pasarme esto a mí?[2] The first child that will bear my name and it is a ... girl! ¡Una chancleta! ¡Carajo![3] *(He storms away, muttering under his breath.)*

MIDWIFE: *(Looks at DON JOSÉ as he exits, then addresses the audience. At some point during the following monologue the Girl will appear. She looks at everything as if seeing the world for the first time.)* He's off to drown his disappointment in rum, because another woman is born into this world. The same woman another man's son will covet and pursue and try to rape at the first opportunity. The same woman whose virginity he will protect with a gun. Another woman is born into this world. In Managua, in San Juan, in an Andes mountain town. She'll be put on a pedestal and trampled upon at the same time. She will be made a saint and a whore, crowned queen and exploited and adored. No, she's not just any woman. She will be called upon to ... *(The MIDWIFE is interrupted by offstage voices.)*

BEAUTIFUL SEÑORITA 1: ¡Cuchi cuchi chi-a-boom!

BEAUTIFUL SEÑORITA 2: ¡Mira caramba oye![4]

BEAUTIFUL SEÑORITA 3: ¡Rumba pachanga mambo![5]

BEAUTIFUL SEÑORITA 4: ¡Oye papito, ay ayayaiiii![6]

Immediately a rumba is heard. The four BEAUTIFUL SEÑORITAS *enter dancing. They dress as Carmen Miranda, Iris Chacón, Charo and María la O. They sing:*

"THE BEAUTIFUL SEÑORITAS SONG"

WE BEAUTIFUL SEÑORITAS
WITH MARACAS IN OUR SOULS
MIRA PAPI AY CARIÑO[7]
ALWAYS READY FOR AMOR

---

2. It can't be! Impossible! How can this happen to me?
3. A slipper (female)! Damn!
4. Look, damn, listen
5. (names of dances)
6. Listen, pops, ay!
7. Look Pops, oh, love

WE BEAUTIFUL SEÑORITAS
MUCHA SALSA AND SABOR[8]
CUCHI CUCHI LATIN BOMBAS[9]
ALWAYS READY FOR AMOR

AY CARAMBA MIRA OYE [10]
DANCE THE TANGO ALL NIGHT LONG
GUACAMOLE LATIN LOVER
ALWAYS READY FOR AMOR

ONE PAPAYA ONE BANANA
AY SÍ SÍ SÍ SÍ SEÑOR
SIMPÁTICAS MUCHACHITAS[11]
ALWAYS READY FOR AMOR

PIÑA PLÁTANOS CHIQUITAS[12]
OF THE RAINBOW EL COLOR
CUCARACHAS MUY BONITAS[13]
ALWAYS READY FOR AMOR

WE BEAUTIFUL SEÑORITAS
WITH MARACAS IN OUR SOULS
MIRA PAPI AY CARIÑO[14]
ALWAYS READY FOR AMOR

AY SÍ SÍ SÍ SÍ SEÑOR
ALWAYS READY FOR AMOR
AY SÍ SÍ SÍ SÍ SEÑOR
ALWAYS READY FOR AMOR
¡AY SÍ SÍ SÍ SÍ SEÑOR!

---

8. a lot of sauce and taste
9. bombs
10. Ay, Damn, Look, Listen
11. lovely girls
12. pineapple plaintains little ones
13. very pretty cockroaches
14. Look Pops Oh Love

The SEÑORITAS *bow and exit.* MARÍA LA O *returns and takes more bows.*

MARÍA LA O *bows for the last time. Goes to her dressing room. Sits down and removes her shoes.*

MARÍA LA O: My feet are killing me. These juanetes get worse by the minute. *(She rubs her feet. She appears older and tired, all the glamour gone out of her. She takes her false eyelashes off, examines her face carefully in the mirror, begins to remove makeup.)* Forty lousy bucks a week for all that tit-shaking. But I need the extra money. What am I going to do? A job is a job. And with my artistic inclinations ... well ... But look at this joint! A dressing room! They have the nerve to call this a dressing room. I have to be careful not to step on a rat. They squeak too loud. The patrons out there may hear, you know. Anyway, I sort of liked dancing since I was a kid. But this! I meant dancing like Alicia Alonso, Margot Fonteyn ... and I end up as a cheap Iris Chacón. At least she shook her behind in Radio City Music Hall. Ha! That's one up the Rockettes!

BEAUTY QUEEN: *(She enters, wearing a beauty contest bathing suit.)* María la O, you still here. I thought everyone was gone. You always run out after the show.

MARÍA LA O. No, not tonight. Somebody is taking care of the kid. I'm so tired that I don't feel like moving from here. Estoy muerta, m'ija.[15] *(Looks* BEAUTY QUEEN *up and down.)* And where are *you* going?

BEAUTY QUEEN: To a beauty contest, of course.

MARÍA LA O: Don't you get tired of that, mujer![16]

BEAUTY QUEEN: Never. I was born to be a beauty queen. I have been a beauty queen ever since I was born. "La reinecita,"[17] they used to call me. My mother entered me in my first contest at the age of two. Then, it was one contest after the other. I have been in a bathing suit ever since. I save a lot in clothes ... Anyway, my mother used to read all those women's magazines—*Vanidades, Cosmopolitan, Claudia, Buenhogar*—where everyone is so beautiful and happy. She, of course, wanted me to be like them ... *(Examines herself in the mirror.)* I have won hundreds of contests, you know. I have been

15. I'm dead, daughter
16. woman
17. "The little queen"

Queen of Los Hijos Ausentes[18] Club; Reina El Diario–La Prensa;
Queen of Plátano[19] Chips; Queen of the Hispanic Hairdressers
Association; Reina de la Alcapurria; Miss Caribbean Sunshine; Señorita
Turismo de Staten Island; Queen of the Texas Enchilada ... and now
of course, I am Miss Banana Republic!

MARÍA LA O: Muchacha, I bet you don't have time for anything else!

BEAUTY QUEEN: Oh, I sure do. I wax my legs every day. I keep in shape. I
practice my smile. Because one day, in one of those beauty contests,
someone will come up to me and say ...

MARÍA LA O: You're on *Candid Camera?*

BEAUTY QUEEN: Where have you been all my life! I'll be discovered, become
a movie star, a millionaire, appear on the cover of *People Magazine*
... and anyway, even if I don't win, I still make some money.

MARÍA LA O: Money? How much money?

BEAUTY QUEEN: Five hundred. A thousand. A trip here. A trip there.
Depends on the contest.

MARÍA LA O: I could sure use some extra chavos ... Hey, do you think I
could win, be discovered by a movie producer or something ...

BEAUTY QUEEN: Weeell ... I don't know. They've just remade *King Kong*
... ha, ha!

MARÍA LA O: (MARÍA LA O *doesn't pay attention. She's busily thinking
about the money.* BEAUTY QUEEN *turns to go.*) Even if I am only
third, I still make some extra money. I can send Johnny home for
the summer. He's never seen his grandparents. Ya ni habla español.
(MARÍA LA O *quickly tries to put eyelashes back on. Grabs her shoes
and runs after* BEAUTY QUEEN.) Wait, wait for me! ¡Espérame![20]
I'll go with you to the beauty contest! *(She exits. The* MIDWIFE *enters
immediately. She calls her* MARÍA LA O.)

MIDWIFE: And don't forget to smile! Give them your brightest smile! As if
your life depended on it!

The GIRL *enters and sits at* MARÍA LA O's *dressing table. During the
following monologue, the* GIRL *will play with the makeup, slowly
applying lipstick, mascara, and eye shadow in a very serious,
concentrated manner.*

MIDWIFE: Yes. You have to smile to win. A girl with a serious face has no
future. But what can you do when a butterfly is trapped in your

18. The Absent Children
19. Plaintain
20. Wait for me!

insides and you cannot smile? How can you smile with a butterfly condemned to beat its everchanging wings in the pit of your stomach? There it is. Now a flutter. Now a storm. Carried by the winds of emotion, this butterfly transforms the shape, the color, the texture of its wings; the speed and range of its flight. Now it becomes a stained-glass butterfly, light shining through its yellow-colored wings, which move ever so slowly, up and down, up and down, sometimes remaining still for a second too long. Then the world stops and takes a plunge, becoming a brief black hole in space. A burned-out star wandering through the galaxies is like a smile meant, but not delivered. And I am so full of undelivered smiles! So pregnant with undetected laughter! Sonrisas, sonrisas,[21] who would exchange a butterfly for a permanent smile! Hear, hear, this butterfly will keep you alive and running, awake and on your toes, speeding along the herd of wild horses stampeding through the heart! This butterfly is magic. It changes its size. It becomes big and small. Who will take this wondrous butterfly and give me a simple, lasting smile! A smile for day and night, winter and fall. A smile for all occasions. A smile to survive ... *(With the last line, the* MIDWIFE *turns to the* GIRL, *who by now has her face made up like a clown. They look at each other. The* GIRL *faces the audience. She is not smiling. They freeze. Black out.)*

In the dark we hear a fanfare. Lights go up on the MC. *He wears a velvet tuxedo with a pink ruffled shirt. He combs his hair, twirls his moustache, adjusts his bow tie and smiles. He wields a microphone with a flourish.*

MC: Ladies and gentlemen. Señoras y señores. Tonight. Esta noche. Right here. Aquí mismo. You will have the opportunity to see the most exquisite, sexy, exotic, sandungueras, jacarandosas and most beautiful señoritas of all. You will be the judge of the contest, where beauty will compete with belleza; where women of the tropical Caribbean will battle the señoritas of South America. Ladies and gentlemen, the poets have said it. The composers of boleros have said it. Latin women are the most beautiful, the most passionate, the most virtuous, the best housewives and cooks. And they all know how to dance to salsa, and do the hustle, the mambo, the guaguancó ...

---

21. Smiles, smiles

And they are always ready for amor, señores! What treasures! See for yourselves! ... Ladies and gentlemen, Señoras y señores ... from the sandy beaches of Florida, esbelta[22] as a palm tree, please welcome Miss Little Havana! *(Music from "Cuando sali de Cuba" is heard. Miss Little Havana enters. She wears a bathing suit, sun glasses and a string of pearls. She sings.)*

CUANDO SALÍ DE CUBA
DEJÉ MI CASA, DEJÉ MI AVIÓN[23]
CUANDO SALÍ DE CUBA
DEJÉ ENTERRADO MEDIO MILLÓN[24]

MC: Oye, chica,[25] what's your name?
MISS LITTLE HAVANA: Fina de la Garza del Vedado y Miramar. From the best families of the Cuba de Ayer.
MC: *(To the audience.)* As you can see, ladies and gentlemen, Fina es muy fina.[26] Really fine, he, he, he. Tell the judges, Fina, what are your best assets?
MISS LITTLE HAVANA: Well, back in the Cuba of Yesterday, I had a house with ten rooms and fifty maids, two cars, un avión[27] and a sugar mill. But Fidel took everything away. So, here in the U.S. of A. my only assets are 36-28-42.
MC: Hmmm! That's what I call a positive attitude. Miss Fina, some day you'll get it all back. Un aplauso for Fina, ladies and gentlemen! (MISS LITTLE HAVANA *steps back and freezes into a doll-like posture, with a fixed smile on her face.)*
MC: Now, from South of the Border, ladies and gentlemen—hold on to your tacos, because here she is ... Miss Chili Tamale! *(Music begins: "Allá en el Rancho Grande".)* Please, un aplauso! Welcome, welcome chaparrita! (MISS CHILI TAMALE *enters. She also wears a bathing suit and a sarape over her shoulder. She sings.)*

---

22. thin
23. When I left Cuba I left my home, I left my place
24. When I left Cuba I left a half-million buried.
25. Listen, girl
26. Fina is very fine.
27. a plane

ALLÁ EN EL RANCHO GRANDE
ALLA DONDE VIVÍA
YO ERA UNA FLACA MORENITA [28]
QUE TRISTE SE QUEJABA
QUE TRISTE SE QUEJAABAAA
NO TENGO NI UN PAR DE CALZONES[29]

NI SIN REMIENDOS DE CUERO[30]
NI DOS HUEVOS RANCHEROS
Y LAS TORTILLAS QUEMADAS

MC: Your name, beautiful señorita?

MISS CHILI TAMALE: Lupe Lupita Guadalupe Viva Zapata y Enchilada, para servirle.[31]

MC: What good manners! Tell us, what's your most fervent desire?

MISS CHILI TAMALE: My most fervent desire is to marry a big, handsome, very rich americano.

MC: Aha! What have we here! You mean you prefer gringos instead of Latin men?

MISS CHILI TAMALE: Oh no, no no. But, you see, I need my green card. La migra[32] is after me.

MC: (*Nervously, the* MC *looks around, then pushes* MISS TAMALE *back. She joins* MISS LITTLE HAVANA *in her doll-like pose.*) Ahem, ahem. Now, ladies and gentlemen, the dream girl of every American male, the most beautiful señorita of all. Created by Madison Avenue exclusively for the United Fruit Company ...ladies and gentlemen, please welcome Miss Conchita Banana! (*"Chiquita Banana" music begins.* MISS CONCHITA BANANA *enters. She wears plastic bananas on her head and holds two real ones in her hands. She sings.*)

I'M CONCHITA BANANA
AND I'M HERE TO SAY
THAT BANANAS TASTE THE BEST
IN A CERTAIN WAY

---

28. Back on the big ranch Where I used to live I was a little dark skinny thing
29. Who used to complain sadly I don't even have a pair of pants
30. Nor leather patches
31. Long live Zapata and Enchilada, at your service.
32. The Immigration Service

YOU CAN PUT 'EM IN YOUR HUM HUM
YOU CAN SLICE 'EM IN YOUR HA HA
ANYWAY YOU WANT TO EAT 'EM
IT'S IMPOSSIBLE TO BEAT 'EM
BUT NEVER, NEVER, NEVER
PUT BANANAS IN THE REFRIGERATOR
NO, NO, NO NO!

(She throws the two real bananas to the audience.)

MC: Brava, bravissima, Miss Banana! Do you realize you have made our humble fruit, el plátano, very very famous all over the world?

MISS CONCHITA BANANA: Yes, I know. That has been the goal of my whole life.

MC: And we are proud of you, Conchita. But, come here, just between the two of us ... tell me the truth, do you really like bananas?

MISS CONCHITA BANANA: Of course, I do! I eat them all the time. My motto is: a banana a day keeps the doctor away!

MC: *(Motioning to audience to applaud.)* What intelligence! What insight! Un aplauso, ladies and gentlemen ... (MISS CONCHITA BANANA *bows and steps back, joining the other doll-like contestants. As each woman says the following lines she becomes human again. The* MC *moves to one side and freezes.)*

WOMAN 1: *(Previously* MISS LITTLE HAVANA.) No one knows me. They see me passing by, but they don't know me. They don't see me. They hear my accent but not my words. If anyone wants to find me, I'll be sitting by the beach.

WOMAN 2: *(Previously* MISS CHILI TAMALE.) My mother, my grandmother, and her mother before her, walked the land with barefeet, as I have done too. We have given birth to our daughters on the bare soil. We have seen them grow and go to market. Now we need permits to walk the land—our land.

WOMAN 3: *(Previously* MISS CONCHITA BANANA.) I have been invented for a photograph. Sometimes I wish to be a person, to exist for my own sake, to stop dancing, to stop smiling. One day I think I will want to cry.

MC: *(We hear a fanfare. The* MC *unfreezes. The contestants become dolls again.)* Ladies and gentlemen ... don't go away, because we still have more for you! Now, señoras y señores, from La Isla del Encanto,[33] please welcome Miss Commonwealth! Un aplauso,[34] please! *(We hear music from "Cortaron a Elena." MISS COMMONWEALTH enters, giggling and waving. She sings.)*

CORTARON EL BUDGET
CORTARON EL BUDGET
CORTARON EL BUDGET
Y NOS QUEDAMOS
SIN FOOD STAMPS
CORTARON A ELENA
CORTARON A JUANA
CORTARON A LOLA
Y NOS QUEDAMOS
SIN NA' PA' NA'[35]

MC: ¡Qué sabor![36] Tell us your name, beautiful jibarita ...[37]
MISS COMMONWEALTH: Lucy Wisteria Rivera *(Giggles.)*
MC: Let me ask you, what do you think of the political status of the island?
MISS COMMONWEALTH: *(Giggles.)* Oh, I don't know about that. La belleza y la política no se mezclan.[38] Beauty and politics do not mix. *(Giggles.)*
MC: True, true, preciosa-por-ser-un-encanto-por-ser-un-eden.[39] Tell me, what is your goal in life?
MISS COMMONWEALTH: I want to find a boyfriend and get married. I will be a great housewife, cook and mother. I will only live for my husband and my children. *(Giggles.)*
MC: Ave María, nena! You are a tesoro! Well, Miss Commonwealth, finding a boyfriend should not be difficult for you. You have everything a man wants right there up front. *(Points to her breasts with the microphone.)* I am sure you already have several novios,[40] no?

33. Isle of Enchantment
34. applause
35. They cut the budget and   We were left without food stamps.   They cut Elena   They cut Juana   They cut Lola   And we were left   With nothing for nothing.
36. What grace!
37. country girl
38. Beauty and politics don't mix.
39. Precious because you enchant, because you are Eden.
40. boyfriends

MISS COMMONWEALTH: Oh no, I don't have a boyfriend yet. My father doesn't let me. And besides, it isn't as easy as you think. To catch a man you must know the rules of the game, the technique, the tricks, the know-how, the how-to, the expertise, the go-get-it, the ... works! Let me show you. (*The MC stands to one side and freezes. The doll-like contestants in the back exit.* MISS COMMONWEALTH *begins to exit. She runs into the GIRL as she enters.* MISS COMMONWEALTH'S *crown falls to the floor. She looks at the girl who seems to remind her of something far away.*)

WOMAN 4: (*Previously* MISS COMMONWEALTH.) The girl who had never seen the ocean decided one day to see it. Just one startled footprint on the sand and the sea came roaring at her. A thousand waves, an infinite horizon, a storm of salt and two diving birds thrusted themselves furiously into her eyes. Today she walks blindly through the smog and the dust of cities and villages. But she travels with a smile, because she carries the ocean in her eyes. (WOMAN 4 *exits. Spot on the* GIRL. *She picks up the crown from the floor and places it on her head. Spot closes in on the crown.*)

As *lights go up, the* MAN *enters with a chair and places it center stage. He sits on it. The* GIRL *sits on the floor with her back to the audience. The* CATCH WOMEN *enter and take their places around the man. Each* WOMAN *addresses the* GIRL, *as a teacher would.*)

CATCH WOMAN 1: There are many ways to catch a man. Watch ... (*Walks over to the* MAN.) Hypnotize him. Be a good listener. (*She sits on his knees.*) Laugh at his jokes, even if you heard them before. (*To* MAN.) Honey, tell them the one about the two bartenders ... (*The* MAN *mouths words as if telling a joke. She listens and laughs loudly. Gets up.*) Cuá, cuá, cuá![41] Isn't he a riot! (*She begins to walk away, turns and addresses the* GIRL.) Ah, and don't forget to move your hips.

CATCH WOMAN 2: (CATCH WOMAN 1 *walks moving her hips back to her place.* CATCH WOMAN 2 *steps forward and addresses the* GIRL.) Women can't be too intellectual. He will get bored. (*To* MAN, *in earnest.*) Honey, don't you think nuclear disarmament is our only hope for survival? (*The* MAN *yawns. To* GIRL.) See? When a man goes out with a woman he wants to relax, to have fun, to feel good. He doesn't want to talk about heavy stuff, know what I mean? (CATCH

---

41. nonsense syllables

WOMAN 2 *walks back to her place. She flirts with her boa, wrapping it around the man's head. Teasing.)* Toro, toro, torito![42]
CATCH WOMAN 3:   *(The* MAN *charges after* CATCH WOMAN 2. CATCH WOMAN 3 *stops him with a hypnotic look. He sits down again.* CATCH WOMAN 3 *addresses the* GIRL.) Looks are a very powerful weapon. Use your eyes, honey. Look at him now and then. Directly. Sideways. Through your eyelashes. From the corner of your eyes. Over your sunglasses. Look at him up and down. But not with too much insistence. And never ever look directly at his crotch. *(She walks away dropping a handkerchief. The* MAN *stops to pick it up.* CATCH WOMAN 4 *places her foot on it. Pushes the* MAN *away.)* Make him suffer. Make him jealous. *(Waves to someone offstage, flirting.)* Hi Johnny! *(To* GIRL.*)* They like it. It gives them a good excuse to get drunk. Tease him. Find out what he likes. *(To* MAN.*)* Un masajito, papi? I'll make you a burrito de machaca con huevo, si?[43] *(She massages his neck.)* Keep him in suspense. *(To* MAN.*)* I love you. I don't love you. Te quiero. No te quiero. I love you. I don't love you ... *(She walks away.)*
ALL: *(All four* CATCH WOMEN *come forward.)* We do it all for him!
MAN: They do it all for me! (MAN *raps the song, while the* CATCH WOMEN *parade around him.)*

"THEY DO IT ALL FOR ME"

(Wolf whistles.)
MIRA MAMI, PSST, COSA LINDA!
OYE MUNECA, DAME UN POQUITO
AY, MIREN ESO
LO QUE DIOS HA HECHO
PARA NOSOTROS LOS PECADORES[44]
AY MAMÁ, DON'T WALK LIKE THAT
DON'T MOVE LIKE THAT
DON'T LOOK LIKE THAT
'CAUSE YOU GONNA GIVE ME

---

42. Come on, Bull, bull, little bull!
43. A burrito (Mexican sandwich) with pork, hash and eggs, right?
44. Look, babe, psst, pretty thing! Look, dolly, gimme some. Ay, look at what God has created In us sinner Ay, babe

A HEART ATTACK
THEY DO IT ALL FOR ME
WHAT THEY LEARN IN A MAGAZINE
THEY DO IT ALL FOR ME
'CAUSE YOU KNOW WHAT THEY WANT
AY MAMÁ, TAN PRECIOSA TAN HERMOSA[45]
GIVE ME A PIECE OF THIS
AND A PIECE OF THAT
'CAUSE I KNOW YOU DO IT ALL FOR ME
DON'T YOU DON'T YOU
DON'T YOU DO IT ALL FOR ME

(CATCH WOMAN 2 throws her boa around his neck, ropes in the MAN *and exits with him in tow.)*

CATCH WOMAN 1: ¡Mira, esa mosquita muerta ya agarró uno![46]

CATCH WOMAN 3: Look at that, she caught him!

CATCH WOMAN 4: Pero, ¡qué tiene ella que no tenga yo![47] *(All exit. The* GIRL *stands up, picks up the handkerchief from the floor. Mimes imitations of some of the* WOMEN'S *moves, flirting, listening to jokes, giggling, moving her hips, etc. Church music comes on.)*

The NUN *enters carrying a bouquet of roses cradled in her arms. She stands in the back and looks up bathed in a sacred light. Her lips move as if praying. She lowers her eyes and sees the* GIRL *imitating more sexy moves. The* NUN'S *eyes widen in disbelief.*

NUN: What are you doing, creature? That is sinful! A woman must be recatada, saintly. Thoughts of the flesh must be banished from your head and your heart. Close your eyes and your pores to desire. The only love there is the love of the Lord. The Lord is the only lover!

NUN: *(The* GIRL *stops, thoroughly confused. The* NUN *strikes her with the bouquet of roses.)* ¡Arrodillate![48] Kneel down on these roses! Let your blood erase your sinful thoughts! You may still be saved. Pray, pray! *(The* GIRL *kneels on the roses, grimacing with pain. The* PRIEST *enters, makes the sign of the cross on the scene. The* NUN *kneels in front of the* PRIEST.) Father, forgive me for I have sinned ... *(The* SEÑORITAS *enter with her lines. They wear mantillas and*

---

45. Ay, babe, so precious, so beautiful
46. Look, that dead mosquito grabbed one already!
47. But what does she have that I don't?
48. Kneel down!

peinetas, holding Spanish fans in their hands, a red carnation between their teeth.)
SEÑORITA 1: Me too, father!
SEÑORITA 2: ¡Y yo también![49]
SEÑORITA 3: And me!
SEÑORITA 4: Me too! *(A tango begins. The following lines are integrated into the choreography.)*
SEÑORITA 1: Father, it has been two weeks since my last confession ...
PRIEST: Speak, hija mia.[50]
SEÑORITA 2: Padre,[51] my boyfriend used to kiss me on the lips ... but it's all over now ...
PRIEST: Lord, oh Lord!
SEÑORITA 3: Forgive me father, but I have masturbated three times. Twice mentally, once physically.
PRIEST: Ave María Purísima sin pecado concebida ...[52]
SEÑORITA 4: I have sinned, santo padre. Last night I had wet dreams.
PRIEST: Socorro espiritual, Dios mío. Help these lost souls![53]
SEÑORITA 1: He said, fellatio ... I said, cunnilingus!
PRIEST: No, not in a beautiful señorita's mouth! Such evil words, Señor, oh Lord!
SEÑORITA 2: Father, listen. I have sinned. I have really really sinned. I did it, I did it! All the way I did it! *(All the SEÑORITAS and the NUN turn to SEÑORITA 2 and make the sign of the cross. They point at her with the fans.)*
SEÑORITAS 1, 3, 4: She's done it, Dios mío, she's done it! Santísima Virgen,[54] she's done it!
PRIEST: She's done it! She's done it!
SEÑORITA 2: *(Tangoing backwards.)* I did it. Yes. Lo hice.[55] I did it, father. Forgive me, for I have fornicated!
PRIEST: She's done it! She's done it! *(The NUN faints in the PRIEST'S arms.)*
SEÑORITAS 1, 3, 4: Fornication! Copulation! Indigestion! ¡Qué pecado y

---

49. And me too!
50. my daughter
51. Father,
52. Hail Mary the Pure born without sin.
53. spiritual help, my God
54. Saintly Virgin
55. I did it.

que horror! ¡*Culpable!* ¡*Culpable!* ¡*Culpable!*[56] (They exit tangoing.
The PRIEST, with the fainted NUN in his arms, looks at the audience
bewildered.)
PRIEST: (*To audience.*) Intermission! *Black out*

ACT II

In the dark we hear fanfare. Spot light on MC.

MC: Welcome back, ladies and gentlemen, señoras y señores. There's more,
     much much more yet to come. For, you see, our contestants are not
     only beautiful, but also very talented señoritas. For the benefit of
     the judges they will sing, they will dance, they will perform the most
     daring acts on the flying trapeze!
Spot light on WOMAN 3 *swinging on a swing center stage. She sings:*

"BOLERO TRAICIONERO"

TAKE ME IN YOUR ARMS
LET'S DANCE AWAY THE NIGHT
WHISPER IN MY EARS
THE SWEETEST WORDS OF LOVE

I'M THE WOMAN IN YOUR LIFE
SAY YOU DIE EVERY TIME
YOU ARE AWAY FROM ME
AND WHISPER IN MY EAR
THE SWEETEST WORDS OF LOVE

PROMISE ME THE SKY
GET ME THE MOON, THE STARS
IF IT IS A LIE
WHISPER IN MY EAR
THE SWEETEST WORDS OF LOVE

DARLING IN A DREAM OF FLOWERS
WE ARE PLAYING ALL THE GREATEST GAMES

---

56. What a sin and what a horror! Guilty! Guilty! Guilty!

LIE TO ME WITH ROMANCE AGAIN
TRAICIÓNAME ASÍ, TRAICIÓNAME MÁS[57]

(Bis)
PROMISE ME THE SKY ...

(During the song lights go up to reveal the other women sitting in various poses waiting to be asked to dance. The GIRL *is also there, closely watched by the* CHAPERONE, *who also keeps an eye on all the other women. The* MAN *enters wearing a white tuxedo and a Zorro mask. He dances with each one. Gives each a flower which he pulls out of his pocket like a magician. The* GIRL *wants to dance, the* MAN *comes and asks her but the* CHAPERONE *doesn't let her. The* MAN *asks another woman to dance. They dance very close. The* CHAPERONE *comes and taps the woman on the shoulder. They stop dancing. The* MAN *goes to the woman singing, pushes the swing back and forth. At the end of the song, the singer leaves with the* MAN. *The other women follow them with their eyes.)*

SEÑORITA 2: I swear I only did it for love! He sang in my ear the sweetest words, the most romantic boleros. Saturdays and Sundays he sat at the bar across the street drinking beer. He kept playing the same record on the jukebox over and over. It was a pasodoble about being as lonely as a stray dog. He would send me flowers and candies with the shoeshine boy. My father and brother had sworn to kill him if they saw him near me. But he insisted. He kept saying how much he loved me and he kept getting drunk right at my doorsteps. He serenaded me every weekend. He said I was the most decent woman in the world. Only his mother was more saintly ... he said.

SEÑORITA 3: He said the same thing to me. Then he said the same thing to my sister and then to her best friend. My sister was heartbroken. She was so young. She had given him her virginity and he would not marry her. Then three days before Christmas she set herself on fire. She poured gasoline on her dress, put a match to it and then started to run. She ran like a vision of hell through the streets of the town. Her screams awoke all the dead lovers for miles around. Her long hair, her flowing dress were like a banner of fire calling followers to

---

57. Betray me, betray me more

battle. She ran down Main Street—the street that leads directly to the sea. I ran after her trying to catch her to embrace her, to smother the flames with my own body. I ran after her, yelling not to go into the water. She couldn't, she wouldn't hear. She ran into the sea like thunder ... Such drama, such fiery spectacle, such pain ... It all ended with a half-silent hiss and a thin column of smoke rising up from the water, near the beach where we played as children ... (*We hear the sound of drums. The women join in making mournful sounds.*)

The mournful sounds slowly turn into the "Wedding Song."

"THE WEDDING SONG"
("Where Have All the Women Gone")

WOMAN:
THERE, THERE'S JUANA
SEE JUANA JUMP
SEE HOW SHE JUMPS
WHEN HE DOES CALL
THERE, THERE'S ROSA
SEE ROSA CRY
SEE HOW SHE CRIES
WHEN HE DOESN'T CALL

CHORUS: WHERE HAVE ALL
THE WOMEN GONE

WOMAN:
JUANA ROSA CARMEN GO
NOT WITH A BANG
BUT WITH A WHIMPER
WHERE HAVE THEY GONE
LEAVING THEIR DREAMS
BEHIND
LEAVING THEIR DREAMS
LETTING THEIR LIVES
UNDONE

CHORUS:
(Wedding March Music.)
LOOK HOW THEY GO
LOOK AT THEM GO
SIGHING AND CRYING
LOOK AT THEM GO

Towards the end of the song the women will form a line before the
CHAPERONE *who is holding a big basket. From it she takes and gives*
each woman a wig with hair rollers on it. Assisted by the GIRL, *each*
woman will put her wig on. Once the song ends, each woman will start
miming various house-cleaning chores, sweeping, ironing, washing, etc.
The MOTHER *sews. The* GIRL *watches.*

MARTYR 1: Cry my child. Las mujeres nacimos para sufrir.[58] There's no
other way but to cry. One is born awake and crying. That's the way
God meant it. And who are we to question the ways of the Lord?

MARTYR 2: I don't live for myself. I live for my husband and my children. A
woman's work is never done: what to make for lunch, cook the beans,
start the rice, and then again, what to make for supper, and the fact
that Juanito needs new shoes for school. *(She holds her side in pain.)*

MARTYR 3: What's wrong with you?

MARTYR 2: I have female problems.

MARTYR 3: The menstruation again?

MARTYR 2: No, my husband beat me up again last night. *(The* GIRL *covers*
her ears, then covers her eyes and begins to play "Put the Tail on
the Donkey" all by herself.)

MARTYR 3: I know what you mean, m'ija. We women were born to suffer. I
sacrifice myself for my children. But, do they appreciate it? No.
Someday, someday when I'm gone they'll remember me and all I did
for them. But then it will be too late. Too late.

MOTHER: Such metaphysics. Women should not worry about philosophical
matters. That's for men. *(She returns to her sewing, humming a song*
of oblivion.)

MARTYR 3: The Virgin Mary never worried about forced sterilization or
torture in Argentina or minimum wages. True, she had housing
problems, but I'm sure there was never a quarrel as to who washed
the dishes or fed that burro.

---

58. We women were born to suffer.

MAMÁ: Such heretic thoughts will not lead to anything good, I tell you. It is better not to have many thoughts. When you do the ironing or the cooking or set your hair in rollers, it is better not to think too much. I know what I'm saying. I know ... *(Continues her sewing and humming.)*

MARTYR 1: And this headache. We're born with migraine. And with the nerves on edge. It is so, I know. I remember my mother and her mother before her. They always had jaquecas.[59] I inherited the pain and tazas de tilo,[60] the Valiums and the Libriums ...

MAMÁ: You don't keep busy enough. While your hands are busy ...

MARTYR 2: And your mouth is busy, while you run from bed to stove to shop to work to sink to bed to mirror no one notices the little light shining in your eyes. It is better that way ... because I... I don't live for myself. I live for my husband and my children, and it is better that they don't notice that flash in my eyes, that sparkle of a threat, that flickering death wish ... *(The GIRL tears off the cloth covering her eyes. Looks at the women expecting some action. Mumbling and complaining under their breaths, the women go back to their chores. The GUERRILLERA enters. She is self-assured and full of energy. The GIRL gives her all her attention.)*

GUERRILLERA: Stop your laments, sisters!

MARTYR 1: Who's she?

GUERRILLERA: Complaining and whining won't help!

MARTYR 3: That's true!

GUERRILLERA: We can change the world and then our lot will improve!

MARTYR 3: It's about time!

GUERRILLERA: Let's fight oppression!

MARTYR 3: I'm ready! Let's go!

MARTYR 2: I ain't going nowhere. I think she's a lesbian.

GUERRILLERA: We, as third world women ...

MARTYR 1: Third world ? I'm from Michoacán ...

GUERRILLERA: ... Are triply oppressed, so we have to fight three times as hard!

MARTYR 3: That's right!

GUERRILLERA: Come to the meetings!

MARTYR 3: Where? Where? When?

59. headaches
60. medicinal tea

GUERRILLERA: ... Have your consciousness raised!
MARTYR 2: What's consciousness?
MARTYR 1: I don't know, but I'm keeping my legs crossed ... *(Holds her skirt down on her knees.)*
GUERRILLERA: Come with me and help make the revolution!
MARTYR 3: Let's go, kill 'em, kill 'em!
GUERRILLERA: Good things will come to pass. Come with me and rebel!
MARTYR 3: Let's go! *(To the others.)* Come on!
MARTYR 2: All right, let's go!
MARTYR 1: Bueno ...
ALL: Let's go, vamos! Si! ¡Arriba! ¡Vamos! Come on, come on!
   MARTYR 3 *picks up a broom and rests it on her shoulder like a rifle. The others follow suit. All sing.*

SI ADELITA SE FUERA CON OTRO
LA SEGUIRÍA POR TIERRA Y POR MAR
SI POR MAR EN UN BUQUE DE GUERRA
SI POR TIERRA EN UN TREN MILITAR[61]

GUERRILLERA: But first ... hold it, hold it but first ... we must peel the potatoes, cook the rice, make the menudo and sweep the hall ... *(The* WOMEN *groan and lose enthusiasm)* ... because there's gonna be a fund-raiser tonight!
   Music begins. The GUERRILLERA *and* WOMEN *sing.*

GUERRILLERA:
THERE'S GONNA BE A FUND-RAISER
THE BROTHERS WILL SPEAK OF CHANGE

CHORUS:
WE GONNA HAVE BANANA SURPRISE
WE GONNA CUT YAUTÍAS IN SLICE
THERE'S GONNA BE A FUND-RAISER
BUT THEY'LL ASK US TO PEEL AND FRY

---

61. If Adelita went with another   I would follow her by land and sea   If by sea in a warship   If by land in a military train

GUERRILLERA:
WE SAY OKAY
WE WILL FIGHT NOT CLEAN
BUT THEY SAY GO DEAR
AND TYPE THE SPEECH

ANITA IS GONNA MAKE IT
SHE'S GONNA MAKE IT

CHORUS:
MARÍA WILL SWEEP THE FLOOR
JUANITA IS FAT AND PREGNANT
PREGNANT FOR WHAT
NO MATTER IF WE'RE TIRED
AS LONG LONG LONG LONG
AS LONG AS THEY'RE NOT

TONIGHT TONIGHT
TONIGHT TONIGHT
TONIGHT TONIGHT
TONIGHT TONIGHT

GUERRILLERA:
WON'T BE JUST ANY NIGHT

CHORUS:
TONIGHT TONIGHT
TONIGHT TONIGHT
TONIGHT TONIGHT
TONIGHT TONIGHT

GUERRILLERA:
WE'LL BE NO MORE HARASSED

CHORUS:
TONIGHT TONIGHT
TONIGHT TONIGHT
TONIGHT TONIGHT

TONIGHT TONIGHT

GUERRILLERA:
I'LL HAVE SOMETHING TO SAY

CHORUS:
TONIGHT TONIGHT

GUERRILLERA:
FOR US A NEW DAY WILL START

CHORUS:
TODAY THE WOMEN
WANT THE HOURS

GUERRILLERA:
HOURS TO BE LOVING

CHORUS:
TODAY THE WOMEN
WANT THE HOURS

GUERRILLERA:	CHORUS:
AND STILL THE TIME TO FIGHT	BORING BORING
TO MAKE THIS ENDLESS	BORING BORING
BORING BORING BORING	BORING BORING
BORING BORING BORING	BORING BORING
FLIGHT!	FLIGHT!

All end the song with mops and brooms upraised. A voice is heard offstage.

MAN: (Offstage.) *Is dinner ready!* (The WOMEN drop their "weapons" and run away.)

WOMAN 1: ¡Ay, se me quema el arroz![62]

WOMAN 2: ¡Bendito, las habichuelas![63]

WOMAN 3: ¡Ay, Virgen de Guadalupe, las enchiladas![64] *(They exit.)*

---

62. Ay, the rice is burning!
63. Gosh, the beans!
64. Ay, Virgin of Guadalupe, the enchiladas.

GUERRILLERA: *(Exiting after them.)* Wait! Wait! What about the revolution! ... *(Black out.)*
   As the lights go up the MAN *enters dressed as a campesino, with*
poncho and sombrero. The SOCIAL RESEARCHER *enters right behind.*
She holds a notebook and a pencil.

RESEARCHER: *(With an accent.)* Excuse me señor ... buenas tardes. Me
llamo Miss Smith. I'm from the Peaceful Corps. Could you be so
kind to answer some questions for me—for our research study?

MAN: Bueno.

RESEARCHER: Have you many children?

MAN: God has not been good to me. Of sixteen children born, only nine
live.

RESEARCHER: Does you wife work?

MAN: No. She stays at home.

RESEARCHER: I see. How does she spend the day?

MAN: *(Scratching his head.)* Well, she gets up at four in the morning, fetches
water and wood, makes the fire and cooks breakfast. Then she goes
to the river and washes the clothes. After that she goes to town to
get the corn ground and buy what we need in the market. Then she
cooks the midday meal.

RESEARCHER: You come home at midday?

MAN: No, no, she brings the meal to me in the field about three kilometers
from home.

RESEARCHER: And after that?

MAN: Well, she takes care of the hens and the pigs ... and of course, she
looks after the children all day ... then she prepares supper so it is
ready when I come home.

RESEARCHER: Does she go to bed after supper?

MAN: No, I do. She has things to do around the house until about ten
o'clock.

RESEARCHER: But, señor,[65] you said your wife doesn't work ...

MAN: Of course, she doesn't work. I told you, she stays home!

RESEARCHER: *(Closing notebook.)* Thank you, señor. You have been very
helpful. Adiós. *(She exits. The* MAN *follows her.)*

MAN: Hey, psst, señorita[66]... my wife goes to bed at ten o'clock. I can
answer more questions for you later ... *(Black out.)*

---

65. mister
66. miss

In the dark we hear the beginning of "Dolphins by the Beach." The
DAUGHTER 1 *and the* GIRL *enter. They dance to the music. This dance*
portrays the fantasies of a young woman. It is a dance of freedom and
self-realization. A fanfare is heard, breaking the spell. They run away.
The MC *enters.*

MC: Ladies and gentlemen, señoras y señores ... the show goes on and on
and on and ON! The beauty, the talent, the endurance of these
contestants is, you have to agree, OVERWHELMING. They have gone
beyond the call of duty in pursuit of their goal. They have performed
unselfishly. They have given their all. And will give even more, for,
ladies and gentlemen, señoras y señores, the contest is not over yet.
As the excitement mounts—I can feel it in the air!—the question
burning in everyone's mind is: who will be the winner? *(As soap*
opera narrator.) Who will wear that crown on that pretty little head?
What will she do? Will she laugh? Will she cry? Will she faint in my
arms? ... Stay tuned for the last chapter of Reina[67] for a Day! (MC
exits. All the women enter.)

DAUGHTER 1: Mamá, may I go out and play? It is such a beautiful day and
the tree is full of mangoes. May I get some? Let me go out to the top
of the hill. Please. I just want to sit there and look ahead, far away.
If I squint my eyes real hard I think I can see the ocean. Mami, please,
may I, may I go out?

MOTHER: Niña, what nonsense. Your head is always in the clouds. I can't
give you permission to go out. Wait until your father comes home
and ask him. *(Father enters.)*

DAUGHTER 1: Papá, please, may I go out and play? It is such a beautiful
day and ...

FATHER: No. Stay home with your mother. Girls belong at home. You are
becoming too much of a tomboy. Why don't you learn to cook, to
sew, to mend my socks ...

WIFE: Husband, I would like to buy some flowers for the windows, and that
vase I saw yesterday at the shop ...

HUSBAND: Flowers, flowers, vases. What luxury! Instead of such fuss about
the house, why don't you do something about having a child? I want
a son. We've been married two years now and I am tired of waiting.
What's the matter with you? People are already talking. It's me they
suspect ...

---

67. Queen

MOTHER: Son, I have placed all my hopes on you. I hope you will be better than your father and take care of me ...

SON: I'm going off to the war. I have been called to play the game of death. I must leave you now. I must go and kill.

WIDOW: He gave his life for the country in a far away land, killing people he didn't know, people who didn't speak his language. I'm with child. His child. I hope it's a son ... he wanted a son so much ...

DAUGHTER 2: Mother, I'm pregnant. He doesn't want to get married. I don't want to get married. I don't even know whether I want this child ...

MOTHER: Hija ... how can you do this to me?! How is it possible. That's not what I taught you! I ... your father ... your brother ... the neighbors ... what would people say?

BROTHER: I'll kill him. I know who did it. I'll wring his neck. He'll pay for this! Abusador sin escrúpulos[68] ... Dishonoring decent girls ... And I thought he was my friend. He'll pay dearly for my sister's virginity. ¡Lo pagará con sangre!

DAUGHTER 1: But I read it in *Cosmopolitan*. It said everyone is doing it! And the TV commercials ... and ...

MOTHER: Hijo, what's the matter? You look worried ...

SON: Mother, my girlfriend is having a baby. My baby. I want to bring her here. You know, I don't have a job, and well, her parents kicked her out of the house ...

MOTHER: Just like his father! So young and already spilling his seed around like a generous spring shower. Bring her. Bring your woman to me. I hope she has wide hips and gives you many healthy sons. (MOTHER *and* SON *exit.*)

The WOMEN *make moaning sounds, moving around, grouping and regrouping. Loud Latin music bursts on. The* WOMEN *dance frenetically, then suddenly the music stops.*

WOMAN 1: Sometimes, while I dance, I hear—behind the rhythmically shuffling feet—the roar of the water cascading down the mountain, thrown against the cliffs by an enraged ocean.

WOMAN 2: ... I hear the sound of water in a shower, splattering against the tiles where a woman lies dead. I hear noises beyond the water, and sometimes they frighten me.

---

68. unscrupulous abuser

WOMAN 3: Behind the beat of the drums, I hear the thud of a young woman's body thrown from a roof. I hear the screeching of wheels from a speeding car and the stifled cries of a young girl lying on the street.

WOMAN 4: Muffled by the brass section, I sometimes hear in the distance desperate cries of help from elevators, parking lots and apartment buildings. I hear the echoes in a forest: "please ... no don't ..." of a child whimpering.

WOMAN 1: I think I hear my sister cry while we dance.

WOMAN 2: I hear screams. I hear the terrorized sounds of a young girl running naked along the highway.

WOMAN 3: The string section seems to murmur names ...

WOMAN 4: To remind me that the woman, the girl who at this very moment is being beaten ...

WOMAN 1: raped ...

WOMAN 2: murdered ...

WOMAN 3: is my sister ...

WOMAN 4: my daughter ...

WOMAN 1: my mother ...

ALL: myself ...

The WOMEN *remain on stage, backs turned to the audience.*

We hear a fanfare. The MC enters.

MC: Ladies and gentlemen, the choice has been made, the votes have been counted, the results are in ... and the winner is ... señoras y señores: the queen of queens, Miss Señorita Mañana! There she is ... *(Music from Miss America's "There She is ..." The GIRL enters followed by Mamá. The GIRL is wearing all the items she has picked from previous scenes: the tinsel crown, the flowers, a mantilla, etc. Her face is still made up as a clown. The WOMEN turn around to look. The GIRL looks upset, restless with all the manipulation she has endured. The WOMEN are distressed by what they see. They surround the GIRL.)*

WOMAN 1: This is not what I meant at all ...

WOMAN 2: I meant ...

WOMAN 3: I don't know what I meant.

WOMAN 4: I think we goofed. She's a mess. *(They look at Mamá reproachfully. Mamá looks apologetic.)*

MAMÁ: I only wanted ...

WOMAN 1: *(Pointing to the* MC.) It's all his fault!

MC: Me? I only wanted to make her a queen! Can we go on with the contest? This is a waste of time ...

WOMAN 2: You and fff ... contest!

WOMAN 3: Cálmate, chica. Wait.

WOMAN 4: *(To MC.)* Look, we have to discuss this by ourselves. Give us a break, Okay?

MC: *(Mumbling as he exits.)* What do they want? What's the matter with them? ...

WOMAN 1: *(To GIRL.)* Ven acá, m'ija.[69] *(The WOMEN take off one by one all the various items, clean her face, etc.)*

WOMAN 2: Honey, this is not what it is about ...

WOMAN 4: It is about what really makes you a woman.

WOMAN 1: It is not the clothes.

WOMAN 2: Or the hair.

WOMAN 3: Or the lipstick.

WOMAN 4: Or the cooking.

WOMAN 3: But ... what is it about?

WOMAN 4: Well ... I was 13 when the blood first arrived. My mother locked herself in the bathroom with me, and recited the facts of life, and right then and there, very solemnly, she declared me a woman.

WOMAN 1: I was 18 when, amid pain and pleasure, my virginity floated away in a sea of blood. He held me tight and said "now I have made you a woman."

WOMAN 2: Then, from my insides a child burst forth ... crying, bathed in blood and other personal substances. And then someone whispered in my ear: "Now you are a real real woman."

WOMAN 3: In their songs they have given me the body of a mermaid, of a palm tree, of an ample-hipped guitar. In the movies I see myself as a whore, a nymphomaniac, a dumb servant or a third-rate dancer. I look for myself and I can't find me. I only find someone else's idea of me.

MAMÁ: But think ... what a dangerous, deadly adventure being a woman! The harassment of being a woman ... So many parts to be played, so many parts to be stifled and denied. But look at so many wild, free young things crying, like the fox in the story: "tame me, tame and I'll be yours!"

---

69. Come here, daughter.

WOMAN 1: But I'm tired of stories!
WOMAN 2: Yes, enough of "be this," "do that!"
WOMAN 3: "Look like that!" Mira, mira!
WOMAN 4: "Buy this product!"
WOMAN 1: "Lose 10 pounds!"
MAMÁ: Wait, wait some more, and maybe, just maybe ...
WOMAN 1: Tell my daughter that I love her ...
WOMAN 2: Tell my daughter I wish I had really taught her the facts of life ...
WOMAN 3: Tell my daughter that still there are mysteries ...
WOMAN 4: that the life I gave her doesn't have to be like mine.
THE GIRL: ... that there are possibilities. That women that go crazy in the
     night, that women that die alone and frustrated, that women that
     exist only in the mind, are only half of the story, because a woman
     is ...
WOMAN 1: A fountain of fire!
WOMAN 2: A river of love!
WOMAN 3: An ocean of strength!
WOMAN 4: Mirror, mirror on the wall ...

*They look at each other as images on a mirror discovering
themselves in each other. The GIRL is now one of them. She steps out
and sings:*

"DON'T DENY US THE MUSIC"

WOMAN IS A FOUNTAIN OF FIRE
WOMAN IS A RIVER OF LOVE
A LATIN WOMAN IS JUST A WOMAN
WITH THE MUSIC INSIDE

DON'T DENY US THE MUSIC
DON'T IMAGINE MY FACE
I'VE FOUGHT MANY BATTLES
I'VE SUNG MANY SONGS
I AM JUST A WOMAN
WITH THE MUSIC INSIDE

I AM JUST A WOMAN BREAKING
THE LINKS OF A CHAIN
I AM JUST A WOMAN
WITH THE MUSIC INSIDE
FREE THE BUTTERFLY
LET THE OCEANS ROLL IN
FREE THE BUTTERFLY
LET THE OCEANS ROLL IN
I AM ONLY A WOMAN
WITH THE MUSIC INSIDE

Alternate Table of Contents by Theme

GROWING UP
Autobiography

Fiction

Poetry

MEN AND WOMAN

Fiction

Poetry

STRUGGLE

Fiction

Poetry

RELIGION AND SPIRITUALITY

Autobiography

Fiction

Poetry

Selected Bibliography

I. Hispanic Literature of the United States

Barradas, Efraín, and Rafael Rodríguez. *Herejes y mitificadores: Muestra de poesía puertorriqueña en los Estados Unidos.* Río Piedras, PR: Ediciones Huracán, 1980.

Bruce-Novoa, Juan. *Chicano Authors: Inquiry by Interview.* Austin: University of Texas Press, 1980.

_____. *Chicano Poetry: A Response to Chaos.* Austin: University of Texas Press, 1982.

_____. *Retrospace: Collected Essays on Chicano Literature.* Houston: Arte Público Press, 1990.

Calderón, Héctor, and José David Saldívar. *Criticism in the Borderlands: Studies in Chicano Literature, Culture and Ideology.* Durham, NC: Duke University Press, 1991.

Candelaria, Cordelia. *Chicano Poetry: A Critical Introduction.* Westport, CT: Greenwood Press, 1986.

Fernández Olmos, Margarite. *Sobre literatura puertorriqueña de aquí y de allá: Aproximaciones feministas.* Santo Domingo: Alfa y Omega, 1989.

Flores, Juan. *Divided Borders: Essays on Puerto Rican Identity.* Houston: Arte Público Press, 1993.

Hernández, A. R., and Lourdes Casal. "Cubans in the United States: A Survey of the Literature," *Estudios Cubanos* 5 (1975): 25–51.

Hernández-Miyares, Julio. *Narradores cubanos de hoy.* Miami: Ediciones Universal, 1975.

Herrera-Sobek, María. *Beyond Stereotypes: The Critical Analysis of Chicana Literature.* Binghamton, NY: Bilingual Review Press, 1985.

Horno-Delgado, Asunción, et al., eds. *Breaking Boundaries: Latina Writings and Critical Readings.* Amherst, MA: University of Massachusetts Press, 1989.

Hospital, Carolina, ed. *Los Atrevidos: The Cuban American Writers.* Princeton, NJ: Linden Lane Magazine, 1987.

Huerta, Jorge. *Chicano Theater: Themes and Forms.* Tempe, AZ: Bilingual Review Press, 1982.

Kanellos, Nicolás. *Biographical Dictionary of Hispanic Literature of the United States.* Westport, CT: Greenwood Press, 1989.

_____. *A History of Hispanic Theater in the United States: Origins to 1940.* Austin: University of Texas Press, 1990.

Lomelí, Francisco. *Handbook of Hispanic Cultures in the United States: Literature and Art.* Houston: Arte Público Press, 1993.

Lomelí, Francisco, and Carl R. Shirley. *Dictionary of Literary Biography: Chicano Writers, First Series.* Detroit: Gale Research Inc., 1989.

_____. *Dictionary of Literary Biography: Chicano Writers, Second Series.* Detroit: Gale Research Inc., 1992.

Maratos, Daniel C., and Manesba D. Hill. *Escritores de la diáspora cubana: Manual bibliográfico.* Metuchen, NJ: Scarecrow Press, 1986.

Martínez, Julio A., and Francisco Lomelí. *Chicano Literature: A Reference Guide.* Westport, CT: Greenwood Press, 1985.

Mohr, Eugene. *The Nuyorical Experience: The Literature of the Puerto Rican Minority.* Westport, CT: Greenwood Press, 1975.

Muñoz, Elías Miguel. *Desde esta orilla: Poesía cibana del exilio.* Madrid: Betania, 1988.

Rodríguez de Laguna, Asela, ed. *Images and Identities: The Puerto Rican in Two World Contexts.* New Brunswick, NJ: Transaction Books, 1987.

Saldívar, Ramón. *Chicano Narrative: The Dialectics of Difference.* Madison: University of Wisconsin Press, 1990.

Sánchez, Marta E. *Contemporary Chicana Poetry: A Critical Approach to an Emerging Literature.* Berkeley: University of California Press, 1985.

Shirley, Carl R., and Paula W. Shirley. *Understanding Chicano Literature.* Columbia: University of South Carolina Press, 1989.

Sommers, Joseph, and Tomás Ybarra-Frausto. *Modern Chicano Writers: A Collection of Critical Essays.* Englewood Cliffs, NJ: Prentice-Hall, 1979.

Tatum, Charles. *Mexican American Literature.* Orlando, FL: Harcourt Brace Jovanovich, 1990.

II. For Further Reading

Algarín, Miguel. *On Call.* Houston: Arte Público Press, 1980.

_____. *Body Bee Calling from the 21st Century.* Houston: Arte Público Press, 1985.

_____. *Time's Now/Ya es tiempo.* Houston: Arte Público Press, 1985.

Baca, Jimmy Santiago. *Immigrants in Our Own Land.* Baton Rouge: Louisiana State University Press, 1979.

_____. *What's Happening.* Willimantic, CT: Curbstone Press, 1982.

_____. *Poems from My Yard.* Fulton, MO: Timberline Press, 1986.

_____. *Martín and Meditations on the South Valley.* New York: New Directions, 1987.

_____. *Black Mesa Poems.* New York: New Directions, 1989.

Cervantes, Lorna Dee. *Emplumada.* Pittsburgh: University of Pittsburgh Press, 1981.

_____. *From the Cables of Genocide: Poems of Love and Hunger.* Houston: Arte Público Press, 1991.

Chávez, Denise. *The Last of the Menu Girls.* Houston: Arte Público Press, 1986.

Cisneros, Sandra. *The House on Mango Street.* Houston: Arte Público Press, 1983.

_____. *My Wicked, Wicked Ways.* Berkeley: Third Woman Press, 1987.

_____. *Woman Hollering Creek and Other Stories.* New York: Random House, 1991.

Cofer, Judith Ortiz. *Reaching for the Mainland.* Tempe, AZ: Bilingual Review Press, 1987.

_____. *Terms of Survival.* Houston: Arte Público Press, 1987.

_____. *The Line of the Sun.* Athens: University of Georgia Press, 1989.

_____. *Silent Dancing: A Partial Remembrance of a Puerto Rican Childhood.* Houston: Arte Público Press, 1991.

Cruz, Victor Hernández. *Rhythm, Content & Flavor.* Houston: Arte Público Press, 1989.

_____. *Red Beans.* St. Paul, MN: Coffee House Press, 1991.

Espada, Martín. *The Immigrant Iceboy's Bolero.* Natcick, MA: Cordillera, 1982.

_____. *Trumpets from the Island of Their Eviction.* Tempe, AZ: Bilingual Review Press, 1987.

_____. *Rebellion Is the Circle of a Lover's Hands.* Willimantic, CT: Curbstone Press, 1990.

Esteves, Sandra María. *Yerba Buena.* Greenfield, NY: Greenfield Review Press, 1980.

_____. *Bluestown Mockingbird Mambo.* Houston: Arte Público Press, 1990.

Fernández, Roberta. *Intaglio: A Novel in Six Stories.* Houston: Arte Público Press, 1990.

Fernández, Roberto. *Raining Backwards.* Houston: Arte Público Press, 1988.

García, Lionel G. *Hardscrub.* Houston: Arte Público Press, 1989.

_____. *A Shroud in the Family.* Houston: Arte Público Press, 1994.

_____. *To a Widow with Children.* Houston: Arte Público Press, 1994.

Hinojosa, Rolando. *Rites and Witnesses.* Houston: Arte Público Press, 1982.

_____. *The Valley.* Tempe, AZ: Bilingual Review Press, 1983.

_____. *Dear Rafe.* Houston: Arte Público Press, 1985.

_____. *Partners in Crime.* Houston: Arte Público Press, 1985.

_____. *Fair Gentlemen of Belken County.* Tempe, AZ: Bilingual Review Press, 1986.

_____. *Klail City.* Houston: Arte Público Press, 1987.
_____. *Becky and Her Friends.* Houston: Arte Público Press, 1989.
_____. *The Useless Servants.* Houston: Arte Público Press, 1993.
Hospital, Carolina, ed. *Los Atrevidos: Cuban American Writers.* Princeton, NJ: Linden Lane Magazine, 1989.
Hoyos, Angela de. *Woman, Woman.* Houston: Arte Público Press, 1985.
_____. *Selected Poems/Selecciones.* San Antonio: Dezkalzo Press, 1989.
Laviera, Tato. *AmeRícan.* Houston: Arte Público Press, 1985.
_____. *Enclave.* Houston: Arte Público Press, 1985.
_____. *Mainstream Ethics.* Houston: Arte Público Press, 1988.
_____. *La Carreta Made a U-Turn.* Houston: Arte Público Press, 1992.
Medina, Pablo. *Pork Rind and Cuban Songs.* Washington, D.C.: Nuclassics and Science, 1975.
_____. *Exiled Memories: A Cuban Childhood.* Austin: University of Texas Press, 1990.
Mohr, Nicholasa. *Felita.* New York: Dial, 1981.
_____. *Rituals of Survival: A Woman's Portfolio.* Houston: Arte Público Press, 1985.
_____. *Going Home.* New York: Dial, 1986.
_____. *Nilda.* Houston: Arte Público Press, 1986.
_____. *In Nueva York.* Houston: Arte Público Press, 1993.
Mora, Pat. *Communion.* Houston: Arte Público Press, 1991.
_____. *Borders.* Houston: Arte Público Press, 1993.
_____. *Chants.* Houston: Arte Público Press, 1994.
Morales, Alejandro. *Death of an Anglo.* Tempe, AZ: Bilingual Review Press, 1988.
_____. *The Brick People.* Houston: Arte Público Press, 1992.
_____. *The Rag Doll Plagues.* Houston: Arte Público Press, 1992.
Pérez-Firmat, Gustavo. *Carolina Cuban.* Tempe: Bilingual Review Press, 1986.
_____. *Equivocaciones.* Madrid: Editorial Betania: 1989.
Piñero, Miguel. *La Bodega Sold Dreams.* Houston: Arte Público Press, 1985.
Prida, Dolores. *Beautiful Señoritas and Other Plays.* Houston: Arte Público Press, 1991.
_____. *Welcome to the Oasis.* Houston: Arte Público Press, 1992.
Ríos, Alberto. *The Iguana Killer: Twelve Stories of the Heart.* Lewiston, ID: Blue Moon & Confluence, 1984.
_____. *Teodoro Luna's Two Kisses.* New York: Norton, 1990.
Rivera, Tomás. *The Searchers: Collected Poetry.* Houston: Arte Público Press, 1990.
_____. *The Complete Works.* Houston: Arte Público Press, 1992.

Salas, Floyd. *Buffalo Nickel.* Houston: Arte Público Press, 1992.
_____. *What Now My Love.* Houston: Arte Público Press, 1994.
Salinas, Luis Omar. *The Sadness of Days: Selected and New Poems.* Houston: Arte Público Press, 1987.
Suárez, Virgil. *Latin Jazz.* New York: Morrow, 1989.
Thomas, Piri. *Saviour, Saviour, Hold My Hand.* Garden City, NY: Doubleday, 1972.
_____. *Down These Mean Streets.* New York: Vintage Books, 1974.
_____. *Stories from El Barrio.* New York: Avon, 1980.
_____. *Seven Long Times.* Houston: Arte Público Press, 1994.

Vega, Ed. *The Comeback.* Houston: Arte Público Press, 1985.
_____. *Mendoza's Dreams.* Houston: Arte Público Press, 1987.
_____. *Casualty Report.* Houston: Arte Público Press, 1991.
Villaseñor, Victor. *Macho!* Houston: Arte Público Press, 1991.
_____. *Rain of Gold.* New York: Dell, 1992.
_____. *Walking Stars.* Houston: Arte Público Press, 1994.
Viramontes, Helena María. *The Moths and Other Stories.* Houston: Arte Público Press, 1985.

Index of Author Names, Titles and First Lines of Poems

Acknowledgments

Miguel Algarín. "Taos Pueblo Indians: 700 Strong According to Bobby's Last Census" by Miguel Algarín is reprinted with permission from the publisher of On Call (Houston: Arte Público Press–University of Houston, 1980).

Jimmy Santiago Baca. "Martín III" by Jimmy Santiago Baca is reprinted with permission from the publisher of Decade II: A Twentieth Anniversary Anthology (Houston: Arte Público Press–University of Houston, 1992).

Lorna Dee Cervantes. "Refugee Ship" and "Heritage" by Lorna Dee Cervantes are reprinted with permission from the publisher of A Decade of Hispanic Literature (Houston: Arte Público Press–University of Houston, 1982). "The Poet Is Served Her Papers" and "Pleiades from the Cables of Genocide" by Lorna Dee Cervantes are reprinted with permission from the publisher of From the Cables of Genocide (Houston: Arte Público Press–University of Houston, 1991). Copyright © 1991 by Lorna Dee Cervantes.

Denise Chávez. "The Closet" by Denise Chávez is reprinted with permission from the publisher of The Last of the Menu Girls (Houston: Arte Público Press–University of Houston, 1987). Copyright © 1987 by Denise Chávez.

Sandra Cisneros. "Ghosts and Voices: Writing from Obsession" and "Notes to a Young(er) Writer" are reprinted with permission from the publisher of The Americas Review Vol. XV, no. 1, Spring 1987.

Judith Ortiz Cofer. "Quinceañera," "Mamacita," "Exile," and "Under the Knife" by Judith Ortiz Cofer are reprinted with permission from the publisher of Terms of Survival (Houston: Arte Público Press–University of Houston, 1987). Copyright © 1987 by Judith Ortiz Cofer. "Tales Told under the Mango Tree" by Judith Ortiz Cofer is reprinted with permission from the publisher of Silent Dancing: A Partial Remembrance of a Puerto Rican Childhood (Houston: Arte Público Press–University of Houston, 1990). Copyright © 1990 by Judith Ortiz Cofer.

Victor Hernández Cruz. "today is a day of great joy," "energy," "The Latest Latin Dance Craze," and "Loisaida" are reprinted with permission from the publisher of Rhythm, Content, and Flavor (Houston: Arte Público Press–University of Houston, 1989). Copyright © 1989 Victor Hernández Cruz.

Angela de Hoyos. "You Will Grow Old," "Lesson in Semantics," and "How to Eat Crow on a Cold Sunday Morning" by Angela de Hoyos are reprinted with permission from the publisher of Woman, Woman (Houston: Arte Público Press, 1985). Copyright © by Angela de Hoyos.

Martín Espada. "Portrait of a Real Hijo de Puta," "Revolutionary Spanish Lesson," and "Colibrí" by Martín Espada are reprinted with permission from the publisher of The Americas Review Vol. 18, no. 2, Summer 1990.

Sandra María Esteves. "Resurrections," "Padrino," "Bautizo," and "Ocha" by Sandra María Esteves are reprinted with permission from the publisher of Bluestown Mockingbird Mambo (Houston: Arte Público Press–University of Houston, 1990). Copyright © 1990 by Sandra María Esteves.

Roberta Fernández. "Zulema" by Roberta Fernández is reprinted with permission from the publisher of Intaglio: A Novel in Six Stories (Houston: Arte Público Press–University of Houston, 1990). Copyright © 1990 by Roberta Fernández.

Roberto Fernández. "Retrieving Varadero" and "Miracle at Eighth and Twelfth" by Roberto Fernández are reprinted with permission from the publisher of Raining Backwards (Houston: Arte Público Press–University of Houston, 1988). Copyright © 1988 by Roberto Fernández.

Lionel G. García. "The Sergeant," by Lionel G. García is reprinted with permission from the publisher of The Americas Review Vol. XV, no. 1, Spring 1987.

Rolando Hinojosa. "Into the Pit with Bruno Cano" from The Valley by Rolando Hinojosa. Copyright © 1983 by Bilingual Press/Editorial Bilingüe. Reprinted by permission of Bilingual Press/Editorial Bilingüe, Arizona State University, Tempe, Arizona.

Carolina Hospital. "Miami Mimesis," "A Visit to West New York," "Alma Mater," "Finding Home," and "The Old Order" by Carolina Hospital are reprinted with permission from the publisher of Paradise Lost or Gained?: The Literature of Hispanic Exile (Houston: Arte Público Press–University of Houston, 1990).

Tato Laviera. "latero story (can pickers)" by Tato Laviera is reprinted with permission from the publisher of Mainstream Ethics (Houston: Arte Público Press–University of Houston, 1988). Copyright © 1988 by Tato Laviera. "AmeRícan," "intellectual," and "boricua" by Tato Laviera are reprinted with permission from the publisher of AmeRícan (Houston: Arte Público Press–University of Houston, 1985). Copyright © 1985 by Tato Laviera.

Pablo Medina. "Madame America," "The Apostate," and "The Beginning," are reprinted with permission from the publisher of The Americas Review Vol. 17, no. 2, Summer 1989.

Luis Omar Salinas. "Ode to the Mexican Experience," "When This Life No Longer Smells of Roses," "My Father Is a Simple Man," and "I Am America" are reprinted with permission from the publisher of The Sadness of Days (Houston: Arte Público Press–University of Houston, 1987). Copyright © 1987 by Luis Omar Salinas.

Ricardo Sánchez. "Soledad Was a Girl's Name" and "Letters to My Ex-Texas Sanity" are reprinted with permission from the publisher of Selected Poems by (Houston: Arte Público Press–University of Houston, 1985). Copyright © 1985 Ricardo Sánchez.

Virgil Suárez. "Dearly Beloved" by Virgil Suárez is reprinted with permission from the publisher of Welcome to the Oasis and Other Stories (Houston: Arte Público Press–University of Houston, 1992). Copyright © 1992 by Victor Suárez.

Piri Thomas. Prologue from Seven Long Times is reprinted by permission from the publisher of Seven Long Times (Houston: Arte Público Press–University of Houston, 1994). Copyright © 1974 by Piri Thomas.

Gloria Vando. "Legend of the Flamboyán" and "Nuyorican Lament" by Gloria Vando are reprinted with permission from the publisher of Promesas: Geography of the Impossible (Houston: Arte Público Press–University of Houston, 1993). Copyright © 1993 by Gloria Vando.

Ed Vega. "The Kite" by Ed Vega is reprinted with permission from the publisher of Casualty Report (Houston: Arte Público Press–University of Houston, 1991). Copyright © 1991 by Ed Vega.

Evangelina Vigil-Piñón. "¡es todo!" by Evangelina Vigil-Piñón is reprinted with permission from the publisher of Thirty an' Seen a Lot (Houston: Arte Público Press–University of Houston, 1985). Copyright © 1985 by Evangelina Vigil-Piñón.

Victor Villaseñor. Excerpt from Rain of Gold by Victor Villaseñor is reprinted with permission from the publisher of Rain of Gold (Houston: Arte Público Press–University of Houston, 1991). Copyright © 1991 by Victor Edmundo Villaseñor.

Helena María Viramontes. "The Cariboo Cafe" by Helena María Viramontes is reprinted with permission from the publisher of The Moths and Other Stories (Houston: Arte Público Press–University of Houston, 1985). Copyright © 1985 by Helena María Viramontes.